PRAISE FOR JOEY E

I heard Joey's story from my friend Darryl in the days before 2017 and I was in awe of what he was hoping to achieve. The thing that struck me most when I met Joey was that he didn't mention a single word about his 'problems' – he was just another guy lining up to do the gnarliest race in the world. To me, that said more about him than anything else. Good job, legend!

Sam Sunderland (overall motorbike winner, Dakar 2017)

Joey Evans is one of the most phenomenal people I have met in three decades of Carte Blanche. His story is one of unbelievable courage, tenacity and belief, blended with a very close bond with his wife Meredith and their four daughters.

Derek Watts (anchor and presenter on *Carte Blanche*)

To
ANDREW

RIDE THROUGH
THE NIGHT!

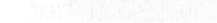

FROM
PARA TO
DAKAR

Overcoming paralysis and conquering the Dakar Rally,
a journey of courage and determination

JOEY EVANS

TRACEY McDONALD PUBLISHERS

First published by Tracey McDonald Publishers, 2017
Reprinted 2018 (twice), 2019
Suite No. 53, Private Bag X903, Bryanston, South Africa, 2021
www.traceymcdonaldpublishers.com

ISBN 978-0-620-75751-5
e-ISBN (ePUB) 978-0-620-75752-2

Text design and typesetting by Patricia Crain, Empressa
Cover design by Ron Olivier, incynq solutions
Front cover photograph of Joey Evans (face) by © Andre Chaco
Front cover photograph of Joey Evans (on the bike) by © Marcelo Machado de Melo
Back cover photograph by © Gustavo Epifanio

Printed by **novus print**, a division of Novus Holdings

For my wife Meredith
and
my daughters Kayla, Jenna, Tyra and Shawna

Joey Evans is a highly sought-after global keynote speaker. He will entertain, motivate and inspire you and your team as he takes you on the journey to realising an impossible dream.

Follow Joey on Facebook: www.facebook.com/fromparatodakar/ and on Instagram: www.instagram.com/joey_evans_132.

For more information and details on how to book Joey for your next event please visit his website: www.joeyevans.co.za.

CONTENTS

Chapter 1   The Beginning of the End   1

Chapter 2   It's a Great Day for Racing   4

Chapter 3   Reality Bites Down Hard   12

Chapter 4   Pain and Passing Lights   16

Chapter 5   Long Days and Longer Nights   22

Chapter 6   A New Line of Sight   28

Chapter 7   Rock Bottom   36

Chapter 8   Riding Again   42

Chapter 9   Wanna Race?   52

Chapter 10   The Race of Crazy People   60

Chapter 11   Pongola Steaks   74

Chapter 12   Finding My Way   81

Chapter 13   Burning Rubber   93

Chapter 14   All In   110

Chapter 15   The Mighty Sahara   124

Chapter 16   June 2016 – 7 Months to Dakar   138

Chapter 17   July 2016 – 6 Months to Dakar   145

Chapter 18   August 2016 – 5 Months to Dakar   152

Chapter 19   September 2016 – 4 Months to Dakar   158

Chapter 20   October 2016 – 3 Months to Dakar   162

Chapter 21   November 2016 – 2 Months to Dakar   169

Chapter 22   December 2016 – 30 Days to Dakar   177

Chapter 23   Dakar Go Time   184

Chapter 24   Stages 1 to 4   192

Chapter 25   Stages 5 and 6 and Rest Day   208

Chapter 26   Marathon Stages 7 and 8   219

Chapter 27   Stages 9 and 10   227

Chapter 28   Stage 11 – End of the Road   238

Chapter 29   Stage 12 and Podium   254

Acknowledgements   261

Chapter 1

THE BEGINNING OF THE END

The alarm on my motorbike burst to life with three sharp beeps. Its sound was clear and distinct even through my earplugs and over the growl of the large titanium Akropovic pipe sticking out the back of my KTM 450RR rally bike.

I was exhausted, my face was raw from wearing goggles caked in mud and dust against my sweaty face for the last eleven days. My lips were weathered and split, my hands were blistered and my body was chafed, dirty and completely fatigued.

The scream of the alarm always sent a shock of adrenalin right through my body, forcing me to pay attention regardless of my mental or physical state. Its penetrating sound meant there was a rally car or truck behind me that was about to overtake me. At least that's how it was explained at the riders' briefing before the rally. In reality, it meant 'get the hell out of the way if you want to live!'

The risks we took as bikers were far more daunting than the rally car drivers in their protective cages. The motorbikes set off first each morning, opening the track, followed shortly afterwards by the cars and then the trucks, both of which were faster than most of the bikers. That meant I was caught and passed daily by at least the leading vehicles. I had heard the alarm many times during the rally and I always chose life.

Once the approaching car or truck starts to see the dust of the bike ahead, they press a button in their vehicle that sets off the alarm mounted on the bike ahead. This system worked well for both parties as the biker would be safer and the car would be able to pass more quickly. As a biker, once my alarm sounded I would look back and see the vehicle usually about 200 metres away and get an idea of how long I had to get off the track before it passed me. Then I picked a spot to pull off the track to safety and stopped. After a few seconds the vehicle would roar past, kicking up fist-sized rocks and dirt in its wake, leaving me invisible in a thick cloud of dust that completely engulfed me.

Once the dust settled, I would look back along the track for other vehicles before racing on, shifting hard through the gears and leaving my own stream of dirt and dust behind me. Of course I had the choice of just pulling to the side of the track and allowing space for the vehicle to pass. I had tried it once, earlier in the race, and found myself completely blinded in the thick dust travelling at 120kph. Not knowing where the gravel road was heading, I ended up in a bush. Lesson learned.

But this time it was different. As the siren went off I turned to see the approaching vehicle through the dust but it wasn't the usual 200 metres behind me, it was a mere 30 metres away and was closing in at twice my speed. I had only three or four seconds to get out of the way before impact. I tried to get out of the deep rut, weighting my right foot peg and pulling hard on the bars, twisting them to the left and keeping the power on. The front wheel just scraped in vain against the left wall of the rut compressing the forks, my wheel unable to climb out. The bike tucked as my body exited left off the track, parting from the bike in a last ditch effort to escape the imminent impact of the car behind me.

The car missed me by millimetres only to drive right over my bike, its two-ton weight crushing the frame as its tyres ripped mercilessly through my tanks and navigation tower. Blinded by the fesh-fesh filling the air, I heard the impact right next to me. I knew exactly what was happening, the crushing sound unmistakable above the roar of the car's engine.

I couldn't believe it! If I had fallen the other way across the track, I would have been dead for sure! The car stopped about 30 metres ahead of me, the navigator opened his door and stood next to the car, one hand still resting on the door frame, and gave me a thumbs up as if to check whether I was alive. I was still on my knees in the dirt right next to the track when my mangled bike came into sight as the dust cleared.

I yelled, 'No! Get back here!'

But he jumped back into the car and they sped off, leaving me stranded next to what had been my bike. I was seething. He had almost killed me, ridden over my bike and then left as though it was an everyday occurrence. I couldn't believe his callous indifference for my life.

Alone, I stared down through tired bloodshot eyes at the wreckage and the horrifying reality hit me. I was out of the Dakar Rally. Words cannot describe the feelings that came over me. It's true that every Dakar competitor makes sacrifices to be there, each one has forfeited holidays, relationships, homes, jobs and worldly possessions to take part in this daring crazy race. All of us have trained for years to reach the level needed to compete. But it felt different for me; it seemed so much more. I'd promised I'd never give up, but this was out of my control, it was the end, a dream destroyed, a fight lost.

It had taken me nearly ten years to recover from the accident that had paralysed me, 51 nights in hospital, over 350 physio sessions, countless hours in the gym, more than 30000 kilometres of hard training, and untold sacrifices – was this how it was going to end?

Chapter 2

IT'S A GREAT DAY FOR RACING

I have always loved bikes. It started with my first second-hand bicycle, a red Raleigh Strika that I got for Christmas one year when I was about six. From grade one I would ride my bicycle to school and back each day along with my brother and friends. We would practise our wheelies, bunny hops and skids on the sandy pavements of Kempton Park.

When I grew up wheelies were always measured in lamp posts, basically how many of them you passed while on the back wheel. Bunny hops were measured by the number of stacked bricks leapt over, and skids by the number of steps measuring the drag line in the sand. These skids were always extra cool if you added the 90 degree turn at the end. As I got older, like about ten, skids were no longer considered cool with someone (no doubt echoing their parents) commenting how it just stuffed up your tyres.

My brothers and I made ramps in the garden from pieces of wood placed on stacked bricks and a track that went through most of the flower beds, much to my mom's despair. The far end of the front patio with its metre drop-off was the biggest stunt in the garden and it would take a serious dare and my buddies' taunts of, 'Are you chicken, boet?' to attempt it.

I also used my bike for my newspaper round. I delivered the *Beeld* newspaper in the early mornings before returning home to get ready for school. The biggest danger in my mind was the dogs that escaped out the yards and chased me down the street. I remember riding for my life, my legs spinning on the pedals at maximum rpm while the dogs snapped at my ankles. At the time it was extremely scary.

There was one house in particular at the top of the road that had a low precast wall which their Alsatian could easily jump over. If he heard me coming, I was tickets. Each morning I would park my bike

4

about two houses away and then creep towards the letter box. Winter was best as I could use the darkness to hide. Then on my elbows and knees I would leopard crawl the last few metres until I was directly under the letter box. I would reach up and carefully slide the rolled paper into the box. It was a delicate operation, making sure I didn't alert the beast. In my mind, I was Indiana Jones, swapping a golden statue for a bag of sand. Then, carefully, back the same way to my bike only to repeat the exercise the next day.

On Wednesday afternoons I delivered the local free newspaper, *The Kempton Express*. I slowly saved up money from my newspaper rounds and pooled the birthday money from my grandparents with the Christmas money from my parents and bought my first BMX – a brand new gold and black Raleigh Racing. The flower bed tracks then started to move into the veld over the road from our house and onto local building sites with their big mounds of excavated dirt. I would ride down the road and meet up with buddies at the back of the old tennis courts and ride the tracks and jumps we made in the dirt. Countless scrapes, bruises and skinless shins from the pedals couldn't dampen our passion for riding.

Like most of us, I always wanted a motorbike, but growing up second oldest in a family of six children it was simply never going to happen. My passion was first ignited when my high school buddy Sheldon Tree, who raced motocross, let me ride his Kawasaki KX125 a couple of times in the veld behind his house. The acceleration as I twisted the throttle sent a surge of adrenalin right through me and although it was scary at first I couldn't help smiling in the helmet and always left wanting more. I remember him trying to teach me to jump a small mound one afternoon after school in the veld behind his house. It took a few attempts but eventually I got it right. I turned around and gave a thumbs up only to hit an anthill in the long grass and fly over the bars. It was my official welcome to the world of dirt bikes.

I often went to the motocross races with Sheldon and his dad. Each time I found myself blown away by the massive scale of the jumps. I stood in awe, watching the brightly coloured bikes fly through the air at insane speeds. I loved standing next to the start as the air filled with the roar of engines and the smell of two stroke, watching the bikes rip away through the dirt as the gate dropped. It was incredible to watch, but watching was not enough.

The next few years went by as I progressed from my BMX to a mountain bike. I also progressed from single to married and then to married with children. I remember the first time I saw my wife

Meredith. She was laughing and to me she just seemed to glow. She was beautiful inside and out. We started dating and I fell in love with her soft gentle ways. We were complete opposites, I was an extrovert and highly competitive; she was shy and didn't care about who won, as long as everyone enjoyed the game. She was thoughtful and kind and in some crazy way we balanced each other out and just clicked. I think her parents felt she could do better, and they were right. I couldn't risk her figuring that out so I made sure I closed the deal. She was only 20 and I had just turned 23 when we were married on 18 July 1998. (For the record I remembered that date without having to check our marriage certificate!)

I was 26 years old before I could afford to buy my first motorbike, a red second-hand Honda CR250 two stroke motocross bike. I started by learning to ride in the veld, taking care to avoid the anthills. I then moved onto motocross tracks, learning to corner and jump, followed in the coming years by a bit of 'freestyle motocross', launching to insane heights off metal ramps combined with tricks. Later I moved onto enduro and hare scrambles where I found my passion racing off road through the ever changing countryside. I loved the places it took me and the challenges of rocky climbs, thick sandy paths, winding through forests, river crossings and the mud pits. The unknown terrain each race held and the varying skills needed to conquer the different natural challenges really appealed to me.

It was around this time that I first heard about a crazy race called the Dakar Rally and I saw some highlights of it on TV. I had always loved camping, hiking and the outdoors, especially the whole wilderness survival side of it. This Dakar Rally seemed to combine outdoor survival against the harsh elements with racing dirt bikes and, added into the mix, faraway mysterious countries and extreme landscapes. To my mind this was the perfect recipe for an amazing adventure. I dreamed of competing in that race and I started to find out more about it.

As I found out more, I began to realise what a massive financial and time-consuming commitment it was. The costs alone of purchasing a bike, sending it to Europe and then racing it across North Africa, combined with the race entry fees and the return airfare were astronomical. It would cost more than my total earnings over several years, making it simply an impossible dream. For the time being, I put my dream of racing from Paris, France, across North Africa and through the Sahara Desert to Dakar, Senegal, on the back shelf. I would think about it each January when I watched some of the highlights.

'One day,' I thought.

Although there was only one Dakar Rally, there were still many other serious, more reachable challenges to conquer in the off-road biking world. I continued to follow my passion, riding as often as I could and racing in club, provincial and national races throughout 2005 and 2006.

One highlight was finishing the Roof of Africa enduro in 2006, staged in the mountain kingdom of Lesotho. I had run several marathons and ultra-marathons before but they paled in comparison with the onslaught of that race. It took months of preparation leading up to it and then three days of racing through the harsh unforgiving Maluti Mountains. Racing up and down the rocky passes worked every muscle in your body, making your arms and legs fatigued to the point where you could simply no longer hold on.

The second and third days each lasted close to ten hours. As the physical exertion compounded, many riders were eliminated from the race. Braving the elements and enduring hours of physical pain, struggling forward to conquer those 3000 metre high mountains felt like a huge achievement at the time. It would, however, be a small ripple compared to the insurmountable mountain I would soon need to face.

It is said that the first bike race took place the moment the second motorbike was made. I can believe it, I loved racing! The 2007 racing season started off well. Meredith joined me at most races and my friends' wives often joined them too. We got to the races in the early hours each Saturday morning and set up the gazebo, the guy ropes attached to bakkie wheels and bike trailers, and then set out the camping chairs for the ladies. We set up our pits with jerry cans full of petrol for filling-up between laps, had some food laid out, spare goggles, gloves and an extra hydration pack filled to save as much time as possible between laps. You didn't want to fight your way past a rider only to lose the position again while in the pits.

The whole morning was filled with banter about how others should move out the way when we lapped them, or why they had even bothered to bring extra petrol when they would be time barred after only one lap. Comments were passed about how their kits seemed to have shrunk in the wash, or how their kidney belts just managed to touch at the front. The morning wouldn't pass without a single glove being hidden away or a stone placed behind the foam lining inside someone's helmet. And there would always be one chop who would try to kick-start his bike for several minutes before realising he still had the exhaust plug in, his petrol tap closed or he hadn't taken the rag out of the airbox since washing the bike. They were good times.

The wives were often rosy-cheeked, dressed warmly and wearing beanies in the fresh winter air, the grass still wet with the morning dew. They laughed and chatted, warning each other not to drink anything because the portable toilets were so dodgy. If they absolutely had to go they would be armed with their own toilet paper, wet wipes and a bottle of hand sanitiser, pairing up to ensure someone guarded the door. They returned looking disgusted, not wanting to talk about it, shuddering, their lips tight and eyes fixed to the ground.

Then it was off to the scrutineering and riders' briefing. The marshals checked your race licence and entry payment, inspected the bikes and issued race numbers. They also confirmed that you had your first aid kit and medical board. These items were often passed surreptitiously between riders like some kind of drug deal to ensure that we all passed the checks. Nerves would run wild as we lined up at the start and went through our individual routines. Huddled together, the wives watched the start as we disappeared in a cloud of noise and dust.

When we arrived between laps the ladies would all be ready to help like a slick Formula 1 pit crew. Bikes were filled, goggles handed over or cleaned, a banana stuffed in your mouth followed by a quick report of how many riders in your class were ahead of you, and then you were off again. Even if you were tired and broken, you sped out of the pits like a mad man only to slow down once out of sight and try to breathe or shake your arms in an attempt to get rid of the arm pump. Every rider suffered this from time to time, when your forearms went solid, almost crippling your hands and making it near impossible to hold on to the bars.

My friend Derek, who was in his late forties at the time, had a different approach. He was there just for a good spin on his dirt bike. He didn't care about the results and between laps would casually take off his helmet, sit down on a camping chair and enjoy a sandwich and cool drink. Once well rested, he would mosey on over to his bike and head off again. He had quite a different approach to the rest of us but enjoyed it all the same.

It was mandatory that whoever finished the race first would strip out of his kit and get back into his shorts as quickly as humanly possible. This ensured that he had maximum ammo while shaking his head as the others arrived and asking, 'Hey boet, are you OK, did you get a puncture or something? What took you so long? I've been asking all over the pits if anybody knew where you were, we were getting ready to send out a search party!' There was usually a slight snigger behind a face desperately trying to fake real concern.

We all loved being there and although we raced on the same track we found our enjoyment in different ways. I was there to compete, I wanted to win or at least podium in my class. This meant riding faster and taking more risks; back then it was all about position for me. I had been very competitive from an early age, winning was everything. Looking back, I now realise that it means nothing in the bigger picture, but at the time it meant everything.

When I raced and started to see dust in the distance when the track opened up, I knew there was a rider not far ahead. I was hunting now! I would push hard, braking as late as possible into each corner and powering out, weighting the rear wheel for extra traction, twisting the throttle hard against the stop and flying through shallow water unconcerned about what might lie beneath.

Slowly I would start to enter the tail of the dust cloud billowing from his rear tyre. As I closed in the dust would swell, getting denser with each metre to the point where I was almost riding blind. No time to back off now, I stretched the throttle cable, keeping the front end light with my weight back, elbows up and the bike tight between my knees, flying through the unknown terrain, hoping for the best. The bike's front end bounced up at me as I caught the occasional half-buried rock or 'lurker', and the branches of thorn bushes whipped at my arms.

Then the light would open up; I was still behind the rider but the dust was now low enough to see over. That's when I started feeling the roost of stone and rocks firing up like shrapnel from his rear tyre as it clawed its way through the stony track. They cut and stung my neck, arms and nose as I closed in, trying to see past him at the track ahead and planning my final move. He had earned his spot ahead of me and wasn't about to give it up without a fight. He glanced back and pushed on faster with renewed motivation. Inside, outside through the corners, swapping lanes back and forth on the jeep twin track constantly crossing the middle mannetjie. Then I'd spot a half gap and, making the move as quickly as possible, I shot past, braking late and locking up the brakes going into the tight corner. My inside leg stretched out and pushing down hard on the bars while weighting the outside peg, desperately trying not to overshoot the corner into the farmer's rusty barbed wire fence. Once past, I spun the back wheel, pulling away and creating as much roost and dust as possible, and even locked it up going into corners to ensure I kept the position

I had risked so much to achieve. On I went, pinned flat out, hunting for the next dust cloud.

The year moved on and I collected the regional championship points as the races ticked by. One of the top riders had crashed hard and was out for the rest of the season which increased my chances of taking the regional open pro championship. I had finished every race; my consistency had me lying second with only two races to go. Winning the championship was within my reach and I was determined to give it everything I had.

MEREDITH:

Before Joey started racing I knew nothing about motorbikes and off-road racing, but it didn't take long for me to get into it. Very few people know how much I love the whole dirt bike racing scene. Watching the AMA Supercross Championship on TV is something I look forward to each January. I'm a huge Chad Reed fan and have his motocross shirt to prove it. When I was growing up I was incredibly shy and quiet, but being married to Joey has changed that, much to my Dad's despair, and I've become quite competitive. I looked forward to supporting Joey at every race and sometimes I think I was more excited and nervous than he was. I would count the riders in his class as they passed each lap, telling him his position and then cheering like a groupie as he passed the chequered flag. Having Joey lying second in the regional championship was something I loved and took pride in.

My life as I knew it would end on a day just like any other race day. That Saturday, 13 October 2007, we headed out to the Heidelberg hare scramble. The pits were on the field of the local high school, from which the route headed out into the fields, small forests and rocky Heidelberg koppies. It was known to be a tough race, the area being full of jagged black rocks and steep technical climbs. We were to race several loops, totalling about 200 kilometres.

We set up our pits as we had done so many times before. Meredith was with me, along with her sister Melissa and some of my buddies, including my brother-in-law Brad, Derek, Tristam and his wife

Tiffany. The mandatory ambulance hadn't arrived, apparently some kind of mix-up with dates so, according to the rules, the race was not permitted to start. Another plan was made and within a couple of hours another ambulance arrived. This one looked about 30 years old and didn't offer much comfort to the riders but the box was ticked and we were just happy we got to go racing. Little did I know at the time that my life would soon be dependent on the treatment that battered taxi could offer.

They started the race class by class and I sat on my bike, lined up shoulder to shoulder with about 20 other riders in the open pro class. Soon they would drop a flag and we would shoot off across the veld, funnelling into the first right hand corner. I had a bad start there the year before and sat frustrated in the dust of the riders ahead through the twists in the first few kilometres of single track, unable to pass. This time I was determined to get a good jump off the line and be one of the first riders, elbows out, in the first corner. I was tense that day, feeling the pressure of the possible championship and playing out different strategies in my mind.

I took a pee in the bushes just before the start then got on my bike, put my goggles on, checked my petrol tap was open and did a few stretches on the bike while shaking out my hands. A couple of kicks down on the starter of my KTM 300cc two stroke and it pinged away, the smoke punching through the air behind me. I blipped the throttle a couple of times, squeezed the front brakes bouncing down on the front suspension, adjusted my helmet, all the usual routine, and was ready for action. Within minutes I would drop the clutch, roaring off to a perfect start and racing towards the end of my life as I had known it.

Chapter 3

REALITY BITES DOWN HARD

And that's the last I can remember. The next thing I knew I was waking up with my helmet off, facing the sky, the faces of paramedics and spectators peering down in a circle around me. The last few minutes were gone from my memory, never to return. It was probably for the best.

MEREDITH:

Normally at the race days I watched Joey's start and then watched our friends start in their classes; this particular race, however, I watched Joey until he was almost out of sight, and so I saw the entire accident happen. Joey was one of the first few riders going into the first corner about 100 metres after the start, when another rider crashed into his swing arm attached to his rear wheel and he was catapulted off his bike. He landed with the initial impact on the top of his head and then, still at pace, was flung like a rag doll through the rocky veld. Then in the reduced visibility of the thick dust he was ridden over by some of the other riders. I started running as fast as I could over the uneven field, panic-stricken, thinking no, no, no, this can't be happening!

When I got to Joey he was unconscious; he came around, realised what had happened and in typical Joey fashion jokingly asked 'Did I win?' I remember feeling enormously relieved and thinking, OK, this isn't as bad as it looks if he can still crack jokes. Joey then started to spit out what he thought were dirt and stones in his mouth but turned out to be pieces of his shattered teeth. He had broken twelve teeth in total, some completely shattered down into the gum. His tongue was shredded and he coughed as his mouth filled with blood. But that would pale in comparison with what was yet to come. Tiffany, who had been standing next to Joey with his bent knees resting on hers stepped back. His legs just dropped to the ground like two pieces of dead meat. I stood next to Joey, crying quietly, allowing the paramedics space to treat him. Joey then pulled the paramedic towards him and whispered, not wanting me to hear, that he could not feel his legs. But I heard Joey and went cold as all hell broke loose around us.

Later I would be told that I would never walk again, but lying there in the red dirt in the middle of the veld I had no idea what a spinal cord injury was. I had seen people in wheelchairs and heard the terms quadriplegic and paraplegic but I didn't really know what they meant. It had never crossed my mind that something like that could happen to me. In my mind, the worst case scenario was six weeks without riding, because that's how long it took a bone to heal. I really had no idea and it was probably just as well. I often think, looking back now, that if I had known the challenges the future held and what this type of injury meant it would have been too heavy a burden to bear.

There were many complications with the treatment I got that day. The organisers first called for a helicopter evacuation which was the standard procedure for spinal cord injuries. My head had also started to swell and it was clear from my broken helmet that I had serious head trauma. Meredith and Brad set off by road so that they would be at the hospital by the time I arrived in the helicopter. Melissa stayed with me.

Meredith had already arrived at the hospital by the time we realised there was a problem and the helicopter would not be coming. The outdated 'compulsory' ambulance that was on site was not equipped to transport a patient with a spinal cord injury so they needed another plan. A second ambulance was called and eventually, after lying paralysed in the dirt for more than three hours, I was loaded into it.

MEREDITH:

I would love to be able to say that I was brave and handled the next few hours of total mayhem like a champion, but I didn't. I was petrified. I was completely overwhelmed by the awful situation we had been thrown into. I was stunned, not knowing what to do or how to help. The medics and race organisers were scurrying about frantically organising a chopper to get Joey to the nearest hospital. I was told to drive as fast as I could to the Glynnwood Hospital in Benoni with Brad, as Joey would be airlifted and get there a lot faster than we would by car. Dazed, we did as they asked.

Brad took this assignment extremely seriously and as a result we were stopped by the police for speeding and driving in the yellow lane. I burst into tears, yelling at the policeman that my husband had been in a terrible accident and we were lost and didn't know how to get to the hospital. I'm sure a lot of what I said was incomprehensible but the policeman took pity on us and we were escorted the rest of the way. As we raced through the traffic following the flashing blue lights, I couldn't believe this was happening. The horrific image of Joey lying in the dirt, unable to move, was burnt into my mind. Tears streaming down my cheeks, I felt completely numb and terrified.

I didn't understand my injury and constantly asked the paramedic what the problem was and how long until the feeling and movement came back to my legs. Would I need an operation to fix it? What I do clearly remember was that he was very vague and wouldn't give me a straight answer. Looking back, I think he really didn't want to be the one to tell me the dark reality of my situation and the near impossibility of recovery. As a result of the head trauma the top of my head had now swollen, changing the shape of my head and causing a lot of concern. I would ask the same questions again and again, sometimes forgetting the answers. I don't remember much of the trip other than the feeling of claustrophobia from spending the last few hours in the uncomfortable headgear, strapped to a board, with painful pins and needles from my chest down. It was incredibly frustrating and I wanted to move on the board to relieve the discomfort. I fought the urge and focused on my breathing, knowing I just had to try to stay calm and still.

In the back of the ambulance Melissa held my hand and did her best to comfort me as the paramedic attempted to keep my body still while the big vehicle rocked and bounced along the dirt road and crawled towards the highway. I lay there with the taste of blood still in my mouth, trying to hold my swollen tongue away from the jagged edges of my hypersensitive teeth. In pain, I stared at the roof of the ambulance, unable to move, hearing the radio comms from the front and the rattle of equipment as I drifted in and out of consciousness. The hospital was still about 60 kilometres away once we reached the tar. My body, as I had known it for the last 32 years, remained behind on that start line.

Chapter 4

PAIN AND PASSING LIGHTS

Once we arrived at the hospital, Meredith was naturally distraught and extremely upset, having been there for three hours already awaiting my arrival. I could see that her eyes were red and her cheeks were stained with tears as her face came into view, peering over me. She was scared, there was so much uncertainty and the full extent of my injuries was not yet known. She held my hand and I squeezed it three times.

'Whatever we have to deal with, it's going to be OK! I can handle this, don't worry.'

I didn't know if I could handle it and I was worried. I'm sure Meredith knew this, but it was what she needed to hear and I made sure for her sake to be as positive and strong as I possibly could be.

MEREDITH:

There were so many problems with getting a helicopter and ambulance for Joey that I reached the hospital nearly three hours before he did. My parents arrived an hour later, my mom hugged me tightly and promised that I wouldn't be alone for a single minute and that they would both be with me for however long I needed them. My dad also hugged me and through his tears told me it would all be OK. He's very British and I had only seen him cry twice before. Once when he watched the Hillsborough Stadium disaster live in 1989, and then again when my mother was diagnosed with breast cancer in 1999. We were all then taken to a private 'trauma' waiting area where Brad and I filled them both in on the few details we knew.

It seemed for ever until Joey finally arrived and was admitted into the high care trauma unit. I wanted to see him so badly, but when I did it became all too real. Joey was competitive and always played rough, and so has had his fair share of scrapes and bruises along the way, but this was different. He was positive and calm, saying all the right things but I knew this was no ordinary bike crash.

I was still in my riding kit, covered in dust, my lips blood-stained. My movement was limited to my face and fingers as my arms were strapped next to my sides and I was unable to turn my head strapped firmly in the headgear. I heard familiar voices as our parents arrived along with my brother Mike and his wife Dee. Their faces appeared into my view of the ceiling, one at a time from different directions. The seriousness of the whole ordeal was written across each teary face that came into view. Many X-rays and MRIs followed over the next few hours.

I was heavily sedated and still disorientated from concussion as I faded in and out of consciousness. Even now most of that time is hazy, waking up now and again and taking short glimpses of my surroundings. One lasting memory for me, though, was being wheeled down the corridors, flat on my back, watching the lights on the ceiling pass overhead, totally unable to move or see where I was going. Another memory was being woken up by the rhythmic grunts of the MRI machine, the tunnel's roof just centimetres from my face. I was still in serious pain and it felt like a coffin. I wanted out! My breathing quickened and my heart was racing. I fought the panic, knowing I needed just to lie still; if there was ever a time to be tough, it was then. I was seen by several specialists whose main concerns were about possible brain and spinal cord injury. I recall the moment they gathered my family around as we were told the spinal cord injury appeared to be 'complete' and I would never walk again. It was all a bit confusing and too much to try to take in at the time.

MEREDITH:

Listening to the doctor telling us that Joey wouldn't walk again was unbearable. I felt the blood drain from my face and I started to shake. My mom could see I was about to break down and put her arm around me and took me for a walk down the hospital corridor. She ushered me to a chair and I sat with my head in my hands and spewed out all the questions going through my mind, ending with 'It's just all too much Mom, how can I cope with all of this?' My mom then gave me some of the best advice I've ever received. She told me that looking at it all right now, it would seem too much to take on, but I should try to take it one day at a time, and if that was too much to handle then take it a morning, afternoon or evening at a time, and if that was too much then an hour at a time. It was exactly what I needed to hear and helped calm my fears that day and for many more days still to come.

Within a few hours Joey was transferred to Wilgeheuwel Hospital, which was closer to our home.

The next day was Kayla's eighth birthday. I had only left the hospital at 2am and had stayed over at my parents' house so I wouldn't disturb our girls, Kayla (8), Jenna (6), Tyra (4) and Shawna (3). I got home at 5am before they woke up. I psyched myself up to try to explain to them what had happened to their dad, being careful not to give too many details that I myself wasn't sure about yet. They handled it amazingly well for such little girls.

We had decided that when our girls turned eight we would buy them a 'big girl's bike'. Joey was adamant that this would not be a pink girlie bike with tassels and a basket but instead a decked-out BMX. When I gave Kayla her red and black bike she told me she couldn't wait to 'ride bikes' with Dad. It broke my heart knowing that Joey might never be able to do this with our girls.

Joey was transferred again, this time to the spinal unit at Muelmed Hospital in Pretoria, about an hour's drive from our home. It was a much older hospital and my heart sank, tears falling silently down my cheeks. Seeing Joey in the spinal rehab centre was very upsetting; the reality of it all was very much in your face, so many people in wheelchairs, but we both knew that this was where Joey needed to be as they offered the best care for his injuries.

Within the first few hours of being at the spinal unit I met the head physiotherapist Melanie, the occupational therapist, the orthopaedic surgeon, and an in-house psychologist. They seemed really geared for my type of injury and we started getting real answers to all our questions, big and small.

I had head trauma with severe swelling and twelve broken teeth, amongst various other smaller injuries. I had broken the T8 and T9 thoracic vertebrae in my back and they had become separated from the ribs, crushing my spinal cord and leaving me completely paralysed from just below the chest. The surgeon was more 'straight out' than the previous doctors and told it like it was, which I appreciated. I couldn't accept it, though; there was no way I wouldn't walk again. I didn't get angry or upset; I just simply didn't believe it. The stark reality was too much to face. I think it's called denial.

A few days later – after more X-rays and MRIs – the surgeon suggested that we fuse my T8 and T9 vertebrae to stabilise my back in an attempt to relieve pressure on my spinal cord. This was a big decision to make, as a doctor at the first hospital had recommended that we leave the area alone to avoid further damage. It was about the same time that we discovered my injury was in fact 'incomplete', meaning I had a small chance of some partial recovery. I had a small 'flicker' in the big toe of my right foot, which gave us some sort of hope. If I focused hard I could make it twitch ever so slightly.

The surgeon left the decision regarding the operation to us; there was no easy answer, both options held huge risks. His opinion at the time was that if the operation was successful, I would have at best a ten per cent chance of walking again. Even then, I would probably walk badly and with serious difficulty. Ten per cent was a very small chance, but it was a chance none the less and that's all I needed.

'You don't know me!' I thought. I was determined to beat the odds.

Having the operation was a massive, life-changing decision. I wanted to take the chance in the hope that the fusion would offer the best long-term possibilities, but it was a decision that would affect the rest of my and my family's life. Meredith was still unsure and we discussed it back and forth, but in the end I decided to go for it and she backed my decision. The operation was booked for early the next day. But it turned out to be one of those days where it kept getting moved later and later in the day because of other emergencies.

That didn't help much with the nerves and the constant wondering whether we were doing the right thing. It was well after lunchtime before they were ready for me. I didn't have too much to lose, but it was still incredibly scary being wheeled into the theatre, once again on my back and watching the ceiling lights pass by. Lying there alone, waiting for the anaesthetist, thoughts raced through my head. I've heard about people saying how their life flashed before their eyes and that's exactly what happened to me. I thought about my life, the places I had been, the things I had done, the people who loved me and those I loved. I felt calm and peaceful. It all seems a bit crazy looking back now, but I knew that if it was my time to go, it was OK. Make no mistake, I definitely did not want to die! I had my beautiful family and so much to live for, but if I had to go, I was ready.

My mind was calm and clear as the mask was put over my nose and mouth and I started counting down: 10, 9, 8, 7…

What seemed like seconds later, I woke up after the surgery. In reality, it had taken more than five hours for me to come round. Something wasn't right and I was in the worst pain I could ever have imagined. It felt as though a heated blade was being twisted in my back, intense and unyielding. I had a morphine button that I pressed like a Nintendo game, but it seemed to make no difference. I had never felt relentless pain like this. When the doctor came to check on me, I could tell he was upset with the nursing staff who appeared not to have followed his instructions. He ensured that I was given the necessary medication, after which (although I was still in excruciating pain) Meredith and her parents were allowed in. I tried to be as brave as I could, telling Meredith I was fine, but the pain was overwhelming.

Meredith, knowing me well and seeing me like this, was visibly upset. We were both teetering on the absolute limit of what we could handle. It was late in the evening by now, I had to be transferred and Meredith needed to go. She kissed me goodbye, trying to be brave herself. I knew she would fall to pieces the moment she left the room and felt comforted she had her parents with her. But I wished I could be by her side. I was pushed down corridors again, staring at those ceiling lights, and was left alone in the ICU ward. It was a long and difficult night for both of us.

MEREDITH:

Seeing Joey in absolute agony after his operation, hooked up to so many beeping machines, and with pipes coming out of his neck, back and arms terrified me and I worried that we had made the wrong decision. I didn't want to leave Joey in the state he was in but we weren't given a choice and were ushered out by the nursing staff. I was told that night that Joey would be in ICU for four days and I was close to collapsing. It had been six nights since the accident and I'd not slept or eaten much in that time so that night I made a concerted effort to try to eat something and get some sleep.

I couldn't get to the ICU fast enough the following morning. I felt sick to my stomach when I arrived and found that Joey wasn't in the ICU ward. I immediately panicked, thinking the worst. The nursing shifts had changed since the night before and we waited for what seemed like an eternity for information – only to find out that he had already been transferred back to the ward because he was recovering so well!

Melanie was with me and she meant business. She had me lying flat in bed, wearing a brace that covered my torso and exercising with dumb-bells in both hands. If I was going to spend my life in a wheel-chair she was going to make sure I kept all my upper body strength. In her mind, there was no time to sit around and feel sorry for myself. She was right.

The flicker in my toe had completely disappeared and with it the glimmer of hope we were clinging to. My legs were now really wasting away; they were so skinny, the bones in my shins stood proud as the little bit of flesh attached to them hung like saggy bags of water. My quads were just about gone and my bum was completely flat. I looked down on a body I couldn't feel or even recognise. The person I was in my mind didn't match the body I was looking at. It was terrifying.

Chapter 5

LONG DAYS AND LONGER NIGHTS

The nights were difficult because every couple of hours the nurses would have to come and roll me over on to one side and then on to the other to prevent me from getting pressure sores. They checked my body daily to make sure that if any had started they were treated in time. An untreated pressure sore was a common cause of death among people with spinal cord injuries.

One of the biggest challenges that haunted me almost every night was the way I dreamed – the way I always had … I was able bodied and strong. I could run and jump, play sports, hike, play with my kids and ride my bike. I was racing through Lesotho, crossing the rivers and climbing mountain passes. Other times I was riding on a Saturday with my buds, racing one another as we flew through the bushveld. But each morning, and often during the night, I woke to the grim reality of my situation, reliving the torment over and over again. It seemed to grind me down each time it happened. I was doing my best to stay positive, but at times I was pushed to my limits. The doctor prescribed sleeping tablets that I took each evening and that helped me get through those very long nights.

I experienced many challenges during my time in the hospital. The bed baths were especially difficult in the beginning. The first week I was there, an older Afrikaans lady was on shift. She came around with a bowl of warm water and face cloth and washed me down from head to toe. I lay there naked, feeling very uncomfortable – especially when she cleaned around the catheter and the family jewels! It was tough, but it was what it was and I just had to deal with it.

The next week the shifts changed and things stepped up a bit. This time the job belonged to a 22-year-old African guy. The fact that he was a guy just seemed to make it worse! The first couple of days with him were something I just suffered through, escaping to the happy place in my mind, distancing myself from the unpleasant situation. But as the week progressed, we began to chat and I learned that he had a young family and was working his way through college, training to eventually become a nurse. I developed a new-found respect for him, learning that often some things just have to be done and there was no use in overthinking it all – just get on with it!

I had what felt like a band around me at the point of my injury where my skin was painful, sensitive to the touch and felt sunburnt. I wasn't digesting food, which meant I hadn't had a bowel movement for 12 days. I was bloated and in even more pain. To try to ease this, the nurses needed to insert a tube up my nose which went down into my stomach. They covered the tube in K-Y Jelly and pushed it up my nose, telling me to keep swallowing, and because I kept gagging and coughing with watery eyes and a burning throat, it took many attempts before we managed to get it all the way in. It stayed in for several days helping to drain my stomach. It was so uncomfortable and it made my throat raw. I lay there frustrated, unable to move, and sucking on cough sweets to try to ease the pain and discomfort.

I was also prescribed painkillers for the daytime, which I took three times a day to try to numb the constant pain in my back. They helped a little, but the pain was always there for 24 hours, seven days a week. The pain eroded my resolve to stay positive. I had never really understood suicide. I had heard of people taking their own lives and had always thought it came down to cowardice. Although I never seriously considered it myself, I now 'got it'. For the first time in my life, I knew how it felt to have no hope for the future, the sure knowledge that my life would be unbearable for ever without any hope of change. I got it; I really, really got it. I would never judge anyone ever again for doing that. I desperately clung on to the positive, focusing on Meredith and my daughters. I didn't have the option of quitting; I had way too much to live for. Pushed forward by my family and friends, I knew I could endure whatever I needed to face.

It was a few days after the operation when the flicker in my toe came back. If I really focused, my right big toe would move. Just a little, but it moved. (Almost like some kind of Jedi mind trick!) Once again, we were thrown a morsel of hope.

The swelling in my head had also started to subside and the MRIs indicated that I would have no permanent damage. (My wife has often specified that they never said I was fine, just that I was the same as I was before the accident.)

About a week after the operation Melanie took me down to the gym area, lying flat on my hospital bed which she parked next to a long thin table. I was carefully slid off my bed and onto the table. She then proceeded to lift up each of the thick straps and strap me down to the table, which to me resembled some kind of medieval torture device. It had me looking around for a guy with a big battleaxe and a black sack over his head with the eyes cut out.

The apparatus was a tilt table and its purpose was to slowly move me into a vertical position so that I could then move on to sitting in a wheelchair. We started with me flat on my back, then she slowly started to rotate the table bit by bit towards an upright position. After the first few degrees she stopped the rotation. Without the muscles contracting in my legs to maintain the pressure, the blood just rushed from my head. I felt nauseous and the room spun around me as I nearly passed out. Then once I had recovered enough, she moved it another few degrees and the room spun again as my head went warm, just like it does before you faint. The process played out several more times, until eventually I was standing – strapped to a board with my feet just off the ground, but standing none the less.

Meredith was there, just as she had been every day from the beginning. She came up to me and put her face, wet with tears, on my chest and hugged me. My own tears rolled off my face and on to her head held firmly against me. In that moment, we knew that whatever happened it would be OK; we were a team, no matter what.

'We've got this,' I whispered. It would become our team motto for many years to come. I had promised her that I would beat this and that everything would be OK. I meant it and put everything I had into my recovery.

I was then transferred into a wheelchair, but without my core muscles I struggled to remain in a sitting position. I kept falling forward, putting my arms against my knees to stop me from falling out of the chair.

I hadn't seen my daughters since before the accident and that had been quite a while. The four of them were still very young, their ages ranging between three and eight. The tube was out of my face and I was at least looking a bit more normal, despite my broken teeth and swollen cone head. I was so excited about seeing them, yet concerned about how they would react to me in the wheelchair. It turned out that for the most part the wheelchair didn't concern them, but it was still a very difficult day because I couldn't pick them up. Even giving them a hug was challenging in the wheelchair.

I unsuccessfully fought back the tears while family members kept them busy playing to distract them from the miserable situation. Jenna, my second oldest, felt there was something wrong because she was clearly concerned and I could tell she knew that this was serious. I decided I wouldn't cry in front of them again. I kept that promise, making sure that if I had my moments of weakness it would never be in front of them.

Looking back now, I don't know whether or not that was a good decision. That same week Errol Dalton came to visit and to pray for my recovery along with some friends from his church group. The only time my children saw me cry again in the next ten years was five years later in July 2012 when Errol died.

Things got really tough from there on and every day was a fight to stay positive and 'keep it together'. But, as I said, I had decided that this was not going to beat me. I would work as hard as I possibly could to recover and walk again. I received so much support from Meredith, my family and friends. Everyone kept pushing me to keep going, rallying around me, praying for me and always full of encouragement. I had visitors every day, for most of the day, week after week; family, friends, people from church, fellow riders and guys from the biking community. I was in for the fight of my life. I knew it would be tough but I had no idea of the challenges that lay ahead of me, my wife and my four young daughters.

A few weeks afterwards, I lay alone in the hospital bed one night and thought about my dream to race in the Dakar Rally and how awesome it would be to come back from my injuries to achieve it. It made me smile, lifting the heavy burden for just a short moment. That would be truly incredible! To my mind it would be the greatest comeback since Lazarus! I had grown up on movies like *The Shawshank Redemption* and *Die Hard*. Nothing beats a great comeback. But this was real life and this time round, it seemed well and truly too impossible even to contemplate. Still, I would allow myself to dream, my body may have been paralysed but my mind was free.

The 2007 Rugby World Cup was being played while I was in the hospital. The final between England and South Africa was about to start and Meredith had bought me a Springbok shirt to wear. I lay there flat in bed, wearing my green and gold shirt, with Meredith and her parents, excitedly watching the game in the hospital room. The final whistle eventually sounded and South Africa had beaten England 15-6. We were the new world champions. The hospital was in the centre of Pretoria – one of the rugby capitals of the world – and the streets erupted! Fireworks, car horns and shouting filled the air. I wanted to join them, but I couldn't even walk over to the window to look out. I thought about my buddies at braais cheering and high-fiving one another. I felt the path of self-pity opening up again, ready to welcome me, but I fought the desire to take it and just enjoyed the moment for what it was.

The six weeks I spent in hospital were difficult for everyone. Each family member helped where they could; Meredith's parents made the one-hour drive to the hospital almost every day, making it easy for Meredith to be with me. Meredith's unconditional support and encouragement every day made a huge difference. Her mom would bring me the fresh fruit that I craved (and sneak in fast food from time to time), as well as rub my feet and make sure my clothes were always washed.

Each morning Meredith's sister Melissa collected the children and took them to school. Then either Melissa or Verity, another of Meredith's sisters, picked them up again in the afternoon and looked after them until my sister Julie arrived home from work. Julie then took over, bathing the children and tucking them in each night. My brother Mike, who worked with me in my small business, took over things at work, often working late into the night and through the weekend to keep up with it all. Brad took care of all the hospital and medical aid paperwork. My buddies Brodwyn and Tristam sorted out my insurance claims and other friends brought round meals for the family. Every detail was taken care of, down to the four little school lunches that were freshly prepared each day.

My parents visited me several times, always offering their own words of encouragement. My mom constantly reminded me that I had always been a survivor and that I was not a quitter. It was something that she had said to me many times since I was young. Many other riders I had raced with came to visit me to offer their support. Friends and family seemed to form an endless queue outside the ward door to help wherever they could. Their support made it impossible to quit. I wish I could name everyone who helped; it would fill all the pages of this book! What I can say is that as difficult as this time was in our lives, the help exceeded our needs. We were blessed with more help than we could ever have needed or asked for.

After the first couple of weeks I think I lost all inhibitions. I could no longer let it all bother me. I had no bowel control, I had a transparent bag of yellow urine constantly strapped to my calf and had all sorts of tests done which involved sticking things up and into every opening in my body – places that up until then I had firmly believed to be 'exit only'. But there was no time to be a wuss about it. I just had to man up and deal with it.

Chapter 6

A NEW LINE OF SIGHT

Over the next few weeks, I gained slight movement in my left ankle and later on I started to feel something slight in my quads. We all cautiously allowed ourselves to hope for a miracle. Each small improvement spurred me on and I became even more driven in my resolve to walk again. I was impatient though and wanted it all just to be right again, but it wasn't to be that easy. It would be a battle in which I would need to fight for every inch of advancement and earn each small victory.

Every day in physiotherapy I got to see other patients. At first they were just handicapped people in wheelchairs – some with brain injuries who would just sit staring into space, unaware of the rest of us around them; others with various levels of spinal injuries caused either by trauma or disease. Like me, most of them had catheter bags strapped to their legs and you could see the nappies and underpants liners sticking out the top of their shorts, just like mine.

In the beginning, they were just a part of society that I didn't belong to. I didn't look down on them or anything like that, it was just that they were different from me. I wasn't part of their group. I had participated in community service projects many times in my life, visiting hospitals and care centres as a volunteer. In Durban, I used to go to a special care unit once a week and play chess with a Muslim guy named Rozaak. He couldn't talk or pick up the pieces, but his brain was perfect. He appreciated the visits and I enjoyed my time with him. He would point awkwardly at the pieces with his clenched, shaking hand and I would move them for him. We got along well and he laughed when I pretended to pick up the wrong piece when he had a good move. Looking back, I wish I had had the ability to see him as the person he was without the disability, not just the man who sat before me unable to move his own chess pieces. It made me see him as different from me, but ten years later I sat in that gym

28

and realised that I was part of that 'other' group now – but, more importantly, that we had all been part of the same group all along.

The spinal cord injury patients were in the hospital for a number of reasons – diving into shallow water, falling from a horse, a car accident, AIDS, a tumour, slipping on wet tiles, being shot, getting stabbed, falling from a roof and a whole number of work-related accidents. I realised how easily an injury could change your life. Many of them were avoidable. The work environment seemed almost more dangerous than dirt bikes. I knew which one I wanted to avoid!

The daily physiotherapy continued at the hospital, where I would be helped onto a plinth and Melanie would move my joints to keep them mobile and to stretch out my muscles. I would have to work on the slight movement I was capable of in order to get stronger. She would sometimes tap my skinny legs rapidly to make them spasm a little to achieve the movement we were looking for. With agonising frustration, I stared down at my legs, my teeth gritted and sweat beading on my forehead as I tried to move them just a little. After each physio session, my shirt was soaked through with sweat but my shorts and socks were bone dry because I was unable to sweat anywhere below my injury line. I fought each day against the physical and psychological pain.

At night I lay in bed, unable to move my legs under the covers, but I could lightly flex what little quads I had left. I wasn't quite able to move my leg yet, but I could feel it and I needed it to get stronger. I would tighten and release, tighten and release, counting out reps while lying there in the dark, desperately praying for a miracle. They became fatigued and stopped flexing, but after a few minutes' recovery I would start my reps again.

I shared a room with other patients while I was in the hospital. In the beginning, I shared with an older Afrikaans guy who had fallen two storeys through a skylight. He had many broken bones but he had arrived a while before me and was coming towards the end of his treatment. Once he had left, I shared with a younger guy who was paralysed as a complication of AIDS and was close to the end of his life. He kept saying that his hands were sore and he needed gloves. I got Meredith to bring him a pair of my racing gloves as I didn't need them any more. He was very grateful. You could tell there was nothing they could do for him yet they still had one of his relatives there training to be his assistant once he got home, just like some of the other patients. This kept him positive and gave him hope, which was the right thing to do in my opinion, but at the back of my mind

I kept wondering whether my situation was worse than they were telling me …

I'm the kind of guy who wants the bad news straight out, don't sugar-coat it. Give me the whole deal right on the chin. Each time I asked how much I would recover and how long it would take, it seemed that no one would give me a straight answer. I wanted to know in days and weeks exactly how long until I could expect to be fully recovered and as I was before. Looking back now, I realise they couldn't tell me because they didn't have a clue – how could they have known?

Each incomplete spinal cord injury is different and how much each person recovers in terms of time and amount differs just as much. This made it very difficult to endure. It reminded me of when I was a kid and my brothers and I would compete with each other, counting how many laps of the pool we could swim underwater with one breath. If you swam first, you didn't know how far you had to swim to win. Swimming last was easy, the goal was set and all you had to do was swim the set distance and you were done. One thing I had been told, and I finally understood it as I lay there, was that the progress would be incredibly slow. Units of weeks and days were wrong – I needed to measure in years.

After being in hospital and indoors for several weeks, I was taken outside in a wheelchair for the first time. I was wheeled past the staring faces in the hospital reception and out the main entrance. Feeling the warm summer sun on my skin and being outside had never felt so good. Outdoors just felt incredible. I teared up, filled with gratitude and emotion. Later, Meredith told me she thought it was because of the realisation that I was wheelchair bound – but they were tears of joy … I was alive! I was still here and even more determined to recover. I wanted to walk in the sun again, go places and do the things I used to. I wanted my freedom!

My occupational therapist's job was to teach me how to function as a paraplegic in the real world. She started off teaching me how to roll over in bed, something that seemed so basic, but it took me a while to master. I practised throwing my arms across my body creating the momentum for my legs to follow. Then she taught me to transfer out of bed into the wheelchair and back again using a short plank of wood they called a transfer board. Then she taught me how to transfer on and off the toilet. Not that it helped much at the time, as I had no bowel control. Nature didn't call, it just rocked up. My digestion wasn't working properly and I was prescribed some pretty serious laxatives to help it along. They tried to get me into a routine, but it was a dismal failure. Let me tell you, trying to balance laxatives with zero bowel control is not a fun game! Throw some painkillers and sleeping tablets into the mix and you have a recipe for disaster.

Some days were harder than others. The lack of bowel control was very embarrassing, sometimes happening in the middle of physio sessions or when I had visitors. Getting dressed each day was difficult and needed to be done by the nurses. I could feel the pressure of touch, so if my shorts were a bit twisted or my shirt bunched up, it bothered me, but there was little I could do about it. The shoes bugged me the most. Wearing the brace and without core muscles, I couldn't reach my feet so I had to rely on the nurses. They forced the shoes on, bunched the toes of my socks up, forgot to pull the tongue out, or tightened the laces too much. I asked them to fix things the first few times, but after a while it seemed better just to try to ignore it. One day my good mate Clint arrived just before a physio session and offered to put my tackies on for me. He did it perfectly, pulling the tongue out and tying the laces just right. I wished he could gather the nurses around and show them how it was done.

My occupational therapist also took me down to the hospital basement, where we practised wheelchair skills with basketballs, learning to hold the ball against the wheel using its revolution to lift the ball up. We would also crank out laps around the concrete pillars in the car park. To be honest, I loved this stuff! I liked training down in the damp dark car park basement, it felt like a Rocky movie, training in the dark and dingy downtown gym. Throw in the *Eye of the Tiger* track and it was a perfect match. I was a fighter on the comeback trail.

When I was in my early teens I had a buddy called Darron who had a rare condition that had him spending weeks at a time in the Joburg General Hospital. He wasn't sickly most of the time he was there, so when my other bud Sheldon and I visited him, we would race the hospital wheelchairs and practise our wheelies. My therapist was most impressed when I wheelied the chair on the first day! Over the next few weeks, I learned to wheelie my chair down steep ramps and wheelie around in circles. I even asked her if it was possible to go down stairs. Her reply was 'It's easy to go down stairs in a wheelchair – the hard part is getting back into it at the bottom!' She had a great sense of humour and spoke frankly about the challenges I would be facing, giving brilliant advice on how to handle them.

One of my first real encounters with how people perceived those with disabilities came one morning as I was on my way to the basement. I was alone in my wheelchair after leaving the ward on the second floor. I pressed the button for the lift which arrived shortly afterwards. The doors slid open and I rolled in, joining a woman already inside. The doors closed and she looked at me and asked very slowly, over-pronouncing each word, 'Which, floor, are, you, going, to?' 'The basement,' I replied, unsure why she was speaking like that. I'm sure she felt a little sheepish at the ease of my response because she hurried out of the lift at the next stop. I couldn't really blame her, though; a few weeks before I myself had no idea what a spinal cord injury was.

One of the biggest frustrations was the lack of information about my injury. I found much information about complete spinal cord injuries, but very little on incomplete injuries. What I did learn was that a year was often considered your cap – what you had achieved by then was probably as good as it was going to get. I spent each day hoping for some improvement, no matter how small, knowing that the days were slowly ticking away.

As the days passed and the physio continued, Melanie put strong plastic back slabs on my legs that went down into my shoes and under my feet. Then the Velcro straps were tightened to hold my legs firmly against them, keeping them locked in a straight position. I learned to stand between the parallel bars with my weight pressing down on my arms, shifting slowly from side to side and allowing my legs to drag ahead of me one at a time in a walking fashion. My legs now started getting stronger, but my hip flexors that brought my legs forward were just not coming back. We continued to work the muscles that we could, but progress was glacially slow.

I had been using the hospital's wheelchairs up to that point, but with the knowledge now that I would need my own I went to have one fitted properly and to choose the colours that I wanted. It was an experience that would change my life. I arrived at CE Mobility and rolled my way in. I sat there waiting for the therapist and started chatting to another guy who was being fitted for his third chair. As it turned out, he had had the same physio as I did a couple of years before me. We chatted for a while then he went back to his vehicle in his chair and was driven away.

I was fitted for mine and, being a biker, I made sure I at least got some cool rims on it! Then we went back to the hospital and I told my physiotherapist about this guy who I had met who had been a patient of hers a couple of years before. She remembered him and asked how he was walking. I told her he wasn't and that he had said that it was just easier in the chair, so he didn't bother trying to move around with the crutches any more. She was upset and said he was one of those guys who possibly could have walked but didn't put in much effort. I was shocked and decided that day that I would make sure nobody would ever be able to say that about me. I promised Meredith again that I would do everything in my power to walk again and recover, no matter what. I was more than ever determined to beat this.

After a few weeks, they said my indwelling catheter could come out and I would finally be rid of the bag of urine strapped to my leg that had been my constant companion since my arrival there. I hated it when people visited and saw me smiling with my shattered front teeth and my skinny, dry legs – not good enough to walk on, but decorated none the less with a bright yellow bag of urine.

I had now graduated to the self-catheter class, not that I knew what that meant. On a day I will never forget, the nurse removed the catheter and bag and then proceeded to explain what I needed to do in future. She pulled out a 30 centimetre long silicone tube which was nearly the width of a pencil, explained to me how to wash it, lube it and push it up my man sausage ...

'Er, push it where?' I exclaimed, hoping I had heard wrong.

My eyes were wide open and my jaw was on the floor. Nope, turned out I had heard her correctly – but wait, it gets better! Because I couldn't feel when my bladder was full, I would need to do it every three hours, day and night.

'On the odd occasion there might be a little blood, but if it happens more than a couple times, let us know,' she told me.

'Hell, yeah, I'll let you know!' I thought. I figured my screams would be notification enough.

Oh, and just for fun, I needed to empty the urine into a measuring jug and write down the quantity. I couldn't believe it at first, but I was committed to this recovery whatever it took. I asked for how many days I needed to do this. The nurse was quiet at first, seeing from my bleak face that this was a big ask. I asked again and she replied, 'Probably for the rest of your life.'

As I said earlier, if I had known everything that lay ahead of me when I was lying there in the dirt after I had broken my back, it would have been too much to handle. This was one of those things that would have tipped the scales for me ...

The only thing I must admit enjoying was telling my buddies and showing them the catheter pipe when they came to visit. Explaining what I had to do and watching them shudder while protecting their crotches, wearing the same expressions on their faces that I probably had when I was told.

The first time I needed to use it took for ever! I tried several times but it wouldn't go all the way into my bladder and the nurse tried too without success. Eventually, it took a couple hours before we got it right. I thought after that ordeal that if it needed doing every three hours, I would spend the rest of my life trying to get that damn tube in and out of me. I look back now, nearly ten years later and it's become easy, taking just a few seconds – even in the dark. I reckon I could even throw it up in the air and get it straight in! OK, not quite.

After being in hospital for more than a month, everything started to bother me. I hated many of the decisions being made for me. I have always been independent and having to rely on people was very difficult. One day, the guy who had AIDS with whom I shared the room soiled himself. It wasn't an uncommon thing and it had happened to me a number of times, but being trapped in the same small room, unable to leave, seemed so frustrating.

I also felt dirty all the time. I couldn't shave my head properly in the wheelchair as I used to do in the shower and lying in bed a lot of the time just felt gross. Out of sheer frustration, I went into the shower with my wheelchair and transferred onto the tiled seat with the hand shower and taps within reach. I managed after some time to get undressed, having taken my shoes off earlier, and placed my clothes on my wheelchair. I then pushed it out of the shower and used the hand shower to shower myself.

It was very difficult and I needed to be extra careful because I couldn't feel the temperature of the water below my injury, but I felt a lot better. That is, until I was finished and realised I couldn't move. I sat there on the tiled seat, getting colder by the minute, looking at my wheelchair only a couple of metres away but unable to reach it. I really hadn't thought this through and now I was stranded. I called out to the nurses as loudly as I could but they couldn't hear me through the closed door. I sat there shivering, holding my core up with my arms for about an hour before I was discovered and helped back into my chair.

There were two other therapists who visited me during my stay in the hospital. The first was the psychologist who had chatted to me a couple of times in the beginning. I'm a pretty positive guy and had a lot of support, so she didn't spend much time with me. Other patients never had visitors and even I could see them quickly heading downhill mentally. You could tell the hospital staff were the only people invested in them.

The other was a sex therapist. Yep, that's what it said on his badge. He joked how his teenage daughter would make him take it off when they were out in public together. In the beginning, I thought, 'Why is this oke talking to me?' I'm all good, ask Meredith! Later, we discovered that there were complications. To be perfectly frank, I could get an erection as per normal, but without proper sensation I would never climax. Sounds like the perfect problem to have for your spouse, but it was incredibly frustrating and psychologically very difficult for me to deal with. I know it sounds stupid, but in a way I felt less of a man. Fortunately, it was one of the things that did recover with time, more than a year later. The night it happened, I distinctly remember seeing fireworks and hearing choruses of angels.

After six weeks in hospital, I was told I could go home in a few days' time. My daughters had struggled with all the changes and one of my good friends, Arthur, made them a puzzle with the number of pieces matching the number of days until I could come home. Each day the girls would add a piece to the puzzle and share the treat that was taped to the piece. It was a small thing to do, but it was big to us and one of the many things people did to lighten the load.

I went home, now in my own wheelchair, to find wooden ramps had been put up in my house by Mike and Brad in order to help me get around. Seeing those ramps was a very 'in-your-face' realisation that life was going to be very different from now on.

Chapter 7

ROCK BOTTOM

MEREDITH:

Having had four children within the space of five years meant that taking care of them was a real challenge at times, and so all our married life Joey and I had tag-teamed each other. I can see when Joey is about to 'lose' it, and he can see when I am, and so we would step in and take over the situation at hand.

There are many positives to having our children all so close together in age, but one of the negatives has got to be that when one got sick, generally the other three would follow suit. Joey has always been the 'vomit cleaner-upper' in our home, because I am so compassionate that if I see someone throw up I tend to join in too.

A stomach bug hit our home soon after Joey was back from hospital and the girls took turns getting sick. The night Shawna, our youngest, had her turn was particularly difficult as it hit the tiled floor and went everywhere. I started to 'lose' it very quickly, lack of sleep and worry can do that to a girl. I cleaned Shawna and put her back to bed and, biting my lip to stop myself from crying, I went to clean the passage floors and walls. Seeing me upset, Joey had got into his wheelchair and came wheeling through holding a cloth to try to help me clean up the mess. This just resulted in him wheeling through the vomit, creating more mess on the floor and a wheelchair that now needed hosing down. The thought of smashing his teeth in again flashed through my mind – no, not really, he was just trying to help me as he'd done countless times before the accident and I could see he was as frustrated as I was. We somehow got through the night but a couple of nights later he too would get the bug.

I had been home for just over a week when I hit rock bottom. I woke up in the middle of the night, and I felt as if I was about to vomit. Meredith rushed to get me a bowl, but the lights weren't working and the smell of burning suddenly filled the house. The main electrical board had a hot connection and had caught alight, burning most of the switches and leaving us in darkness. Luckily, nothing else had caught alight.

Before the accident I could easily have bypassed it and made a plan for the night, but the board was at head height and there was nothing I could do. Meredith gave me the bowl, but this was an attack at both ends for me. She grabbed my wheelchair and we struggled to get me in it while vomiting and holding the bowl. Eventually we got to the bathroom where I transferred onto the toilet with seconds to spare. I still couldn't sit up properly on my own because of my weak core muscles, so I leaned forward against the back of my wheelchair with the bowl on my lap while sitting on the white throne.

Another of the injury complications was terrible haemorrhoids. Some of the children had woken up crying and Meredith was desperately trying to get them back to sleep. There I was, at two in the morning, unable to sit properly on the toilet with bleeding haemorrhoids, and diarrhoea just trickling out – my body lacked the ability even to push it out properly – vomiting into a bowl while leaning against the back of my wheelchair in the darkness, the smell of burnt wiring in the air and my children's crying in the background. Without any muscles on my bum and thighs, the toilet seat was hard against my bones. I remember smiling briefly at the time, thinking how this was stuff you couldn't make up! This had to be rock bottom! If I survived this night from hell, then it could only get better.

Derek who, along with Tristam, had brought all my stuff and my bike back from the race the day I crashed, came round in the morning. He had struggled to visit me in the hospital in the first week, finding that witnessing the whole incident was really traumatic. He's an electrician and he spent that morning sorting out the DB box, replacing the burnt switches and wiring, all at no charge.

The next year, 2008, was by far the most difficult year of my life. My body from my chest downwards wasted away completely and my skin hung loosely from my bones. I could feel touch, but not any hot or cold or pain sensation on the skin below the injury. My feet and legs constantly felt as if I had pins and needles and I still had the wide band around my torso where the skin felt burnt and hypersensitive. I had constant pain in my back, still had no proper bowel and bladder function, making daily life very difficult for me and my family. My body didn't sweat below the injury and my legs would often spasm, bouncing around and making it difficult to use what basic functions I had. I struggled to digest food, playing the ongoing game of chance, trying to balance laxatives and diet.

Then there were the many trips to the dentist for my teeth to be fixed as best as possible. The first time Meredith and I arrived at the dental rooms, the wheelchair ramp was so steep that we struggled to get up it together. Before my accident I hadn't realised how low the gradient needed to be in order to realistically get a wheelchair up a ramp. Then when we got to the top, the wheelchair didn't fit through the doorway. The receptionist ran around trying to find the key for the other door, as we waited in the sun, perched at the top of the ramp. It was a rough day at the dentist.

I have fairly long canines and I had broken all four of my front teeth between them. The dentist who fixed my teeth the first time round, made all four of them the same length as my canines and I looked like a horse. (Meredith, just so you know, cannot be trusted to give you an honest opinion. Worried about hurting my feelings, she kept telling me that they looked great and not to worry so much. The fact that she wouldn't kiss me should have been a dead giveaway!) About a week later I couldn't take it and we went to a different dentist with a photo of me smiling before the accident. She sorted them out and the relief on Meredith's face was apparent. We've laughed about it many times over the years since then. The dentist visits were ongoing, as we did the best repairs we could while keeping within the medical aid's limits.

I realised daily how little society accommodates for people with disabilities. Everything seemed to be a battle, from narrow parking bays to the steepness of ramps and paraplegic toilets where the seat wouldn't stay up or the toilet door didn't close once a wheelchair was inside. The everyday world is a challenging place for people with disabilities. My family and many of my friends noticed this and able-bodied people using parking bays for the disabled were sure to get a mouthful. The support from Meredith, our girls, family and friends never wavered and I persisted with my determination to make a full recovery.

It was still incredibly tough, but things started to get better. I began to get more movement in my legs and was learning to stand without the back slabs. Then, slowly, I went on to start to walk again. I went from walking in parallel bars with back slabs on my legs, to removing the slabs one at a time. Then onto crutches, then to one crutch, although I often ended up in a heap on the ground. When I collapsed, I could hear the sound of my kneecaps colliding into the tiled floor and although I couldn't feel the pain, I knew it should've hurt. The purple bruises that showed up the next day often confirmed it. The improvements were tremendously slow but I had no room to complain. Many of the other patients who I had met during the physio sessions had 'complete' injuries and had made almost no improvement in months. I felt almost guilty about my recovery when I was with them. I certainly felt blessed and had a lot to be grateful for. I was walking badly, but I was walking!

Each day was still a struggle and having people constantly staring at me just added to the weight of the burden. Sometimes I'm sure people just thought I was drunk, tripping on stairs and staggering around. However, I was determined this would not be my fate forever. I would insist on walking through the mall with Meredith and my girls, dragging my feet and losing my balance, but I did not want to be in that wheelchair, despite the fact that it would have been much easier at the time. I always took the stairs, even though they took for ever to climb, often testing my family's patience. There was still daily physiotherapy and so many unforeseen physical complications – stuff that I always took for granted which I couldn't do now. Simple things, like picking up my kids, kicking a ball or driving my car.

I slowly began to understand my new body. My left side was stronger than my right – the opposite of how I had been before. I learned to understand my bowels better and I began to feel when my bladder was full. I would try to measure my physical progress with the reps of a particular exercise I could do, or timing how long it took me to get dressed on my own. They were small things, but they helped me to stay positive and know that, although slow, I was moving forward. It wasn't enough just to move forward physically. I realised early on that it was as important to work on my attitude and positivity. If you're constantly miserable and complaining about your lot in life you make things difficult for everyone around you. Relationships became strained very quickly and people would begin to distance themselves from you. I needed not only to endure, but to endure with a smile.

I also knew I needed to get off the painkillers and sleeping tablets and that was difficult. I started first with the sleeping tablets, learning to accept the dreams. Over the next year they began to change to match the reality of who I really was. I cut down the painkillers to just one dose at night, eventually getting to the point where I took them only a couple of times a week.

People had many different responses when we met. Some would just hug us and we could feel their love and support without a word being said. Others tried to encourage me. Some were philosophical and some told me about their own injuries, saying that they knew exactly how I felt. One guy said he had a scar on his knee that had no feeling, so he knew how my legs must feel. I just smiled; it was probably the kind of thing I would have said a couple years before. An older lady gave me a brief lecture about 'murdercycles' and how she hoped that I had learned my lesson. She meant well but I wanted to punch her in the face, to be honest, but I smiled and nodded, although I was boiling on the inside. She had no idea where my motorcycle had taken me, the places I had been and the people I had met. My life was rich with experiences and it filled needs I couldn't explain in words. How dare she judge my life based on her life paradigm?

Gary and Lynne Franks from *Enduro World* magazine started a fund which was supported by many bikers and friends and helped to raise money for additional therapy not covered by my medical aid. Many people called to encourage me. Most of the time I was bulletproof and motivated, working like a machine on my recovery. I was optimistic and pumped to succeed and beat this, whatever it took.

I would like to say that's how it always was, but the truth is different. There were times when I would lie in bed at night and just cry; sometimes it all seemed just too much to endure. Meredith was a huge support in getting me through those low times. Sometimes she could no longer handle it either and I would be the one comforting her as she cried, telling her it was all going to be all right. Other times, we would lie in bed holding each other and just cry together. All the stupid things we thought were important before the accident now seemed so trivial. Suddenly we valued our relationship more. Our children seemed more precious and monetary items lost their value.

Meredith took on many of the jobs I had done before. She would carry the heavy bags and drive the car when we were together. When we got home after dark she would make four trips to the car to carry in sleeping little girls. I had always had a tradition with them called the 'Tickle Test'. Everyone who's been a kid knows that if you fake sleep when you got home you will be carried in. I would perform the test. I would whisper in a funny sing-song voice 'I'm gonna tickle you!' If they could keep a straight face they got a free ride to their bedroom, but if they smiled or laughed they failed the test and had to walk in themselves. It didn't really work, as they always insisted on 'do-overs' until they got it right.

Meredith also needed to lock up the house at night and set the alarm. I remember feeling very vulnerable, especially while I was in the wheelchair. I worried constantly about the house being broken into at night or being hijacked. Both had happened to us before. Less than a year earlier I had been held up by four armed men as I had pulled into my driveway and a gun was held to my head as I was forced into the back of the car. On two other occasions, we had some guys try to break into the house while we were asleep. If anything like that happened now, I would be a sitting duck along with the family that I was supposed to protect.

I hated feeling that way. It wasn't me!

Chapter 8

RIDING AGAIN

The first time I rode a bike again happened a bit by chance. It was probably close to two years since the accident. I was with my family pulling up to church one Saturday when I saw my buddy Neal across the road in the veld with a mate he was teaching to ride on an older KX250.

I walked back to him and we chatted about bikes and rides we had done together just a few years back – which now seemed like a lifetime ago. I watched him showing his mate how to pull off, releasing the clutch smoothly and keeping his weight central. It was all the basic stuff that I had learned years ago. It was difficult to watch them, aching to be able to ride again myself.

Over the past couple of years I had heard about the places my friends had ridden and their preparations leading up to the Roof of Africa enduro. It hadn't been easy sitting at the braais with mates and hearing about all the stuff I was missing out on.

Neal joked, 'You should give it a try, Elvis. It's not that hard!' He called me Elvis because of the way my legs went into spasm when they got tired – the kind of comment only a buddy could get away with.

'Cool, let's do it,' I replied, unable to resist the opportunity to throw my leg over a bike again. Neal was a bit taken aback – it wasn't the response he had anticipated. 'Come on, help me get on,' I said quickly, before we both changed our minds. Neal and his buddy held the bike and pushed down on the rear suspension to lower the seat and helped me slowly lift my leg over the bike. (It wasn't exactly the 'throw my leg over a bike' moment that I had anticipated.)

With a little trouble, I was on. I pulled the kick start out with my right hand – as I had done a hundred times before – and pulled on my cargo shorts to help lift my right leg up onto the kick starter to fire it up. But now the difference came in … I found that I couldn't hold the weight of the bike with my left leg and I fell over to the left with the bike on top of me.

Neal did a poor job of stifling his laugh while he picked the bike off me and helped me up. Once again, they helped me back on. This time they were holding tightly on to the bike, looking around to see if Meredith had seen what they were encouraging. It was clear there was no way I could kick-start the bike myself so while I sat on the bike balancing as best I could, Neal gave it a couple of good kicks. The engine burst to life with the familiar two stroke pinging. The two of them held the bike firmly, now well aware of my lack of leg strength.

Neal held the rear mudguard and back wheel between his legs as I clumsily clunked it down into first gear using the heel of my left foot. My knuckles were white as I held tightly on to the bars. Twisting the throttle, I slowly released the clutch and took off. It felt good, really good! I clumsily clicked up the shifter into second gear using my whole leg and twisted the throttle wide open. The hard acceleration made the front wheel lift up off the ground as the bike surged forward pulling on my arms. I rode only about a hundred metres before I turned around and headed back. I knew not to push my luck. I stopped next to the guys who were wide eyed and grinning as they grabbed hold of the bike firmly to keep me up. The surge of adrenalin flooded through my veins making my legs spasm and jump around. No doubt it was a perfect Elvis impersonation in Neal's eyes. The two of them needed to help me off the bike – but I was back on the horse and I wanted more.

The moment I returned Meredith knew by the grin on my face that I had ridden the bike. Together, we had been through hell the last couple of years and she wanted me to recover and do the things I used to just as much as I did. She definitely worried about me getting on a bike again but she knew me well enough to know it was just a matter of time. She smiled at me, shaking her head in disbelief. The thought of being able to ride again flooded through my mind. Suddenly the grey future was wide open, the places I would go and the freedom it would give me made my heart swell. My mind immediately raced towards my Dakar dream, once again I smiled at the vision of lining up at the start of that race, 9000 kilometres of hostile environment spread out ahead of me. The dream was carved into my soul.

'One day,' I thought.

A couple of days later I was at my usual weekly session with my physiotherapist Sharne at the local Virgin Active gym. Over the last few years we had spent countless hours working on my recovery with strength and balance exercises, balancing on bosus, catching balls while standing on one leg, moving up and down steps, core work, walking in the pool with flotation belts – just about every exercise you could imagine.

But this time I had a special request. I asked her to train me to be able to throw my leg over a bike again. With a raised eyebrow, she questioned my request. As a medical professional she knew full well it was against her better judgement to help me ride again. But from our many conversations over the years together, she knew how I felt about riding and the hole in my life now that I was not able to do it any more. She agreed to help me and I explained how I needed to be able to lift my leg and pivot on the other foot. I'm certain it was the first time she had had this request. Luckily, she was not one to shy away from a challenge, so she proceeded to build a 'bike' out of some gym equipment and Reebok aerobic steps stacked up on top of one another. I would practise lifting my leg over it and bringing it back, much to the amusement of the other hard-core guys in the gym. You know the kind of guys who needed to walk closer to their arms. But I didn't care about them. I had stopped worrying long ago about what others thought of my condition. The bottom line now was that I was learning to ride again.

It was more than a year before I was ready to get on a bike and actually go for a ride again. Several years after the spinal cord injury I was walking without any aids but my legs were still not very strong. I borrowed a bike from Brad and Tristam organised a day to ride. We had chosen to ride in Maraisburg, to the west of Johannesburg. The area consisted of veld with paths and the huge sandy mine dumps. I expected a couple of mates to be there, but more than 20 guys showed up for the ride, all there to support and cheer me on.

I was shocked once again by the amount of support I was being given. To be honest, it was daunting. There I was, kitted up in my riding gear last worn several years ago while I was lying in the dirt with a broken back, now about to head out on the trails. I felt physically sick. All the memories of what I had endured over the past few years came flooding back. I started second guessing myself. Was this really brave or just plain stupid? Luckily, my buddies were there to ease the strain: Tristam, Brad and Derek had been there the day I was paralysed. Neal, Andre and Clint were mates from racing with whom I had bantered while setting up the gazebos years earlier. We were all there with a group of other riding buds and I knew they were all rooting for me to succeed. I pushed the doubts to the back of my mind and, using a kerb for some extra height, I climbed on the bike and we finally set off.

Although the ride was slow, it was an unbelievable feeling for me. I couldn't run, or jump, or play any of the sports I had enjoyed before the accident, so to be there riding a dirt bike – flowing along the sand and gravel, moving freely with my mates – was just incredible.

It was such a feeling of freedom! Alone in my helmet I swallowed deeply and felt my eyes well up, knowing that it was truly a miracle to have come what seemed like full circle and be back on the bike again. This was never supposed to happen! I was filled with gratitude.

MEREDITH:

Joey telling me a couple years after the accident that he wanted to buy a bike again was frightening for me to hear. It scared the living daylights out of me, and it wasn't an easy thing for me to wrap my head around. My first instinct was to shout 'HELL NO!' A million 'what ifs' came to mind – surely this was just too crazy even to consider? It wasn't something I would even consider doing if I was in his situation.

So many things that made Joey who he was were taken away from him after the accident. He had always been so active, constantly outdoors and involved in one sport or another, and now he was unable to do the majority of those things. Although I knew agreeing to it would give me many sleepless nights, I totally got that it was what he needed to do. I understood that getting back on a bike again would be the healing for his mind that he so desperately craved.

After that first ride, I knew I wanted to ride again, so I bought a second-hand KTM 250 XCW enduro bike. I had the suspension specially lowered by Hilton Hayward and I cut the foam in the seat down to help my legs reach the ground. That way, I could hold the bike up with my legs which were still quite weak. I continued to ride on the weekends with my mates, no doubt stretching their patience at times on the rocky climbs, where I fell over time and time again. We laughed about how well I was riding, only to fall right over as soon as I stopped and often needing someone to lift the bike off me. Other times, I would need to stop mid-ride and use my catheter to drain my bladder, amongst the usual chirps of 'Are you finished yet?' and 'This isn't a five-day game!' I had to remind them how, when I was able-bodied, I whipped them at the races, just to keep them in their place.

I loved riding again but it wasn't easy being slower than all my mates. Sometimes it was physical and emotional torture. Riders I didn't know would catch up to me on the rocky climbs at De Wildt and their frustration was obvious as I tried to battle my bike out of the way, constantly falling over and dropping it. I felt like an idiot! I wanted to explain that this wasn't really me. I watched them push past, no doubt wondering what this hacker was doing in the mountains. Other times I would find myself at the back of my own group struggling through terrain that would have been relatively easy before. Feelings of self-pity flooded my mind as I compared my feeble efforts with those of the guy I used to be. It took everything I had to fight the constant temptation to walk the dark downward path. If I compared myself with how I was before the accident, it was dreadful, but if I compared where I was now to being completely paralysed in hospital, it was incredible. It was all a matter of perspective.

Without a doubt one of my favourite places was the mountain kingdom of Lesotho, home to the Roof of Africa enduro race. There were a few good places to ride around Johannesburg, but we needed to get out of town for the best terrain. We organised a couple of short trips over the next year, squeezed in between our commitments to family and work, generally trying to be away for no more than 48 hours.

One trip in particular was a pilgrimage that Clint, Neal and I made together. It was 2am on a cold winter morning when we tied our three KTMs down on the trailer and loaded our kitbags into the back of my grey double-cab Toyota bakkie. The usual banter followed, with comments about one another's weight, riding skills, levels of baldness and the condition of the others' bikes. It didn't take long before someone piped up to remind the rest of us how lucky we were to have such a skilled rider accompany us. But before long we were off on the four-hour drive to the border.

The small border post was still quiet and after sharing the only pen we had to fill in the forms, we were granted entry. We drove to a small rather dodgy guest house where we parked the bakkie and offloaded the bikes. By about 8am, we had kitted up and headed out into the surrounding mountains. That day it was fairly warm and we rode the dirt roads and donkey paths used by the local Basotho people. We waved at the kids who ran out of the round mud-walled and grass-roofed huts as we passed through each small village.

The mountains seemed to roll into one another, constantly revealing more peaks as we rode on. Each time we stopped in the mountains, a young local herder seemed to appear magically out of nowhere in his gum boots with a grey blanket tied around him, often riding on a rough-looking donkey. I was always amazed at the tender age of some of the boys, alone and far from home, entrusted to watch the livestock in the harsh, unforgiving mountains. At that age, I wasn't even allowed to cross the road without holding my mom's hand! We rode close to 100 kilometres, until we decided to ride up Belakoma Pass in the mid-afternoon, an infamous route that formed part of the Roof of Africa course.

We were a long way from the so-called guest house, but we still had about four or five hours of light left in the day, so we decided to start the climb. The pass started off gently with winding tracks that lulled us into a false sense of confidence. Then it gradually got rockier and the gradient increased. The track now switchbacked on itself, as it climbed higher and higher. We crossed over small clear mountain streams as we climbed, watching the water cascade down the sheer drops. Some of the rocks were wet, which sapped our energy as our tyres spun, fighting to cross over them.

Clint was better at this type of riding and he often rode ahead and waited until Neal and I caught up. I was slow because of my dodgy legs, but I don't know why Neal was so crap. Both of us often dropped our bikes and the rising fatigue with each metre we gained in altitude wasn't helping either. Clint helped me get through the gnarly sections and past the steep ledges. It was hard going, but we were having a blast. The views were fantastic which made the physical effort worthwhile. At about 4 o'clock that afternoon Clint decided that it was time to head back, realising that at the pace we were going, we weren't going to make the top and get back down again before nightfall. Neal and I weren't about to give up on making it to the top, it surely couldn't be much further now? So, mumbling under his breath, Clint reluctantly rode on.

A short while later Clint, now clearly serious, recommended we go down. Neal and I again insisted that we could still do this and kept pushing upwards. We continued against Clint's recommendation as the sun sank lower and lower. The top of the pass just never seemed to get any closer and so Neal decided to call Errol Dalton to see how much further it was.

*

Sadly, Errol passed away racing Supermotard bikes about a year later, but at the time he was the go-to man for anything related to Lesotho. He was a multiple off-road and enduro national champion and had raced the Roof more times than I could remember – probably more than he could remember either! We used to take our bikes to him to be serviced in the workshop at his home, guarded by the meanest looking cross-breed dog I had ever seen. But more than that, Errol was a tough guy with a soft heart, who, as I have said, came with some mates to pray at my hospital bedside when I was lying there paralysed. I will always remember and be grateful for that.

*

Neal explained on the phone to Errol where we were on the mountain and I could hear Errol laughing. The feedback was that we were nowhere near the top, and also unlikely to get back down before it got dark. I could imagine Errol hanging up the phone shaking his head and chuckling at those hackers stuck in the Maluti Mountains in the middle of Lesotho.

This was the ammunition Clint needed, now justified in his earlier demands to descend. 'I told you okes!' he insisted, clearly annoyed by now. 'Do yous know how cold it gets in the mountains at night?'

Neal and I found the whole situation rather funny and our stifled laughter and quips about combining body heat just worked Clint up even more.

We immediately started the descent, but Neal and I were physically wasted. We could fill our hydration packs in the streams but our rations of energy bars, nuts and biltong were long gone. We slowly crept down the mountain but by now the sun was setting and the light was fading. I stopped, exhausted, resting my helmet on my handlebars and Neal, his arms too fatigued to steer or even brake, rode into the back of me at walking pace and we both fell over. We lay there, laughing at our predicament.

Then Clint had total sense of humour failure. 'Were either of yous in the military?' he barked. 'Best you start collecting sticks!' Neal and I heaved the bikes up, trying our best to hide the smirks on our faces – like schoolkids in the principal's office with a bad case of the giggles. I think the most frustrating part for Clint was that he could easily have left us and made it down in time on his own, but the thought

48

of having to explain to our families how we died was probably what kept him loyal.

Somehow, we eventually made it to the bottom of the mountain, but by then it was dark. The small lights on the enduro bikes were like a little torch flickering all over the place as we rode over the rocks in the dark.

'Which way now?' Neal asked at a split in the path.

'JUST RIDE!' Clint shouted back over the sound of the engines, his anger fuelling the humour of the situation for Neal and me.

When we finally got back to base camp that night our fingers and faces were freezing and our stomachs were growling with hunger. We sat in silence around the fire that night as we braaied the fillet steaks Meredith had packed for us and heated up the cheese sauce in a cold drink can on the open flames. Clint was tight lipped, while Neal and I exchanged smirks out of his sight.

The next morning, all was forgiven and we laughed about Clint's heated words and my and Neal's unprecedented confidence, combined with epic lack of skill. Neal – whose top priority was always food – headed off for breakfast at the main house. Clint and I were about to follow, but remembered the three steaks left over from the night before. We put them on rolls, smothered them in cheese sauce and greedily downed one each. There was one left. We looked down at the last delicious steak roll and then at each other. Back at the roll and then back at each other. Finally we had one last quick look over in the direction Neal had gone to make sure he wasn't on his way back and we split the last one between us, knowing full well it was totally wrong but chuckling as we ingested the last steak.

Then we headed to the main house and joined Neal for scrambled eggs on toast and some black looking boerewors that none of us had the courage to eat. It looked more like it belonged in a Bear Grylls episode than a good piece of boerie! We finished up and were walking back to our room, when Neal remembered the leftover steaks.

'Ah, I'm going to murder that steak roll now,' he said, with visible excitement on his face.

Clint struggled to hold back his laughter, desperately trying to conceal it with a cough. I joined him with a stifled cough.

'No, you didn't!' exclaimed Neal. 'Are you kidding me? You okes are just wrong, man!'

I felt a tinge of guilt, but it was suppressed by my full stomach. Clint loved the moment, no doubt enjoying the revenge owed him from the day before. We rode again that morning, returning at lunchtime to load the bikes and head home.

It was good to be riding again and hanging out with my buds, but the physical challenges continued. I struggled constantly with my teeth. At the time of the accident all the focus was on my spinal cord injury and although my twelve shattered teeth were serious, it wasn't a priority for a long time. Most of my teeth were filled and crowned, many of them breaking again and again, resulting in numerous trips to the dentist. It was very frustrating. I eventually had to have a maxillofacial surgeon remove some of the most damaged teeth and fit titanium posts in my jaw.

Then there were the visits to all sorts of specialists. My feet were changing shape and my toes were becoming deformed with the lack of muscles operating in my feet, so I had to see a podiatrist. He gave me inserts for my shoes and braces to wear on my feet each night to slow down the changes. Then I had the awesome urologist and bladder tests, where two tubes were put up my urethra. One was to pump water in and the other to measure the pressure in my bladder. And, finally, I had another sensor pushed up my anus to measure something else as well. The first time they did those tests was really tough, but after a while I came to terms with them. They were what they were. If I was determined to recover, it was all part of the process so I just sucked it up and got on with it. I still needed to self-catheter several times a day to ensure my bladder emptied properly. As a result I dealt with urinary tract infections from time to time, which was never fun. Then there were the ongoing weekly physiotherapy and exercises to top it all off.

One major challenge came one year when I was sick for several days. Meredith had told me to go to the doctor a number of times, but I was just being a typical, stubborn guy, insisting I would soon be fine and that I didn't need help.

I knew I was in trouble and that it was something serious when I could hardly stand up one night because of severe stomach pain. It was late at night and I needed to get to the hospital urgently. Meredith said she would take me, but it meant waking up four children and having to take them with us. So I insisted on driving myself, promising that I would be back later that night. The ten-minute drive to the hospital seemed to take for ever – the pain had me close to passing out.

I arrived at casualty and worked through the ridiculous pile of forms before they admitted me. After that, the doctor saw me and he pressed around my stomach asking where I felt the pain. It was really difficult to say because, with my spinal cord injury, I didn't always feel pain and to pinpoint it was nearly impossible. To cut a long story short, the doctor was convinced it wasn't my appendix, as I couldn't feel the pain where he expected me to. A couple of days later, after seeing another two doctors, I had a barium meal X-ray where the appendix showed up to be the problem. I was rushed in to theatre to have the appendix removed. As it turned out, my appendix was gangrenous and the condition quite serious. I ended up staying in hospital for just over a week. Lying in bed for that week set me back again, as my legs were very weak when I was eventually up and about again. But over the next month they became stronger and I was back on my bike again.

Each time I rode my bike I would think about my Dakar goal and the odds of actually achieving it. It still seemed impossible, but then again, riding my bike had seemed impossible just a few short years ago …

Chapter 9

WANNA RACE?

I missed the days of heading out to race in the dark early hours on Saturday mornings, the setting up of gazebos in the crisp morning air on the wet veld grass, the smell of petrol wafting from the jerry cans.

Until it was all snatched away from me, I never truly appreciated how fortunate I was to be young and healthy, racing dirt bikes in amazing places. It had been a very long three years and 136 days since the day I had broken my back and my life changed for ever. Physically, I wasn't even close to how I had been before the accident, but I felt I was ready to go back and the time had finally come to race again. I applied for my racing licence, making sure as I filled out the form that I was a bit vague about my medical history … It was granted! I filled out the race entry form, paid the entry fee and got my kit packed and ready. On Saturday, I was going racing.

The race was organised by Gary and Lynne Franks from *Enduro World* and was held at Arrow Rest near Hartbeespoort Dam. They had given me great support when I needed it most and it seemed only right for one of their races to be the first one back for me. For the other riders it was a normal sunny Saturday and just another race. They put up their gazebos, joked with their mates and set out their fuel cans, spare goggles and drinks.

For me it was different, this race was everything. I had thought about this day many times. Most of the racers there didn't know about my accident or, better yet, had forgotten. I was just another rider standing around at riders' briefing, being told about the track and the terrain that lay ahead. But I wasn't alone. Neal was there for me in the pits and Tristam and Johan were there to shadow me. The format of the race was to complete about four to six laps of the sixteen or so kilometre course – depending on your class – with a time limit of about three hours, after which the remaining riders would be time barred. Once riders' briefing was over I walked back to the pits to fetch my bike and head to the start line. I would be lying if I told you 'all was well'. I tried not to show it amidst the words of encouragement from my buds, but I was scared and anxious about how this would play out.

I lined up at the start along with the other riders. It was a dead start with engines off our hands on our helmets. I straddled my 250cc KTM enduro bike with the lowered suspension and the cut down seat, the sound of my heart pounding in my chest. I felt physically sick. There were no thoughts of getting to the corner first or championship points. It was all too familiar and a little too close to home. I swallowed, gritted my teeth and took a deep breath, fighting the fear that was biting at my resolve. My bike was in neutral with my kick-start out to the side, the piston at top dead centre.

Then Gary dropped the start flag and the sounds of the engines firing up smashed the silence. Gear levers stomped down into first, riders' wheels spinning off the line, dirt and stones flying out behind them, their front wheels light with acceleration. I joined in out of instinct and was mid-pack, holding my position through the first corner. I held my position during the first few hundred metres of the narrow, rutted twisting track, the air thick with dust and adrenalin. I strained my eyes, peering through the dust.

The track opened up and a rider passed me, followed by another, their roost pounding my body as they passed. It didn't bother me, I could take it and I realised in those first few hundred metres that I was no longer racing the other riders. The days of chasing clouds of dust and positions were gone. I was racing my injury, every metre I rode, every lap I completed, was me beating it. I wasn't supposed to be there racing again, this was not the expected outcome. In my mind, I was winning.

The other riders became almost invisible. We raced through the mounds and gullies, and the rocky koppies drew nearer, until we started to climb their stony sides. I lost momentum on the rocky climb and, unable to hold the bike up, it crashed into the ground. I slid and struggled as I picked it up and pushed on. Many times on the rocky slopes, unable to support my own weight and that of the bike as it tilted over, I dropped it again and again. Each time I had to stand the 110-kilogram bike up again was pure torture. First I had to stand up myself and I battled on the loose rocky slope, looking like a wounded boxer, semi-conscious and trying to beat the ten count. Then I regained my balance and grabbed on to the handlebars of the bike. The correct way is to use your knees and squat the bike up but I couldn't even squat my own body weight. I stood almost upright, with my knees only slightly bent, and relied just on my arms and shoulders. It took every ounce of strength I had each time I needed to do it.

Every time the bike fell was soul crushing – the sound of the steel frame, bars and foot pegs banging as they smashed against the rocks, often sliding backwards down a ledge or over a large rock I had just conquered. As the race continued, I slipped further and further back in the field until I was the last rider. Well, not quite. Behind me I had Tristam and Johan following me each metre of the way. I had given them strict instructions not to help me and it must have been killing them. Theirs was a test of patience that day. I struggled along clumsily, metre by metre, and as time went on exhaustion set in from the constant fighting with the bike. It wasn't pretty and I knew it. My legs kept going into spasm, jumping up and down, making it difficult to control the bike or even to stand. On one of the times I fell over I put my hand out and it connected hard with the rocky slope, injuring my left wrist as I landed. After that, the pain shot through my arm with each rock I rode over jarring the front suspension. It throbbed and made using the clutch even tougher.

This was not as much fun as I had remembered. I used my 'race survival strategy'. If I rode until I got stuck and then stopped, by the time I got going again I was already tired. So I changed it up and rode a few metres and then stopped at a spot from which I would be able to pull off again. There I rested for a few seconds. Then I picked a spot again a few metres further up, rode there and stopped again. That way, I dropped the bike less, because instead of just smashing my way through, I was choosing the best lines to ride, being as efficient with my energy and strength as possible. Despite all my clever plans, my pace was such that my bike often overheated, making the radiators boil due to my lack of speed restricting the airflow through them. I would have to stop for a few minutes every now and again to allow them to cool before continuing.

It wasn't long before riders started to lap me, some of them were the same guys I had raced against just a few years earlier. It was tough to watch and in my sorry state I wanted it to end. Tristam and Johan could see my fatigue and the pain I was enduring and encouraged me to continue, pushing me on. The goal they set for me was to try to get to the lap halfway point that passed near the finish, before winding back out again over the koppies. I kept going, pushing through the pain, watching more riders lap me, some now for the second time. I had been riding (if that's what you can call it) for a couple hours by now. I was breathing heavily, struggling to get enough breath while trying to drink from my hydration pack. The sweat soaked my helmet lining and fogged up my goggles, my eyes were stinging and wide. I came up to the halfway point completely broken physically and the escape out to the pits was visible, I just needed to turn left. I couldn't do it ... I hadn't quit a race since I was a kid!

When I was about 11 years old in primary school, I competed in the 1200m running event. I had trained hard with the team each morning before school for weeks and was fit and ready when the inter-house athletics day arrived. I won the race that day with my mother watching from the stands in a moment that I would look back on with pride for the rest of my life. I went on to be chosen to represent the school. A couple of weeks later I was at an inter-school athletics meeting, competing now against some other schools. The start gun went off and in the excitement, bunched up with the other runners, I headed out on the first lap way too fast. By the middle of the second lap I was in trouble. My heart rate was through the roof and I had a stitch like a dagger in my ribs. Instead of slowing right down and giving up my position and finishing the race, I pulled out of the race on the back straight, on the opposite side to the spectators, hidden behind the field events. It was a cowardly move and one of my biggest regrets to date. I should have accepted my poor judgement and finished the race, even if I had to walk across the finish line long after the other runners had finished. I never forgot that feeling and I vowed never to do that to myself again. I would always finish the race, no matter what!

So there I was, now in my thirties, ready to quit on the back straight. I remembered the day at the primary school athletics track. I simply couldn't turn left and leave the track. I kept right, missing the early exit and just kept going. Tristam shouted that I had missed the turn, but I already knew it. I was OK with being time barred or even having a mechanical breakdown, but I couldn't just quit because it was too difficult. I was sure that by now my two guardians were pretty fed up with their babysitting duties, but they didn't show it and continued on with me, constantly encouraging me and offering help that I refused.

I would like to say they never helped me the whole way, but it wasn't true. As we continued into the third and fourth hour, I really needed them. I can honestly say I rode every metre, but they ended up helping me to pick my bike up and pushing me up the rocky steps while my back wheel spun, showering them with dirt and stones. They stood next to the bike to prevent me from falling over as we edged along paths with sheer drops down the loose rocky face. It was hot, the air was still and the sun was beating down from above with the rocks reflecting the heat back up towards me. The sweat dripped from the chin guard of my helmet. I was lapped again and again by other riders who seemed to skip over the rocks with ease.

I thought about how I had been before the accident and found myself comparing that to how I was now. But then I stopped myself. I had to! I knew that dark path of thought only too well – it was the path of self-pity that ended in no good place. Instead, I thought about all the other patients at the hospital with spinal cord injuries, still unable to walk or even to care for themselves. Others, with brain injuries, were locked out of the world. Here I was, riding my bike through mountains overlooking the Hartbeespoort Dam. I had to keep going. It was simply the right thing to do.

Eventually, I left the last koppies behind me and zigzagged through the final chevron-taped flatter section. There was still one final challenge – to get over the tractor tyres and through the log pit. The log pit was a section about eight metres long filled with cut up logs ranging in thickness and length. It was easy to get it wrong and end up going over the bars or looping out the back and landing under the bike. Tristam and Johan went ahead, cheering me on from the finish line.

I stopped in front of the half buried tyres with arms like jelly and cramping forearms. I shook them out, took some deep breaths, peeled off my goggles to strap them backwards over my helmet. With my hydration pack empty and my mouth dry, I put in one final effort powered by will alone. I dropped the clutch, lifting the front wheel on top of the tyres and rolled the back wheel over with the momentum. I somehow managed to get through the log pit unscathed and, with the clutch in, I revved the bike on the limiter as I finally crossed the 'finish' line.

Gary stood there smiling, waving the chequers. Lynn, his wife, was emotional, smiling with tears running down her face. They knew what had just happened. I was time barred after only one lap! That meant that I was prevented from starting another lap and it could not have been more welcome. I was overcome by a sense of achievement and total exhaustion. I stopped next to Neal, who held my bike as I awkwardly climbed off and collapsed to the ground. He helped me onto the edge of the steel bike trailer, where I sat fighting back the tears, unable to talk.

I was physically and emotionally drained. I didn't have to say a word, Neal knew. He undid the buckles on my boots and pulled them off slowly, one at a time. With a hard pat on the shoulder, he handed me a cold drink and then he, Tristam and Johan gave me some space. I sat there silently, staring at the ground a couple of metres ahead of me, my eyes filled with tears. I was covered in dirt, my lips were cracked and caked in a mixture of sweat and dust, my body ached, my hands were blistered and my wrist throbbed. But that day, after finishing only one lap, I had won the race.

There were other races that followed, where I was time barred again and again after only one lap. One race I particularly remember was an enduro held at Pilgrim's Rest. Neal and I raced it together this time, helping each other along as we both struggled through. We laughed together at our exhausted states, barely able to get out of the way as other racers lapped us.

The first race I managed to finish was a local club race, hosted by the Gauteng Off-Road Club (GOC). Once again, to every other rider there I was just another guy on the start line, so I'm sure my victory shouts and air punches as I crossed the finish near the back of the pack probably seemed a bit of an overkill. I didn't mind, to me it was huge, a major milestone on my journey towards my dream.

Then in 2012 I raced the Botswana Desert Race – my first two-day event since the accident. The full Botswana Desert Race covers 1000 kilometres, all of it off road and through some of the harshest terrain Africa has to offer. The landscape is jam-packed with every thorn tree and thorn bush you can imagine growing out of the dry sandy ground. As if the distance and terrain weren't difficult enough, live-stock, donkeys and wild animals roamed free through the homelands, adding to the dangers of the high speed race. I entered the silver class where we had to race only 500 kilometres as supposed to the full 1000 kilometres. On each of the two days we needed to cover a different 250-kilometre loop through the untamed bush.

I made the seven-hour trip over the border alone and set up my tent right there in the Botswana bush. I met up with some guys from Pretoria in the pits. They helped me out during the race and, in the biker's way, really made me feel part of their team. The route was dry with thick sand, the dust often cutting visibility down to just a couple of metres. It was dangerous and the first day felt really long. My legs struggled over the long distance and I battled to grip the bike between my knees, making it more difficult and dangerous over the whooped out tracks. I somehow got through it and that night I prepped the bike myself next to my tent in the light of my head torch.

The second day was a cold early start and I headed out with a marathon mentality, trying to ride smoothly and conserve my energy and the fleeting strength in my legs. Early on I caught the tube of my hydration pack in a thorn bush, ripping the rubber bite valve off the tube. The next time I tried to drink, I held the hard plastic valve in my mouth and cleverly managed to break a front tooth – again – which had originally been broken on the day I broke my back. The cost of repairing all my teeth properly was huge, so I just had most of them filled. Other than that, the race went relatively well and the kilometres ticked by.

Most people think that you sit down when riding a bike and for street bikes and smooth terrain it's mostly true. However, when racing off road in rough terrain the bike bounces and bucks as it goes over the obstacles. You need to stand 90 per cent of the time, absorbing the movement with your legs if you want to stay on the bike. By the end of that second day, my legs had just about given up. I had to sit down on the bike most of the last 50 kilometres because my legs were useless. Now, moving at a slower speed over some of the bumps, my foot bounced off the peg and I struggled to pick up my leg and get it back on. I had pushed my legs hard to the point where it was simply physically impossible to remain standing. I wasn't going to quit and just did what I could to get through the final kilometres to the end. Once again it wasn't pretty, but a finish is a finish! I even managed to take first place in the senior silver class, and gave my wide hillbilly grin at the prize-giving that night.

I continued to enter other one-day races until 2013 when I entered the full 1000 kilometre Botswana Desert Race. I had trained hard and knew I could cover the distance. Because it was part of the national off-road series and I didn't have any championship points, I was forced to start near the back on both days of racing. I was started in row 28, with each row made up of four riders side-by-side. That year was particularly dry and dusty, making passing another rider near impossible and really dangerous. I managed to get through the first 500 kilometres on day one, but I was time barred on the second day, unable to go out on the second 250-kilometre lap. The time bar was harsh, as not a single rider after row eight had made the cut, so sitting back in row 28, I didn't stand a chance.

For the first time since the accident I was genuinely disappointed to be time barred. I knew I could have ridden the full distance. It was really tough to accept and I felt as though I had been robbed, but no amount of self-pity or complaining was going to change it. I parked my bike in the pits and sat quietly in my camping chair, still in my riding pants and boots, but with my shirt off. I held my head in my hands and stared down at my boots, half buried in the red Kalahari sand, and took stock of the whole situation.

A year ago I had barely made 500 kilometres, this year I had covered 750 kilometres and could go longer. It was a step in the right direction. I thought of how I literally used to count steps when I was learning to walk again, each time going for just one more. Every time I got despondent with my progress Meredith would remind me how far I had come, how I had taken more steps than the previous week or climbed an extra flight of stairs, constantly recounting the milestones I had passed along my journey of recovery. I was getting stronger and was reminded that I needed to measure my recovery in years, and it had been a good year. Sometimes it's not what you achieve but what you overcome to get there that matters.

I knew exactly what I wanted to achieve and that day I inched a little bit closer.

Chapter 10

THE RACE OF CRAZY PEOPLE

had now finished a number of races, and as much as that gave me great satisfaction, my Dakar dream was always there. I dreamed about it as I raced, imagining I was there racing high speed through the desert. It became a challenge and an obsession that I started to prepare for with the same obstinate determination that I had focused on my recovery and return to racing. But Dakar was no ordinary race ...

The Dakar Rally was originally started back in 1978 by a Frenchman called Thierry Sabine with the traditional route going from Paris, France, to Dakar, Senegal, on the west coast of Africa. The race was about 10000 kilometres long and crossed, along with the Sahara Desert, some of the harshest terrain in Africa. One hundred and eighty-two vehicles consisting of motorbikes, cars and trucks started in that first race, of which only 74 reached the end in Dakar. A race was born where to just finish and survive would be the goal of most entrants.

The race grew and Thierry ran it with huge success until he was killed during the 1986 rally when his helicopter crashed into a dune in Mali during a sudden sandstorm. The race was taken over by his dad Gilbert, aided by Patrick Verdoy, and continued to grow. Over the next 21 years the rally route was changed many times including the start, beginning several times in Portugal, Spain and Senegal. The finish also changed on several occasions to the pyramids of Egypt, Cape Town as well as back in Paris. As the race continued to grow it was bought and run by ASO (Amaury Sport Organisation), the same company that owns the Tour de France.

The rally had faced many challenges over the years but in 2008 it faced its biggest challenge yet when, along with three Mauritanian soldiers, four French citizens were murdered in the final days before the start. The French Ministry for Foreign Affairs warned the rally organisers not to go into Mauritania and direct threats were also made against the event by Al-Qaeda related organisations. Unable to protect the competitors spread out over thousands of kilometres, the organisers were forced to cancel the race the night before the start.

A terror attack three weeks later in the heart of Nouakchott justified the wise decision. The rally had changed the route many times over the years but 2009 would take that to a whole new level when it was decided that the race would be held in South America. It would cross through Argentina over the Andes Mountains to Chile and then back across the width of the continent to finish in Buenos Aires. The response was huge with more than four million spectators lining the route.

From 2009 onwards the route through South America changed each year to include countries like Peru, Paraguay and Bolivia. The Atacama Desert along with the high altitude dunes of Bolivia and the dry arid wasteland of Argentina, coupled with the cold, wet trails crossing the Andes Mountains became the new challenges of the two-week race.

Apart from the founder of the race, there have been many more deaths on the Dakar Rally, totalling almost 70, including both competitors and spectators. The bikers ran the biggest risk, with deaths resulting from injuries in crashes, dehydration, heart attacks, heat exposure and over-exertion. Safety was a massive concern for the organisers and they had become very strict with regard to who they allowed to race in the bike category, wanting to ensure that each rider held a high level of skill and experience in cross country rally racing.

In order to race the Dakar on a bike, six months prior to the start you needed to submit a rider proposal. This would contain your medical history, as well as a comprehensive list of all the racing you had done – complete with results and championship points. You also needed to state your cross country rally results, including the completion of at least one international rally from the World Rally Championship calendar.

If I wanted to reach my Dakar goal, I needed to get some proper races and results on paper. There were no cross country rally events in sub-Saharan Africa until the Amageza Rally came along. It was to be held right here in South Africa, at a fraction of the price of an overseas rally. I needed to enter and finish this race to begin building my Dakar proposal.

OK, now here's the deal.

You need to understand that all this time I'm still dealing with the normal pressures of everyday life. There were bills to pay and deadlines to meet. I had swimming galas to attend and school projects to help with. I dealt with theft at work, absent employees, meetings with suppliers and with customers. Not forgetting date nights and family holidays. Finding the time and funds to race was always a challenge. So making the time to race a three-day event in the Cape, with an extra three days for travelling from Joburg during my company's busiest season, was near impossible. But this was a step towards my big goal. I had to make a plan. Nothing about this was easy, but I just closed my eyes and thought, 'Stuff it, let's do it!' I paid my deposit and it was game on.

The Amageza Rally in 2013 was a 'Dakar style' race which started in Cape Town and then wound its way off road 1884 kilometres northwards to just over the Namibian border, then moved eastwards through the Richtersveld, ending up in Kakamas near Upington.

'Amageza' means 'crazy people', which gave a sense of the toughness of the race and terrain. Like the Dakar, you not only had to race but navigate your route as well. Each evening racers were issued a long scroll of paper called a roadbook which was fitted above your handlebars. The roadbook had navigation clues on it, kilometre markings, rough sketches of road turns or splits and French symbols indicating warnings or terrain changes, which was useful if you knew French! The roadbook would also warn of dangers in the track, such as washouts, deep holes, cliffs and fences. These dangers were graded as either a single, double or triple caution. Singles you could often almost ignore, doubles you needed to slow down and be very careful, and triples were basically life threatening. Missing one on the roadbook meant a trip to the hospital or worse.

Each day of the rally was called a 'stage'. These daily stages consisted of 'liaisons', or connecting sections which you had to ride but were not timed. Basically they got you through to the 'specials' which were high speed racing sections. They were timed and totalled up to determine an overall winner. There were time penalties for navigational errors and speeding in controlled 'sensitive' zones, like urban areas, during the liaisons. You camped in a designated area each night called a bivouac and had only the tools, spares and clothes you could fit in a steel trommel, plus two spare tyres. You had to do your own service work on your bike each night – including tyre changes – and only breakfast was provided.

If that sounded like fun, then you'd come to the right place! It was designed to be rugged, raw and tough, a race for crazy men, and I qualified.

Anyone who rides off-road bikes knows that if racing motorbikes is your sport, then working on them had better be your hobby. I basically needed an enduro bike that was roadworthy and had a range of 300 kilometres off road. I also needed all the navigational equipment used for this style of racing. This included the roadbook reader, which was basically an aluminium box with two spindles and a small motor operated by a switch on your handlebars. You loaded the paper rolled-up roadbook into it and use the toggle button to move it forwards or backwards as you raced along.

I also needed two 'ICOs' – one was a digital odometer that you could adjust up or down to match the route on the roadbook; the other was a digital compass that numerically displayed the direction you were travelling in. I had just bought a KTM 450 EXC enduro bike and decided this would be the basis of my rally bike. Luckily, it wasn't too difficult to register for road use, since the bike came with a basic roadworthy kit. But I still needed to get all the navigation equipment, as well as a bracket to mount my GPS.

I searched the internet, checking out all sorts of rally kits and decided in the end to go with the rally lite kit from Rally Raid in the UK. It was nothing too fancy, just the basics that I needed and it seemed easy enough to install. I ordered it online and it arrived within a couple of weeks. The timing was good, there were still about five weeks to the race. I opened it up about a week later only to realise that it didn't come standard with the bar clamps I needed for the whole thing to be attached to the bike. So I got back online and sent the order in with a big ASAP on it. The clamps arrived about a week later and I started the build with only three weeks to go. I changed the sprockets ratios from a 13/50 to a 14/48 which gives a better top speed that would be important in the open desert sections, and put on some new tyres and mousses. I neatened up the back with some smaller indicators higher up and mounted the number plate. Next, the big 19-litre long-range tank from Raceworx KTM arrived. I moved the fuel pump into it and got it all mounted up. I added some foam grips and then got started with the navigation stuff.

I was down to about two weeks when I realised that I had to drop my bike off in Pretoria a week before for it to be transported with Kevin and Vernon – some buddies of mine – so that I could just fly down in an effort to limit my time away to as short a time as possible. Then, as always seems to happen, things got really hectic at work. This meant a lot of late nights running into the early hours of the morning in the garage getting everything built up.

Loctite on every screw, joining and extending wires. Basically, trying to get all that stuff to fit on the handlebars. Eventually, I finished the night before I had to drop the bike off. I hopped on and test rode it around the neighbourhood in the dark for about ten minutes to make sure it didn't explode and then loaded it up with my trommel (which I had packed and unpacked more times than I care to remember). I added my spare wheels and the next morning I dropped everything off.

The next thing I knew, I was on a plane to Cape Town. I arrived in Gordon's Bay on the Saturday morning amidst gale force winds that were blowing the tents away. It was so bad that the organisers decided to change the starting line to a guest farm a few kilometres inland. Here, they held the registration and scrutineering in a large warehouse where there was a long line of some very cool looking rally bikes. We all had to have a medical examination (nothing they made you cough for!) and you had to show them your essential medical and survival equipment, including two-way radios, hand-held flares, paper maps, a standard compass, water purification tablets and a full first aid kit, to name just some of it.

It seemed a bit overboard at the time, but these guys weren't messing around and, after experiencing the remoteness in the days to come, I could see why. After registration, I enlisted the help of my buddy Mark Campbell to explain how my ICO worked and Kevin sponsored some batteries for it which I had forgotten (he was clearly far better prepared than I was). Everyone was doing last-minute things to their bikes and packing and repacking their trommels. I did the same – not wanting to feel left out.

Then we all headed over to riders' briefing where Alex, the race organiser, gave us a lecture that – well, let's be honest – scared the crap out of us. My mind was filled with memories of mornings spent in bed when I should have been in the gym and of eating those large pizzas, just because no self-respecting man orders a medium! Then we were given our roadbooks and we were officially rally racers. There was really something cool about getting that first roadbook which promised danger and adventure. I couldn't help smiling as I pictured the places it would take me. I loaded the visual waypoints into my GPS and marked up the roadbook with my coloured highlighters, as I had seen other experienced riders do on the internet. The idea was that you would colour code the route and warnings, making it easier to read while racing full speed through the harsh terrain. I then loaded it into my roadbook holder, after spying on others to see how it was done, and headed off to bed.

DAY 1

The next morning was an early start. We were up at about 4am. I'm sure that, like me, most of the guys hadn't slept much. We ate a basic breakfast and started in the dark just before sunrise. You could feel the air buzzing with anticipation. Most of these guys had spent months building their bikes and finally the day had come to let them race. We were set off in twos, a few minutes apart, as we started our 451 kilometre liaison to the start of the special or racing section. Now don't be mistaken, this wasn't some easy road trip to the start. You were given a time to get to the start of the special, so you couldn't waste any time. It was pretty much all off road, winding through forests, up and down mountain passes and across farmland through the Overberg, Breede River Valley and into the Karoo.

I really struggled to stick to the speed limits in places and had to constantly check my GPS speed to ensure I didn't get any penalties. But in other places it was a challenge to get anywhere near the speed limit because the route becoming a lot rougher and more technical. There was a ferry crossing that day on a small barge over the Breede River next to Malgas, which was a first for me at the time and added nicely to the whole adventure. I felt pretty good and my bike was running well, despite my not having an opportunity to give it a proper shakedown beforehand. I tried to stand up as much as I could while riding, knowing full well from past experience what multiple day races can do to your butt ... something I don't care to dwell on.

Eventually I arrived at the start of the special. It's not often you ride 451 kilometres off road and *then* start a race of a couple of hundred kilometres. The special started in proper enduro style, with the first part through a sandy river bed full of ponds of varying depths. I went through one that was way deeper than I expected and came very close to not getting out the other side. The murky water covered my wheels and the wake they created reached way up over my head. Others would not be as lucky, with several motors being lost to the river that day.

After several attempts, I managed to find the point where I was supposed to exit the river. Thereafter, the track became very rocky and as my bike shuddered through the sharp loose rocks, I was worried about how my navigation was going to hang in there, as the ten minutes around my quiet, well tarred neighbourhood had not been much of a reliability test. This was soon answered when I realised my GPS was dangling off my handlebars by a lanyard. I had put the lanyard on as a backup in case something went wrong with the brackets and I was really glad I had, or I would have been involved in an (unwelcome) impromptu game of hide and seek. As it turned out, the inserts in the rubber grommets had been put in backwards in the factory, so I had to strip the whole mounting down and reassemble it. This probably took about ten minutes and it made me pretty frustrated.

Once I had sorted it out, I headed off at a really quick pace in an attempt to make up for lost time. The navigation was challenging as I raced along tracks that zigzagged through the stark landscape. A section would then come up on the roadbook where I needed to leave the rough track and head in a compass direction for a few kilometres, pushing though the brush and around ruts and rocky outcrops. Then I would join another track, often barely visible in the remote locations which a famer's bakkie used only every few months. Again, I would follow the rough track for several kilometres to be once again sent in another direction where there would be a junction of five or more paths, of which only one would match the CAP heading or compass direction on the roadbook.

It was easy to miss the turns as the tracks blended into the terrain. At one point I missed a turn by just a few metres, so I stopped and did a pivot turn. I would always pivot to the left planting my stronger leg on the ground as I wheel spun the back wheel and whipped the bike around. However, this time I managed to fall over and, putting my hand out to break my fall, I landed on some short, hard plant stalks. One of them went into my wrist, taking out a chunk of flesh and opening up a fair-sized hole. I could see the exposed artery wall and realised that if it had been a millimetre or so deeper I would have been in serious trouble.

You are so alone in this race. To give you an idea, I had seen only two riders during the whole special which lasted a few hours, one right at the beginning and another just before the end.

I thought to myself, 'Stop being an idiot! This is a marathon and you're about to throw it away on the first day!'

I decided to forget about the time and race positions, took out my medical kit, washed my wrist out and bandaged it up properly. I felt like a real chop for being so stupid. I got back on my bike and rode smooth and smart, focusing more on exact navigation and learning to match my riding speed to my ability to navigate. A few hours later the marshal came into sight at the end of my first rally special section. I pulled up, punching the air and skiing to a stop in a cloud of dust alongside the startled marshal. I had survived and I knew that was another step on the path to my Dakar dream.

After that, there was still another 82-kilometre liaison to the bivouac in Sutherland. A couple of kilometres later I came across a cobra in the track, standing up with its hood fully extended. I almost didn't see it and had to swerve, missing it by millimetres. I stopped and watched it slide off into the brush. As I continued, the heavens opened and I felt the large raindrops stinging my face. I pulled my buff up over my nose closing the gap between my goggles and the helmet chin guard to protect myself from the drops that whipped at my face as I sped along.

Towards the end of the day I noticed that my back wheel was moving around so I stopped and checked, only to find my rear tyre mousse had collapsed. Mousses are like big foam doughnuts that a lot of racers fit into their tyres instead of inner tubes. The advantage was you would never get a puncture, but the downside was that they were expensive, and in extreme heat they would become soft and sometimes collapse. Mine had been brand new that morning! I nursed the bike through the remaining kilometres, rolling slowly in to the finish. Despite the challenges, I had managed to reach the end of my first rally day in the Karoo town of Sutherland.

It was cold and raining heavily as I sat on the Sutherland school's grandstand, wrapped up in my bike's waterproof cover and watching the staff trying to put up the tents in the rain and mud. It was going to be a long night but there was nowhere else I would rather have been. This was what I had come for and I was getting my money's worth. I had asked for adventure and it was being served up by the bucket load. I changed my air filter, lubed my chain and swapped my back wheel with my only spare hoping it would last for the next two days.

In true Amageza fashion, there was a Plan B and the nightly riders' briefing was held at a small local restaurant-cum-bar. Here we heard, at almost 10pm, that there were still some riders battling away in the racing special. Stories had started to come in from riders of punctures, drowned bikes, smashed engine casings, navigation towers breaking off and one guy, Donovan, had even cut his neck open on a wire strung across a path.

I soon realised that I had had a good day compared with most of the guys. I'm not sure of the exact numbers, but about 47 guys had started that morning and 15 were already out of the race after the first day. We were then given our roadbooks and I marked mine very differently now that I knew a bit more about how they worked. I also had to work somewhat faster because of my desperate need for sleep. Some guys slept in the outdoor covered area under the carports, right there in the open. Others slept in the ablutions at the bivouac which was based at the Sutherland school. I opted for my pop-up tent which I pitched on the hard, wet concrete and had no problem falling asleep.

DAY 2

It was another early start. I put on my wet kit, sliding my feet into my cold boots. I packed away my tent and ate a good breakfast supplied by the Sutherland school staff. I went back to the bathrooms which were quieter now that the riders were heading to the start and I cleaned my catheters and changed the sterile solution in the tubes. The other riders didn't know about my challenges from the spinal cord injury and I was happy to keep it that way. It was the same reason I had brought my own tent as opposed to sharing the tents supplied by the organisation. In my own tent at night I had the privacy to use my catheter. I have said before that I didn't care what others thought, but in a way I guess I did. It was always an awkward conversation so it was just easier if I could avoid it.

I then moved off to the start where I had a couple of minutes, so I stopped at the ambulance to get my wrist treated properly and bandaged again. Then I was off! The day started cold and wet, but little did I know that this was going to be one of the best riding days of my life!

It started with more river crossings than I could count – and they were all flooded (with the occasional farmer's 4x4 stuck along the way). I stopped behind some guy on a big rally bike just before a big muddy river. It would happen that at that exact moment he grabbed a fist full of throttle and blasted his way through the mud ahead of him, leaving me covered in about 10 kilograms of the Northern Cape. I must have looked like a cartoon when you can only see eyes blinking after an explosion. I was scooping mud off the top of my helmet by the handful!

After that ordeal, we went through some amazing passes often on 'twee spoor' dirt tracks with sheer drops down to the ravines below. One in particular was very steep and wet, with small pockets of snow in places. The area was slate and the slick and disintegrating surfaces offered little traction in the wet. I locked up the rear wheel on a steep downhill switchback and dropped my bike. Luckily the bike and I were both undamaged. I gave myself a good telling-off before I picked up the bike and carried on riding.

That day was 731 kilometres in total, so I really didn't need any problems. It was 394 kilometres to the start of the special which was then a further couple of hundred kilometres. All went smoothly, apart from wishing I had made the effort to get some more foam on my seat – 'the knife's edge', I liked to call it. A good enduro bike has a hard narrow seat, perfect for racing and handling the bike in rough terrain where you are standing most of the time. However, on a rally there was a lot more sitting each day on parts of the liaison and the enduro seat was not your friend. To top it off I had very little muscle on my butt since my injury and the seat felt as though I was sitting on a roof truss.

As I came up to the start of the special on the West Coast, the sun out now, I had the most incredible view of the vast blue sea that just suddenly seemed to appear before me. I'm sure the Cape Town riders thought nothing of it, but I was like an excited kid arriving at a holiday destination, this was so cool! I stopped alongside the marshal standing next to his 4x4 in the hot sand. It was a lot warmer now compared with our cold, wet start that morning, so I took off my jacket and put it in my backpack. The marshal counted me down and I was off racing!

The special had started and it took us right down onto the beach. I gave a huge 'woohooo' in my helmet, even though there was no one to hear for miles around. For the next 100 kilometres, I rode up the West Coast. I raced past lonely white beaches broken by dark black rocky outcrops and the cold dark blue Atlantic, the white sandy track stretching out, twisting and turning like a long white snake ahead of me. The thick sand grabbed at my tyres and my bike wobbled and wove crazily until I got up to speed, after which your bike floats over the sand, almost skating, as a plume of white sand from my wheel chased along behind me. I raced along that Atlantic seashore, all alone, winding along the thick sandy beach tracks. What an experience! At one point, even though I was racing against the clock, I had to stop to take some photos – it was just so incredible. It was the first time I had seen the West Coast and I fell in love with its desolate beauty.

There was a point at which I went down the wrong turn and got stuck on a small beach full of washed-up kelp with only steep thick sandy paths out. I went back into the wet sand at the edge of the lapping waves for some run-up and managed to get up and over, despite adding a good few hours on my motor in the process. Towards the end of the special the route took a sharp eastward turn inland for about 50 kilometres on a wide dirt road in good condition. I opened the throttle wide and tucked down behind my navigation tower. The bike screamed and shuddered under me, as I managed to get up to 160kph and was quite proud of myself until I heard of other guys going over 190kph on their larger bikes. A screen would have come in handy on those sections, because my neck was worn out after fighting against my helmet which was being whipped around by the stream of air coming in through the front at high speed.

There was another 189-kilometre liaison to the end of that day's stage in the town of Springbok. While on the track coming through some mountains, I came across Adrian Storm. The suspension link on his bike had broken clean off and his race was undoubtedly over. He had tried to make a plan but it was just too serious. He had sent guys ahead with his GPS location and had plenty of water, so he sent me on my way. I felt really bad for the guy. He had been riding so well – amongst the leaders – and his bike was clearly well prepped. Shortly after that I came across Thomas Eich who had a flat front tyre and was trying to nurse his bike in. I gave him all my big cable ties to help keep the tyre on the rim and was off again.

At the end, I went into Springbok to fill up with petrol and used the tap at the garage to give my bike a wash in an attempt to get rid of the mud still weighing it down from that morning. Once I was satisfied, I grabbed a quick burger and made my way to the bivouac. It was after dark and riders' briefing was about to start. There were going to be two specials on the last day and we were given strict instructions: 'Be careful not to crash in the first 80 kilometres of that special! It is extremely remote and it will be near impossible to get any medical assistance to you.'

I was starting to get used to going to bed like a scared little girl each night, falling asleep to the sound of soft crying from the other tents. After riders' briefing, I did an oil change and ended up prepping into the late hours of the night, only managing to get to bed well after midnight.

DAY 3

Day 3 started with the – now usual – 4am alarm. My body ached as I tried to get up. The last two days were taking their toll. For a while

I had been taking a daily anti-inflammatory tablet prescribed by my doctor. It helped to manage the pain but I could tell I wasn't doing my body any favours. My walking was worse that morning because of my fatigued legs and I stumbled my way to breakfast in the dark. There was no time to feel sorry for myself, today's goal was simple: just finish. It was pretty cold and I was glad my kit was dry for a change.

I lined up on the gravel start and the marshal held out his hand and counted me down. I hadn't managed to enter all the waypoints into my GPS the night before, so I pulled over just after the start and took about ten minutes to put them all in. I figured rather safe than sorry! My focus needed to be on finishing, not on the times and positions. We filled up with fuel early on in the stage and then the start of the first special arrived. I could still hear Alex's voice in my head from the riders' briefing the night before about the dangers of this stage and I was determined not to throw it all away as I had nearly done on Day 1. It started off easy, but before long the track deteriorated and became unbelievably rocky with loads of square edges, steep ups and downs that were actually quite technical – more like an enduro race than a cross country rally. Although I couldn't reach the speeds of the guys on the bigger bikes the day before, I was glad I was on the smaller bike now which was easier to handle along the jagged pathways.

I could not believe the vastness of the area. It was so barren – just rocks, sand and mountains – and we rode for about 80 kilometres without seeing anyone or anything even close to civilisation. It was like being on another planet. I had no idea these places even existed in South Africa! I would later be told it was the Richtersveld, an arid and harsh area that felt almost Martian. The volcanic rock and craggy mountains were as beautiful as they were desolate. Only small pockets of vegetation survived there, clearly evolved over thousands of years to handle the harsh climate. The whole racing special went really well for me and my suspension worked great over the rocks.

My hands and arms still felt fine but my legs were tired and went in and out of spasm as the first special wound down. I struggled to use the back brake with my foot and relied mostly on the front hand-operated brake, occasionally managing to stamp on the rear brake with my heel when I came in to a corner too fast. My back ached and my stomach kept cramping. My spinal injury level meant my two upper stomach muscles worked fine but the lower two didn't. If I sneezed or tightened my stomach muscles quickly the lower two would just stretch out and the upper two would over-contract and cramp. The only way to release it was to stand up and stretch over backwards with my hands above my head. It would have looked funny to anyone watching me, as a random cry of pain from my helmet was followed by an emergency stop in a cloud of dust. Then, while trying to balance the bike against me, I did some bush yoga to release the cramp before getting back on the bike and racing off in a spray of dirt and stones from my back wheel.

That first special ended with us having to cross over into Namibia to fill up with fuel, and as the attendant filled my bike there were a couple of minutes to grab a bite to eat and take off the outer sleeves of my rally jacket. Then back into South Africa and on to the final special. The next 200-odd kilometres were basically all semi-desert landscape, lots of red Kalahari sand and some rocky sections, but it flowed beautifully and you could just twist the throttle and hold on. It was what I enjoyed the most – pure riding bliss!

I caught up with Peter How, a vet from Durban, and we rode together for kilometres through the dry Kalahari. It was like being with my buds on a Saturday morning, the riding felt awesome, kilometre after kilometre! We swapped positions back and forth for more than 150 kilometres, until suddenly in a split second, I caught a ditch with my bars slightly turned. I tucked the front and exited right over the bars! It was a really rocky area and one of those crashes when the bike seems to whip you to the ground. I wasn't going too fast, but it totally winded me and I was seriously sore. Peter came up behind me within a couple of seconds after witnessing my fall and said something to the effect of 'Damn, are you OK?' Being winded, I could barely manage to get the words out, but managed to croak, 'Can you pick my bike up?' He appreciated the true racer attitude and we laughed about it later. I got back on and rode out the rest of the special, although a little tentatively at first.

The special ended near the bustling metropolis of Pofadder. It had been a long day already, but there were still about 200 more kilometres of liaison before it counted as a finish. I grabbed a quick bite to eat with Andrew Johnstone and Willem du Toit, a couple of good mates who were also racing, and then we hit the tracks for the last stretch.

But I still had one final scare waiting for me. Probably daydreaming, I managed to miss a turn-off by a good couple of kilometres. Once you go off the roadbook, it is a mission to find your way right again, as your ICO meter is thrown out and it all gets messed up really quickly. Luckily I didn't panic. I just pulled over, called on my

Standard 6 maths (lower grade) and managed to work out by how far I had passed the turn, reset my ICO and headed back to find the turn. Then it was all the way home to Kakamas.

It had been a tough three days, with only 16 finishers from the 47 racers who had started which meant that this finish had not come easily, making it all the more sweet for me. I was even more surprised to finish in fifth place overall.

I had one final night in my tent at the finish, with my bike parked right outside as I enjoyed a beautiful Northern Cape sunset reflecting off the dam. It certainly felt good to finish and add the race to my budding Dakar proposal, but I also felt gutted that it was all over. After that race, I knew I had discovered my passion in cross country rally racing. There were the many different terrains I got to ride and the truly remarkable places I got to see. On top of that was the camping and sense of roughing it, the endless challenges I would face and, above all, there was always that sharp racing edge that constantly reminded me that this was no tour. I had pushed past the pain and physical challenges and this rally made me believe that Dakar was possible despite my physical limitations, not easy but possible. All I needed was to believe it was possible; I would fight to make it real.

Above all, it confirmed that the Dakar goal was the perfect dream for me and I left Kakamas more determined than ever to achieve it.

Chapter 11

PONGOLA STEAKS

Up in northern KwaZulu-Natal, South Africa, near the Swaziland border, lies the small town of Pongola, where you will find Dallie Terblanche, a friendly guy often seen laughing and joking with his mates. He comes across as a typical cheerful farmer, always dressed in shorts and driving his white, single-cab 4x4 Land Cruiser, complete with black steel cattle rack. The cab would probably contain some tools, a tow rope, an old hat, a small part of some farm machine or motorbike, and some padkos. But under that farmer exterior, lies a tough – and, to be honest, a little crazy – dirt bike racer, the kind of guy you hear stuff about before you get to meet him.

He's a guy built for Africa, a tomato farmer by trade, but in his heart he's a hard core racer. He's competed for national titles in quad bike racing and can ride a bike just as well. His wife Maryanne is, if it's possible, even friendlier than Dallie. A small, pretty blonde lady who at first seems far too good for her rough, wild outdoor husband. Somehow, Dallie had managed to get her to marry him; no one knows what sorcery he used to pull it off, but good on him. However, as you get to know them, you realise they were made for each other. Completing the family is their young son Dallie-Boy. The wild adventurous streak from his dad was already apparent at his young age, the kind of kid you wouldn't be surprised to see catching snakes barefoot in the veld or, at five years old, racing around on his little KTM motorbike. Between them, each August they put on the annual Pongola 500 Challenge event.

Throughout the years, finding the balance between quality time with Meredith and my girls and fulfilling my riding and adventure needs has always been a delicate task. At times I've been selfish to the detriment of my family, and at other times I've been frustrated and edgy because of not enough 'guy time'. When racing bikes, it's difficult to involve the whole family. The locations are often distant and remote with just the bare minimum of amenities.

The Pongola 500, however, is different from most other events. It's an event we all love and gets everyone's vote. It's a great family event based at the Jozini Tiger Lodge, an upmarket hotel on the banks of the Jozini Dam where the wives and families get to enjoy the pool, spa and spectacular views of the dam and nature reserve, while their husbands and dads get their fix of adrenalin. In the evenings, around the large crackling fire, the boma fills with the smell of braaivleis and the sounds of the riders laughing and sharing their war stories. There are novelty awards and prizes.

The time had come and as a family we booked early for the 2014 leg and were looking forward to the weekend away. The date arrived and on the Friday, Meredith and I, along with our four daughters, excitedly loaded the car and headed off on the four-hour drive to the event.

The event is a 500-kilometre one-day route split into green, red and black routes which vary in difficultly. Strictly speaking, it's not a race, but I think someone forgot to tell the riders. Naturally, I needed to do the toughest black route; the 500-kilometre distance in the remote wild areas covered in one day was the perfect training. Don't be fooled by the cushy hotel it starts at. This is a proper adventure, with riders leaving at sunrise and often arriving back way after dark, dirty and exhausted, with broad grubby smiles, sore bodies and tired eyes inside their dusty helmets.

Early that Saturday morning before sunrise, I quietly kitted up in my riding gear and leaving my wife warm in bed, I headed off to riders' briefing in the main car park. Dallie showed us a map of the routes and explained the challenges the day held. The route passed along the borders of Swaziland and Mozambique, past the Tembe Elephant Park, down the sandy East Coast tracks past Lake Sibaya and then wound through the rocky Lebombo Mountains. The terrain consisted of whooped-out thick sand, hard pack forestry roads, winding jeep tracks, dry river beds, river crossings and rocky mountain switchbacks. We would travel through rural villages with their chickens, goats and cows roaming free between the subsistence crop patches, the eroded red sand huts and slick black mud.

I couldn't wait to get going; we were in for an epic day of riding! The usual emergency procedures were covered, the refuel waypoints pointed out and a word of prayer offered. Then it was go time. About a hundred bikes started firing up their engines and the noise filled the area. I'm sure the other hotel guests were happy to be woken up by the song of my people.

The riders started out, some in groups, others alone. Not wanting to sit in the dust of other riders all day, I headed out fairly quickly. The tracks were fast and open to start with and the speeds were high. I had the track downloaded on my GPS and was chasing the imaginary line, missing the occasional turn, whipping around and heading off in a new direction. I kept glancing down at the small GPS screen and back up while racing along the narrow, hard packed, stony track. Small thorn bushes and occasional trees whizzed past.

Nothing too out of the ordinary was happening as I flew past Johan and Erika van der Merwe manning a back-up point on the route. I was flying along at high speed along the narrow gravel and stone track and I did another routine check of the GPS. As I looked back up, a cow ran out from behind some bushes just a few metres in front of me. I think it must have been startled by the bikes riding ahead of me. In a split second, at well over 120kph, my bike collided with the side of the cow running across the track. It all seemed to happen in a flash and I didn't even have time to hit the brakes.

As my bike ploughed into the flank of the cow my body parted from the bike and, after connecting with the top of the solid brown hide, I was sent flying over the cow at what felt like the speed of light. The impact spun the cow around as my bike cartwheeled down the track behind me. Sky-ground-sky-ground flashed past my goggles as my body crashed and bounced into the hard packed stony red surface. Gritting my teeth, I felt myself being flung like a rag doll down the rocky track, coming to a stop a good 40 to 50 metres down the road.

Unconscious, I lay there in a cloud of dust, the blood trickling through the tears in my shredded rally jacket. As I came round, my ears ringing, I was winded and in searing pain, unable to breathe. I gasped and gasped for air and after what seemed like an eternity I eventually got that first, sweet breath. The pain was intense and all-consuming. I had been there before, lying in pain in the blood-soaked red dirt. My first thought was to wiggle my toes. Surely I couldn't go back to that dark place that I had fought so hard to escape? My toes moved. I knew whatever else was damaged I could deal with, just not back there again.

Erika, now about a kilometre back, had heard the impact and the sudden silence, and she and Johan got into their bakkie and raced to my aid. Riders behind me had started to arrive and, as is the biker's way, each one stopped to assist where they could. The looks on their concerned faces told the story of my condition. For some, it no doubt brought back awful memories of their own past injuries. I could see the cow lying in the distance, unable to stand; my mangled bike and broken bike parts were lying between us. The cow's fate was to be worse than mine. Because it was unable to stand and was in pain, it had to be put out of its misery shortly afterwards.

The dust settled and I lay there with the sun beating down on my broken body which was slowly revealing where the pain was coming from. It was my entire right side. My head was pounding and my helmet was smashed, the peak was nowhere to be seen. My mouth was dry and I needed to drink, so the other riders put my hydration pack mouthpiece into my mouth, warning me to take just a tiny sip as I would likely be in theatre within hours. I sucked on the tube but no liquid came out. My hydration pack bladder had burst on impact with the ground; it was in shreds and almost torn off my back, so one of the other guys let me take a sip from his hydration pack. My gloves were torn and bloodied, and there were deep cuts in my palms and fingers. My right forearm was ripped open to the bone and there were numerous other gashes where the rocks had torn into my flesh. After calling the medical response ambulance, Johan cut my jacket open and used the riders' medical kits to try to stem the bleeding as best he could. I had crashed in a remote location, far from the main road, and it would take the medics well over an hour to reach me.

I didn't want Meredith to hear from anyone else that I had crashed and was injured, as I knew it would be extremely difficult for her to hear the news. I seemed always to do a proper job when I crashed, no half measures here. I wanted to call her, but my phone had been smashed to pieces. So another rider contacted Meredith and handed me the phone. Although in serious pain, I put on the most upbeat voice I could muster, explaining that I had hit a cow and would be unable to continue because my bike was damaged. I would see her at the hotel later that day once I had been collected by the backup marshals. She was cool with that and I hung up.

The truth was a little different. When the ambulance arrived, the paramedic cut the remains of my jacket off and bandaged the lacerations. I was placed in the all too familiar headgear and was drugged because of the pain so that I could be placed on the board and loaded into the ambulance. It was a long drive to the nearest hospital, more than an hour away in Richards Bay. En route, we were met by Dallie's wife Maryanne, along with Meredith who had my medical aid card and ID book. Naturally, Meredith was shocked when she realised my true physical state after my 'small' crash. Unable to come with me, she went back to the hotel to be with our girls.

When we arrived at the hospital, I was still drugged and really fuzzy about what was happening. I didn't even realise that I had seen my wife. X-rays were taken and it was found that I had broken several ribs and torn the ligament between my shoulder and collar-bone. Amongst many other injuries, I had deep lacerations down to the bone in my right forearm and elbow which were still full of dirt and grit. I was taken through to theatre where they operated, cleaned out my forearm and stitched me up. I came out of theatre with my arm bandaged from the shoulder and with a back slab to be worn for the next six weeks.

The next day, Meredith's parents drove to Pongola with her sister Verity and my brother-in-law David. Verity and David took care of the kids, taking them back to Joburg so that they could be at school on the Monday. Meredith and her folks continued on to the hospital in Richards Bay, arriving on the Sunday afternoon. They booked into the Road Lodge next door and stayed there for the next six days until I was discharged.

The five-hour drive home to Joburg was painful and long with a damaged shoulder, forearm and broken ribs. I sat with a pillow on my lap trying to rest my arm on it and take the weight off my shoulder. My elbow was so painful and each bump in the road had me scream-ing inside. On the outside I was a little tougher – you can't show the in-laws any weakness!

Eventually, the torture trip ended and we arrived home, but over the next three weeks the pain in my elbow just got worse and worse. Finally, I went to my local orthopaedic surgeon and he sent me for X-rays and a sonar. The tests showed up dense matter just off the back of my elbow, so it was back to theatre to find out what it was and get it sorted. I came out of surgery with my arm in a cast from my wrist to my shoulder set at 90 degrees. The stuff on the X-ray turned out to be bone still attached to my triceps that had been torn off my elbow in an avulsion fracture. No wonder the pain had been unbearable! The surgeon reattached my triceps with a titanium anchor and placed the bone fragments back as best he could – a bit more complicated at that stage since it was four weeks since the injury.

I was so frustrated! My 2014 Amageza Rally was coming up in six weeks' time! It was the next step towards my Dakar dream and I was desperately trying to work out a way to make it possible, but the cast wouldn't even be off by then. So, painful as it was to accept it, I knew it was not going to happen for me that year. I had already paid the entry for the five-day Amageza Rally, so I would need to try to sell my entry. I called Alex, the organiser, to see if it was transferable and he said it was and even helped me find a buyer. He invited me to come anyway and help with the organisation. But the thought of being there, my arm in the big awkward cast, watching others live my dream, was the last thing I wanted to do at the time. He understood my logic, often being frustrated himself at not being able to race his own race and he wished me well.

I ended up sitting at home and following the race online, watching the daily updates and chatting each night to my buddies who were there. The photos of the tracks and terrain and the familiar faces in the background were all over social media. Stories about the route along the Botswana border through the Kalahari red sand dunes (with one particular five-storey high dune climb that guys struggled to get up), the spectacular finish on the beach in Cape Town under the inflatable arch with Table Mountain in the background, it was all just too painful to hear. It sucked! I wanted to tell them to stuff off! I was miserable, this was not the plan!

Once again – as if it was even possible – my Dakar dream was pushed further out of reach.

I had a lot of time to think about my dream and the price I was paying to get there. I second guessed the sanity of the whole thing and the risks I was taking. Was it time to give up? Did I need to find a new dream? The questions swam around my head and in those difficult moments I considered calling it a day on my dream. But I still had fight in me! I still wanted to race, I wasn't done yet.

'You won't break me!' I thought.

I knew that if I ever managed to get to Dakar there would be times when I wanted to give up, when it would seem like the right thing to do. I knew it made no sense, but I was not going to quit because of this setback, I had been through worse. I didn't know if I would ever make it to that Dakar start line but I knew I could go another round. I was ready to fight.

The next few months were tough. My elbow wasn't healing well, my shoulder was painful, I could only sleep lying on my left side, so I wasn't sleeping well either. There was even more physiotherapy than my usual weekly visit. My physiotherapist Sharne just shook her head when she saw me at the first session after I got back. The way I was going, she wouldn't need any other patients. Taking anti-inflammatory tablets and painkillers messed with my digestion. As a result of my spinal cord injury I still needed medication to help me digest food and now all that was out of whack. Still not having proper bowel control complicated things even more. I was frustrated, miserable and grumpy. About six months after the 'cow attack', as I like to call it, my arm now out of the cast, but still healing, my wife had had enough.

She took me by my shoulders, looked me in the eye and said, 'Go ride your bike for a few days and come back the man I married!'

I had an adventure to plan.

Chapter 12

FINDING MY WAY

This adventure needed to be something a little bit crazy to really get the juices flowing – but also not too hectic, as my body had to survive (this was one of the conditions Meredith had strictly laid down). The other condition was a daily call to let her know I was still alive and where I was sleeping. I had decided to ride my KTM 450 XCW to Cape Town, on dirt. My bike was an enduro bike, built for off road and not really the right weapon for an assault on such a massive distance. But it was the only bike I owned so, like me, it needed to adapt and survive.

I had never really done the long distance adventure riding thing before, but I figured how hard could it be, right? I've seen those old guys on their heavy beasts with the protectors to protect the protectors that protect the extra lights above the backup lights, on a bike that already weighs half a ton.

So here we go. I went to see the helpful guys at NavWorld in Strydom Park and got them to load the Garmin Basecamp software on my laptop and give me a brief lesson on how it worked. Next, I fitted a new back tyre more suited to the longer distance and a new rear mousse from Raceworx KTM just up the road from me. I fitted my long-range tank, my softer and wider rally seat (which I had recently imported after learning the hard way), a GPS mount, an aftermarket front LED light and some bags, so things were looking good.

Neal was keen to join in and made a plan to buy a second-hand bike because, for some reason, he felt his 250 two stroke might not be up to the task of the 2700 kilometre ride. My brother-in-law Bevan was also keen to join on his CRF250L, but as a newbie to riding he knew that the full deal off road to Cape Town was a little out of his depth. I came up with a plan. We would trailer the bikes to Underberg, KwaZulu-Natal, do a loop through Lesotho with Bevan, then he would return to Joburg in the bakkie and Neal and I would continue to Cape Town. This way I avoided the first 400 kilometres boring part on tar and Bevan got to see the mountain kingdom of Lesotho on a bike. Great plan!

Now although Neal is never prepared, has zero first aid knowledge and has a general disregard for rules and authority, my wife somehow felt that I would be safer with him at my side. So once he was fully on board her mind was put at ease. For the next few days, I played on Google maps and Basecamp, searching for as many dirt roads as possible, including as many passes and epic routes mentioned on the Wild Dog biking forum. After a few late nights of planning and dreaming about my adventure, I had my route sorted and I was ready to roll.

Then things went a bit pear shaped. Neal's second-hand bike was in worse shape than he had anticipated. There was a lot to fix and we were out of time. He had no choice but to pull out. He was gutted (I could tell from the way he was crying, it wasn't pretty, the kind where there is a lot of snot and coughing). Fortunately, I didn't care how Neal felt. The bigger problem was that I had lost my riding partner and so the mission might be deemed too dangerous by Meredith and was at risk of being aborted. However, I played the depression card once again. I started wearing a lot of black and spoke about cutting myself. My wife figured I was no use to her in this state anyway, so she might as well go along with the idea of a solo ride. Naturally, solo riding increases the risks all round, but although I love riding with mates, there is something about riding all alone on the desolate, inaccessible tracks that just speaks to my soul.

DAY 1

Finally, the day came and Bevan arrived in the dark autumn air at 3am. We quietly loaded up the bakkie with the two bikes, packed our heavy bags filled with riding kit on the back seat of the double cab and quietly snuck out of Joburg. We had been driving for about four hours when the sun came over a small guest house in the farmlands, just outside Underberg and near the bottom of the infamous Sani Pass. The smells of the countryside filled the air as we crossed a small stream and rode along the dirt track towards the wooden gate.

We checked in to the fairly basic accommodation in beautiful rural surroundings, telling the owner to expect us back later that afternoon. We could see the sharp tops of the Drakensberg Mountains to the west and thought about the ambitious expedition we were about to embark on. We dumped our stuff in the room and quickly kitted up in our riding gear, anxious for the adventure to begin.

We fired the bikes up and headed back down the dusty road towards the base of the Sani Pass, the gateway to Lesotho. The pass itself began in 1913 as a bridal path, used for trade between Natal, South Africa and Mokhotlong. Over the years, it had been widened to accommodate 4x4 vehicles and some crazy Basotho taxi drivers in their vans who risked their lives, along with those of their passengers, on each trip. It's a pass steeped in history and tales of tragedy and with the talk of it possibly being tarred soon, we both felt it was one we needed to ride. We were off and headed along the smooth tar road towards the base. We stopped at the border post and had our passports stamped. Although it is a fairly 'soft' border between South Africa and Lesotho, each time I cross an African border I get excited. I often wonder what it must have been like to explore this continent before all the borders and man-made lines were established.

We continued up the zigzagging dirt road which showed off more beautiful vistas with each turn. The sky was fairly clear, so we had great views and looking back down at the pass once we had reached the top was totally incredible. Now at an altitude of 2874 metres, the air was crisp and we took the mandatory photo in front of the Sani top chalets. I filled up my hydration pack and we grabbed a quick cold drink before pushing on, knowing we still had about 400 kilometres to cover that day.

Now, don't ask me what I was thinking when I thought we could cover that much distance in Lesotho in one day, going through dirt passes with sheer drop-offs, and with Bevan who was still new to riding any kind of off road. But we set off feeling positive and blissfully unaware of the mammoth task that lay ahead. The route I had plotted was circular and I estimated it would be about eight hours of riding.

As the day went on, I did the maths in my head and slowly came to the realisation that we were never going to make the border cut-off time of 6pm at Ramatseliso's Gate. We weren't even going to get close! We stopped and took stock of the situation at about 4pm and had the choice of either trying to find a place to stay, or just keep going and sleep at the border, if necessary. We both had lights on our bikes, plenty of warm clothes and more than enough food, so we decided that we might as well just keep going.

Then things started to go wrong. First up, Bevan hit a lurker, a large half buried sharp rock, and his front tyre went flat immediately. He had some tyre weld, but I knew from past experience that it wasn't going to do much other than make a huge sticky mess on this kind of impact puncture, let alone last another 200 kilometres. Although I was running mousses, I had spare tubes and tyre levers on me just in case, so we decided to change the front tube. By some amazing chance, my KTM wheel spanner fitted his Honda front axle bolt only to find that it was over-tightened and we struggled to get it to budge. But, after shouting a few words that are not in the Bible and a running kick or two, we managed to get it off. We spent another half hour getting the tyre off, on again and re-inflated with a ridiculously small bike pump I had with me. But now we had lost even more time.

Next, using my clearly flawed maths skills, I realised that we were going to run out of petrol, which meant a 74-kilometre detour to the nearest town to get more. To top it off, it was at this point that it started to rain. Bevan's tank held only about 7 litres, but mine held 19 litres. Naturally, my pace was a lot faster than his and so, in light of the time pressure we were under, we decided to split up – the one thing I know you should never do, but if we rode together we would lose another hour at least, so we decided to risk it. I filled his tank from mine and then raced the 74-kilometre round trip to get petrol, then another 20 kilometres to catch up with Bevan. The rain was falling and it had started to get dark. Man, was I glad to see him again! My mind had been going on about what my sister would do to me if I lost or damaged her husband. It would not have been pretty!

By now night had fallen and we still had another 150 kilometres to the border. The pace we managed to maintain on the dark rocky track was only about 20 to 30 kilometres per hour, so we knew we were in for a long, cold night. Luckily, we were in good spirits and loved the adventure this was growing into. I've found over the years that when things start to go a little wrong, that's when the fun really starts! That's where the stories to share around the campfire come from! We trekked on in the dark through the rocky basalt and sandstone mountains.

In the daylight the Lesotho landscape is spectacular, with streams flowing down the steep rocky faces and the occasional flock of sheep or goats being tended by a lone young boy. The views were amazing because you could see valleys and mountains rolling out in every direction. Riding at night our visibility was reduced to just a circle a few metres ahead of us lit up by the lights on our bikes. It danced around as our wheels navigated over and through the rocks. Whenever we stopped, the motors would go quiet and as the bike lights automatically switched off, we were immediately engulfed by a thick blanket of silent darkness. It felt so remote and isolated.

Although we were really tired, we were having a blast! There were a couple of muddy sections where Bevan dropped his bike, but after riding for about ten hours on just a couple of hours' sleep the night before I couldn't fault him. He had the right mindset and was never going to quit – which in my opinion was all that mattered. I knew we would eventually get through this. It was about midnight by the time we reached the small border post and obviously it was deathly quiet with not a soul in sight.

We parked our bikes in front of the locked gate and weighed up our options. The idea of waiting there, cold and wet, until the morning when the border opened, was not very appealing. We took a walk around and noticed that we could get through the border between two fences. We had a choice: either sleep there in the veld with just a silver survival blanket for another six hours, or just go for it. We decided to go for it. We pushed our bikes past the border check in the sort of stealth mode that would make some Mexicans proud!

Feeling relieved to be back in South Africa and on our way home, we continued to bounce down a rough 4x4 track descending out of the Lesotho highlands. The track was rocky and steep, dropping off small rock ledges and twisting as it wound downwards, kilometre after kilometre. In the early hours of the morning Bevan and his little red CRF250L were really starting to take strain. It was tough even for me and we needed to stop more often. Bevan was determined not to give up, but we had been on the bikes for 16 hours at this stage and he was no doubt cursing my choice of route. Eventually, the track levelled out to a pretty good dirt road and we managed to go a little faster. At this point Bevan, totally exhausted, started to fall asleep while riding. Instead of riding ahead and waiting as I had been doing, I decided to ride behind him, then next to him, accelerating and braking randomly in an attempt to break the monotony.

Finally we reached the tar road, which meant we had a final 75 kilometres to go to Underberg. It must have been the first time in my life that I was genuinely glad to see tar. We rode for a bit and then stopped because my fuel light had come on and Bevan's had been on for a while. So there we were, in the dark at about 3am, trying to decide on the best plan. We didn't know if either of us would make it, even combining the fuel from both bikes. If we tried that, we may well both have ended up stranded, 40 kilometres apart, in the pitch dark, and still in the middle of nowhere. I wasn't comfortable towing

Bevan, as he had never done that before and we weren't even sure if it would help us conserve petrol.

So we just decided to ride as conservatively as possible, for as long as we could. At that time in the morning it seemed like the best option. Eventually, I ran out of fuel with about 24 kilometres to go. We looked in Bevan's tank and it was completely dry, with only what was left in the fuel pump. Then I realised the shape of my long-range tank meant that there was about a cupful on the other side, so I lay the bike on its left side to shift the petrol over to the fuel pump. We got only about one more kilometre before Bevan was dry. With no more options, we decided that I should just ride on alone until I ran out. After that, I would walk the rest of the way until I got petrol, no matter how long it took. So off I headed, leaving Bevan alone for the second time, this time in utter darkness.

I got up to the highest gear and, with as few revs as possible, just kept the speed constant at about 100kph. This proved to be very dangerous in the thick mist and darkness, as I could see only a few metres in front of me and my light seemed just to light up the fog, which made it worse. I took my goggles off in an attempt to see better. My eyes were like slits, strained with trying to make out the broken centre line in the road at those high speeds. At the top of each hill, I pulled in the clutch and killed the engine, rolling until the road turned upwards. Then, while still keeping momentum, I started it up again and continued, keeping the revs as low as possible. Naturally, each time I killed the engine, the headlamp went out within a few seconds, and in order to keep on the road I could only stare about a metre ahead of my front wheel at the white line that I could barely make out.

I entrusted my hearing to warn me of any cars coming from the other direction, but luckily there were none – it was about 3.30am and not a soul was around. Eventually, by no small miracle, my bike running on the memory of petrol, I made it to the Shell garage in Underberg with only fumes left in the tank. As I stopped at the pump, I punched the air in victory, noticed by no one in the still, predawn hours of the morning. The attendant looked at me in surprise, probably wondering where I had come from at that bizarre hour. I filled up and rode the 20-odd kilometres back to Bevan who was slowly pushing his bike in the darkness. He was surprised to see me so soon, convinced I wouldn't make it on the petrol I had. With a sense of pride, I transferred some fuel into his bike and we returned to the farm guest house which we had left many hours earlier. We were completely exhausted, it was 5am and we had been riding for 19 hours and been awake for 27 hours since 2am the previous day.

We slept for about four hours and then woke up feeling very rough. The guest house owner greeted us and wondered what had happened after hearing our bikes arriving in the early hours of the morning. After telling him our wild story, he just shook his head, mumbling something about being crazy. In spite of the marathon ride and insane happenings in the last 24 hours, I know Bevan was disappointed he wasn't continuing the adventure on to Cape Town, but I'm sure he was looking forward to getting home and having a proper sleep.

In my weary state I felt I had had my fill of adventure and the option of joining Bevan and heading back home seemed inviting, but I knew that sitting at work a couple of days later I would regret it. Together we loaded his bike on to the bakkie along with my wet gear and our bags. I took only the essentials; my tent and sleeping bag strapped to the back of the bike. I rinsed the mud off my bike with a bucket, changed my air filter, lubed the chain and made sure all my kit was secure. I said cheers to Bevan and headed out on my bike alone. I had four days to get to Cape Town.

DAY 2

Now, I get that riding on your own is dangerous and there are certainly more risks, but there is something really free about being on your own, far away from people, with just your thoughts and incredible country surrounding you. I made a plan to get all my stuff on the bike, only to realise that now I couldn't get my leg over it! So every time I stopped, I had to swing my leg over while still moving, and when pulling off I had to place one foot on the peg, pull off and then swing my leg over. I like to think of it more as the way the Lone Ranger got on and off his horse, and less of the way a decrepit guy with dodgy legs climbed on a big bike. Originally, I had hoped to get an early start and go quite far on that first day, but after the Lesotho 'adventure', I settled for about 300 kilometres.

I rode the Pitseng Pass in the foothills of the mighty Drakensberg, a rough, gravel road pass where I was alone the entire time. This was followed by Naude's Nek Pass, which was hauntingly beautiful and dangerous. I rode the slippery flat black rocks, accompanied by some light rain, avoiding the sheer drops to certain death alongside the road. I wound my way down the pass, ending up just as night fell in Rhodes, where I found an old school that had been converted into a cheap guest house to stay the night. The cut sandstone walls, high pressed ceilings and red painted cement floors all bore witness to a bygone time. I put my stuff down in my room, which was an old classroom, complete with the chalkboard up at the front. I had a quick shower in the old bathroom and then walked across the short crusher rock parking area to the small dining room. I had a tasty burger and a great chat about bikes and riding with a friendly guy who worked at the Tiffindell Ski Resort and who enjoyed riding himself. It was a good evening, until I went back to my room …

I opened the door, only to realise that someone had broken into my room and taken some of my clothes and all of my money, apart from the couple of hundred rand I had on me. I had brought a fair bit of cash with me, knowing I would be out in the sticks for most of the time and probably wouldn't be able to use a card much.

Man, I was mad! I was angry at myself for being so stupid. I like to think I'm pretty street smart, living in Joburg and having experienced a serious hijacking at gunpoint and been the victim of crime several times in my life. I guess being in a small picturesque town made me let my guard down. After inspecting the room, I noticed that none of the window latches locked and they could easily have been opened from the outside. There were no burglar bars and, when opened wide, the windows would easily allow someone to climb through.

I went back to the manager and told her what had happened, but there was nothing they could do. They did say that it had happened once before. Thanks! A heads-up would have been nice. At the end of the day, my stuff was gone and, as we all know, no amount of regret would bring it back. At least I was now a bit wiser. I decided to roll my bike into the room instead of leaving it outside, as I couldn't afford any more problems. I closed all the windows and placed various items on them, so that if anyone tried to open them, the items would fall and make a noise. I placed a can on the door handle as well. A little home-made booby-trap-alarm-system, just to be sure! Then I climbed into bed and after a lot of thinking about what I should have done, combined with a fair amount of self-recrimination, I fell asleep.

DAY 3

The next day I woke up at about 5.30am and, determined not to let the previous night's problems dampen my adventure, I put it all behind me. I kitted up and headed out as the early morning sun began to rise. The riding was fantastic! I rode along dirt roads and tracks

My first BMX, feeling extra cool with my A-team cap and really short shorts

Big wheelies with my pants tucked into my sock, and my bike lock around me

At the motocross track, 2004

The Roof of Africa finish line, 2006

A proud dad and five beautiful girls, 2005

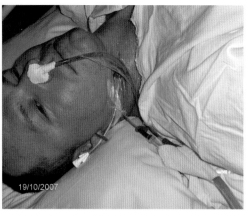

19/10/2007

At the Muelmed Hospital with the hated tube going into my stomach, October 2007

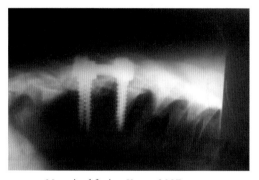

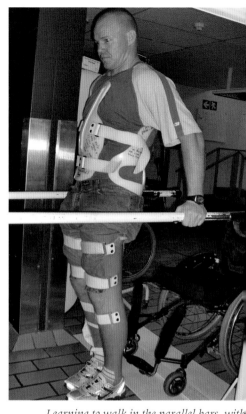

My spinal fusion X-ray, 2007

Learning to walk in the parallel bars, with the back slabs on my legs

In the hospital wheelchair

Still in the back slabs but now on the crutches, with sweat pouring through my shirt

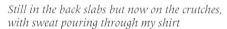

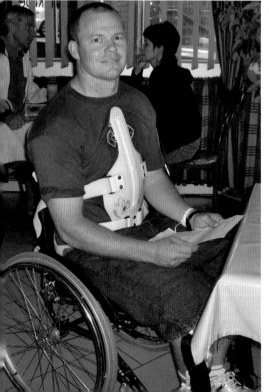

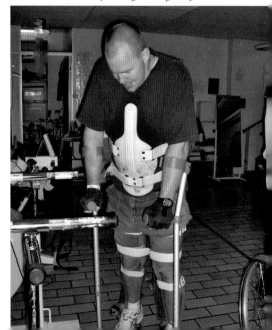

Late at night, fitting the navigation equipment onto my enduro bike, with wires like spaghetti, August 2013

Crossing the Breede River at Malgas by ferry

Leaving Die Hel early in the morning

My destroyed tyre on Day 6 of the 2015 Amageza Rally

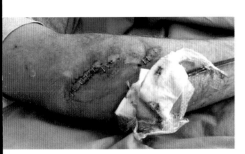

My right forearm after the 'cow attack'

Arriving late at night at the checkpoint, complete with wire marks from the fence across the top of my front number board   (Photo credit: Oakpics)

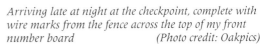

Sunset wheelies on the Hakskeen Pan, 2015 (Photo credit: Oakpics)

Training on the mine dumps at Maraisburg, west of Johannesburg   (Photo credit: Alan Robert)

Me and my beautiful Meredith, North Coast, KwaZulu-Natal, 2014

Racing the KTM 450 Rally Replica in the Northern Cape, 2016 (Photo credit: Eugene Botes Sports Photography)

Just a couple minutes before all hell broke loose at the Merzouga Rally final day mass start

Even the camels find it tough out there at the Merzouga Rally, Morocco, 2016

winding their way through the Drakensberg Mountains and valleys. Fairly early on, while on a jeep track, there was a beautiful black, grey and dark orange puff adder in the track, I just missed it, but did a mad scramble to try to turn around while taking my camera out of my jacket pocket. I got the shot, but the moment he entered the grass he immediately disappeared – his camouflage was just incredible!

I rode over 600 kilometres on dirt that day, including the Otto du Plessis Pass, De Beer's Pass, Suurberg Pass and Doring Nek. Almost out of petrol (again) I arrived in Addo and decided to stay at the Orange Elephant Backpackers. (I really screwed up on that petrol planning thing!) I was busy booking in at the reception when the owner John arrived back. He's a biker and when he saw I was on a bike he gave me a room at about 30 per cent of the normal cost! It was a welcome gesture after having most of my cash stolen the previous night. Then to top it off, he gave me a big braai pack on the house and cooked the meat for me.

We sat around the braai talking and laughing with some other travellers. It had been a great day's riding but being on my enduro bike I wanted to make sure I looked after the motor. So I did an oil change that night, along with a normal service routine. John came over and offered to help and let me use some of his tools when he saw that I had stripped a nut while doing the oil change. It's the kind of service and generosity you don't find every day but, as I had discovered over the years, most bikers were like that.

DAY 4

The previous night I had noticed that my front tyre looked a bit flat. The old mousse inside was worn and collapsing, so with more than 1000 kilometres still to go to Cape Town, I had to make a plan.

I headed to Port Elizabeth and the KTM dealer to which John had given me directions. I arrived just after 8am and the guys were super helpful. Within about half an hour, I had a new front tyre and mousse fitted, they even set and lubed my chain on the house. The mechanics asked about where I'd come from and were clearly intrigued about why I was doing such a trip on the enduro bike. We spoke for a few minutes and laughed like old buddies – it's just the biker way. Great guys and more great service!

I then said 'cheers' to my new mates and did the required wheelie up the road (to look at my new tyre, obviously) before heading off to Patensie and through the Baviaanskloof. What a place! There were lots of river crossings varying in depth and width, I came across plenty of game, including kudu, small buck, a big monitor lizard and tons of baboons. I wished I had more time to stop and take it all in. I could have spent days there admiring the vistas. The dark damp dirt road wound its way from the lush bush at the start up and over the mountains with steep rocky tracks bleached pale by the sun, the dust clouding up as I rode past. I stopped at the top of one peak and looked back down the track that I had just ridden and I couldn't help being reminded of how fortunate I was to be there. I was seeing places that millions of people living in the country never even knew existed. My self-pity regarding my injuries was slowly evaporating. I had a lot to be appreciative about!

The terrain became more arid and dry as I continued on towards the small town of Uniondale. The vegetation became sparser and the plants changed to suit the harsher environment. I was entering the Klein Karoo. I rode on, alone with my thoughts and the sound of the engine below me, gliding effortlessly as the dirt road wrapped its way through the dry, dusty habitat. Then the road became much steeper, as I started the climb up the south side of the Swartberg Pass. Along the way I passed two adventure riders with panniers covered in flags and stickers of their travels. I waved and they waved back, then I shot on ahead, leaving them trundling up the pass on their heavy bikes, proud of my 'light' adventure rig. We were on different bikes and different adventures, but we were all part of the same biker family.

I reached the top of the pass and took a left, entering the Gamkas-kloof road. This weaving dirt track has 'adventure bike legend' status, a must-do for anyone who has thrown their leg over an adventure bike. A 37-kilometre rugged gravel road, it twists and drops its way downwards through a narrow isolated valley, ending in the final oasis, the valley floor surrounded by wild olive and thorn trees and ironically nicknamed 'Die Hel'. I arrived in the old seemingly forgotten community just as it was getting dark. My plan was to set up my compact one man tent and camp, but there were small old caravans to rent for the same price, so I figured that that option would be much easier after riding another 600-odd kilometres that day. How they got the old beige caravans there in the first place was a mystery to me. I opened the small wonky door of the caravan, brushing a few cobwebs aside, and stepped onto the vinyl floor which was lifting at the edges and creaked under my boots. I put my bag and jacket on the old veneer countertop – the chipboard exposed and swollen at the edges. It was perfect! It fitted the adventure and added to the strange, eccentric surroundings.

There were a couple of other bikers there – I'm embarrassed to say I can't remember their names – who asked me to pull in for a braai with them that night. The kind lady who ran the small shop there put together a braai pack for me, even though they were already closed. I took a quick shower and joined the other guys at the fire, the bush dark and quiet around us.

I could tell they'd had their own 'adventure' that day when I noticed that one guy's BMW bike had a car battery strapped to the back of it. His battery had failed and they had managed to get a spare one from a passing 4x4. Strapped to the back of the bike and connected with dodgy looking wires, they had made it in earlier that day. Both of them had pillions; one was riding with his daughter and the other with his wife. I found the hairpin mountain bends that day intimidating enough on my own and couldn't imagine having someone on the back with me. It was a good evening sitting under the stars, surrounded by the Swartberg Mountains and, with the smell of sizzling meat on the fire, we swapped stories and added firewood to nature's TV.

DAY 5

I woke up early again in the dark, just after 5am. Early morning, when everything feels quiet and untouched, is my favourite time of the day. I kitted up quietly and rolled out of the camp at first light. As I headed out, I saw the two other bikers that I had passed on the climb the previous day. They had their bedrolls out and were sleeping under the stars. I can only assume that they were doing some really big trip and to see them sleeping under the stars made me feel as though I had been a bit of a softie staying in the old caravan. Next time I'm doing the million star hotel for sure!

Coming out of Die Hel alone, as the sun rose to meet me in the crisp morning air, was certainly a highlight of the trip. I stopped on several occasions and just sat quietly for a few minutes, in awe of the valley with its dirt track twisting its way through the mountains. My heart swelled with gratitude for the opportunity to be there. I was alive and, in spite of my physical challenges, life was good. I felt I could do anything I put my mind to. I thought about my Dakar goal, how crazy and ridiculous it seemed, but it was *my* dream and I was going to do it. It was that simple.

I passed lots of small buck as I exited Die Hel that morning. I headed south, back down the Swartberg Pass which was now enveloped in thick fog. I was sopping wet by the time I reached the bottom. I really didn't want to be wet all day, but the Klein Karoo dried me out soon enough. I rode many dirt passes that last day, including Huis se Hoogte Pass, Seveweekspoort, Koueveld Pass, Langkloof Pass and Ouberg Pass. The incredible wide open spaces of the Klein Karoo seemed to speak to me. It's a dry, wide open, harsh environment, but it just drew me in. I felt safe and in control there. Well, at least until my GPS decided to stop working …

Suddenly the barren wilderness was not so inviting. The thought of being lost there, alone and with a dwindling water supply, was a much less heart-warming vision. Luckily, I had brought some paper maps as a backup, so I managed to work out my route and pushed on. As the day went on, I saw what looked like a big stick on the dirt road. I rode around it and as I passed it hooded up and turned out to be a long brown Cape Cobra. The same crazy braking and fumbling for the camera followed. Once again, it amazed me how well it blended into its surroundings.

Finally, after riding 2700 kilometres over the last few days, I rode my enduro bike into Cape Town early that evening. The Cape winds were blowing so strongly that it had me knee dragging while riding in a straight line. Although it was Sunday evening, my mates Neal and Eddy from Eddy2Race, the local Husqvarna dealer, went the extra mile and opened up the workshop for me to park my bike. I got a bed at Neal's place that night. Eddy serviced my bike over the next couple of days and between them they arranged for it to be crated and sent back to Joburg for me. They were just two more brothers in the biking family, happy to help wherever they could. I flew back to Joburg the next day, exhausted, sore and worn out, but happy to be home again with my family and in my own bed.

I was done with my self-pity and frustration. I had a Dakar goal to chase. It was time to get busy!

Chapter 13

BURNING
RUBBER

I joined a few local races after getting back from Cape Town, but the big one coming up was the 2015 Amageza Rally. This year they had once again upped the game to a distance of 5000 kilometres spread over seven days. The route started in Kimberley and wound its way through the Northern Cape Kalahari, crossed the border into Botswana with its thick sand, cut lines, beautiful wildlife and endless miles of thorn trees, before crossing the border back into South Africa, where it finally finished back in Kimberley. It was a big one for my Dakar rider proposal and I needed to get a finish to add it to the list. I sent in my entry and, to make it even tougher, I entered the Malle Moto class.

Anyone who's a Dakar Rally fan will have heard of the 'Malle Moto' class – a rough-looking group of guys who do the Dakar without any team support or mechanics to assist them. Directly translated, 'Malle Moto' means 'trunk motorbike', which is basically all you have. When you see them on TV, they don't look like the clean stage winners in the Red Bull kit or the factory riders with the shiny bikes. These guys are in dirty kit with bikes that don't get a proper wash for 14 days, they have facial hair like steel wool, bugs in their teeth and have that crazy 'I'm on the edge' look in their eyes, like a guy in a fight with nothing to lose.

The rules for that class are that you put your stuff into two standard metal trunks that get transported on a truck to the next bivouac each day. Once you've arrived each night, after riding 750-odd kilometres off road and generally after dark, you have to set up your own tent, service your own bike, fix anything that was broken or crashed, attend riders' briefing, eat some food, try to rehydrate, mark and load your roadbook, enter the essential waypoints on your GPS, and then maybe shower and possibly get some sleep.

When other racers asked me what team I was with at documentation and I replied 'Malle Moto', their response was generally, 'Why did you do that? You know what it is, right?' followed by 'Good luck' and a snigger. By the time documentation and scrutineering was over, there were eight guys out of a total of 86 riders who had entered in the Malle Moto class, each of us wondering what lay ahead. What had we got ourselves into?

It was a crazy race and these are the stories of each of the Malle Moto riders.

First up was Jonathan Lewis, a veterinarian from Shelly Beach. He was a keen biker who loved adventure riding and had a passion to race in a cross country off-road rally. Although at the time he had no previous racing experience, he was determined to get out there and learn the ropes of off-road rally racing. Day One was a baptism of fire for Jonathan, handling his heavy bike for hundreds of kilometres and arriving in the bivouac long after dark. It left him unable to continue on Day Two, partly because of the strict medical clearances required for the high safety standards set by the organisers. It was all over too soon, but he was determined to return with more sand training under his belt and to be better physically prepared.

Next was Rikus Botha, a 48-year-old dairy and beef farmer from the Eastern Cape and father of three. He'd been riding bikes since he was 13, had raced the three-day Roof of Africa enduro in work overalls in 2003 and was here for an adventure. He certainly got that! Halfway through Day One, after several hundred kilometres and shortly into the first special stage, he stopped to help a fellow rider and noticed oil all over his boot. It turned out that the insert on the clutch cover was missing, spewing out most of his engine oil and the inside of his clutch was now full of sand.

Now we have all heard that a 'boer maak 'n plan' and I think this oke was the original boer that we all talk about. He took the perspex screen off his roadbook, cut it to size with his Leatherman, and then using Pratley Putty, wire and duct tape, he made a plan to close the gaping hole. The oil was really low, but he pushed on in the thick river bed sand for more than 20 kilometres, trying to keep the revs low. Anyone who has ever ridden slowly in sand will know that it is just simply torture. Eventually, the river bed ended and he managed to get some car oil at a small shop. He filled up the bike and put the hammer down to make up as much time as possible. As the sun set, alone and physically exhausted from the slow soft sand riding, he continued to push on. By 7pm, with still a long way to go, he decided the safest and smartest thing to do was to stop and spend the night in the bush.

Now for most city guys, the thought of surviving a night alone in the bush right on the Botswana border, with only what you have on you, is enough to make you soil your linen. But he tells his story as if it was a normal Tuesday. He made a fire, dried his clothes and slept on his large paper map of the Northern Cape, with only a thin foil survival blanket to cover him. At 4am the next morning, the sweeper truck arrived fully loaded. They gave him five litres of water and told him to stay put, as they had been recovering many riders throughout the night.

More than five hours later, he got the chance to pay a local guy to retrieve him on an old bakkie and take him back to the tar road with his bike. He decided to call the ops room and make his own way back on his bike to the start at Kimberley. After several oil top-ups and more putty and wire, and several hundreds of kilometres later, he arrived that evening back at the start in Kimberley and found a place to sleep. The next morning, without any spare clothes (they were all in his trunk on the Malle Moto truck, now in Botswana), he went to a local mall to buy some clothes wearing the same clothes he had been sleeping and riding in for more than 48 hours, and without shoes. No doubt the looks he got were priceless! Then, feeling that he needed more adventure, he decided to get into his Hilux bakkie and drive about 650 kilometres to Hakskeen Pan, where he met up again with the rally at the end of Day Five. Without hesitation, he joined the recovery crew to help for the next two days using his own vehicle. He covered more than 1500 kilometres of racing stages, helping stranded riders. Unfortunately, there was no finisher's trophy for him that year, but he left with a bucketful of adventure and respect from racers and marshals alike. He is tough as they come!

Then there was Niel Kruger. He was also on his first rally, riding a modified WR450 – which he had done entirely on his own over many late nights in his garage. He probably knew his bike better than any of us did and was very well prepared. His race started off well through the first few hundred kilometres, which saw a lot of guys with inferior builds take a hammering on the corrugated surfaces. He then entered the dreaded river bed section on the first special stage and rode it fast – the only way you can ride that soft sand – dodging washouts, trees and the hidden holes dug by the locals for water. He took a fall fairly early on and dislodged his fuel lines, which was not a major problem for him, as he sorted them out fairly quickly. He continued his race, only to have problems shortly afterwards because he had picked up some sand in the lines during his previous stop. Still not a major problem for Niel! He reverse bled them and was off racing again.

The next challenge, however, was a bit more serious. Over a small jump, the back completely locked up and he lost the use of his gears. After some heavy blunt force trauma, he managed to get the bike in a gear, but still unable to change. Still, this wasn't a problem; he would just ride it in that one gear! The problem with cross country rally racing is that time is your enemy and every problem robs you of that precious commodity.

His situation then unfortunately snowballed when he found himself trying to navigate as night fell, making matters not only more difficult, but more dangerous too. Now in pitch black darkness, he and two other riders were completely lost with no way to work out the correct route. They managed to text their situation to race head-quarters and were recovered via their Spot trackers at 3am. It took them until 11.45am to reach the bivouac, from which the race had moved on. He had no choice but to stay another night, as he couldn't get to the border in time. Getting a lift on a bakkie, he managed to catch up with the race two days later. It turned out that his gearbox was a complete mess and impossible to fix, which put him out of the race. Still keen for adventure, he joined the Malle Moto truck and travelled with the rally where he helped many of the riders. He was a great guy to have met and share the adventure with.

The next Malle Moto rider was Antal Verschuuren from The Netherlands. After riding and racing all over Europe for the last five years, he had decided that he needed an African adventure. He shipped his bike over for the rally and arrived in South Africa shortly before the start. Since his bike had been on a ship for the previous six weeks, he had a lot of last-minute hassles to sort out. Despite all this, he made it to the start ready to roll, as calm as ever. Nothing seemed to stress this guy out. He handled every challenge like a champ. He played it cool and calm, navigated well and got through the first few days really well. The long heavy days of riding and some injuries took their toll on him, though, and saw him miss Day Four in order to recover.

By Day Five he was back and fighting again – only to be hounded by motor problems this time. He got some help on the side of the road near Pofadder. He raced again on Day Seven, only to have to deal with motor problems that put an end to the day. He was collected by the sweep vehicle about 225 kilometres in. It was a disappointing end for such a dedicated and positive rider who showed perseverance and composure in the face of many challenges. Still, it was clear that he had loved his time in Africa and would return to race again.

Then there was Gerrit du Toit, the only guy to have ridden in every Amageza for the past five years. The guy is a machine! He doesn't care about positions and times and has probably helped more fellow riders stuck out in the bush than anyone else. He raised money to race by selling space on his shirt and bike, where people could 'gooi a selfie', so his bike and shirt were filled with pictures of all his friends, family and sponsors – very cool indeed!

Luck dealt him a hard blow on Day Two, with his foot peg break-ing clean off. But in true Gerrit fashion, he made a plan with a stick and rode the last 50-odd kilometres to bring it home. Then he strug-gled with battery issues on Day Three, making it difficult to start the bike. This also snowballed when, along with several other riders, he arrived at a petrol station in one of the villages in Botswana where they were supposed to fill up, only to find that it had run out of fuel. The entire area was clean out of fuel and it was just before sunset.

He made a plan, somehow managing to get a police officer to take him and fellow rider Claude in his own personal car 15 kilometres across the border from Botswana into Namibia and back to get fuel. Later that night, they set off for another 120 kilometres in freezing weather, with their space blankets under their jackets to try to retain some body heat. Despite helping many riders and with his fair share of challenges, including some very late nights fixing his bike, he went on to finish the full seven days and received his coveted finisher's trophy.

Also riding with Gerrit that evening was Quintin du Plooy, the owner of Outdoor Escape in Stellenbosch and another Malle Moto guy who had been struggling with his clutch and electrical problems since the first day. He finally had to call it quits when his bike completely died. On top of that, he had a collapsed rear mousse and was out of petrol. It was obviously difficult for Gerrit to leave a man behind, because it isn't in his nature. But Quintin, a keen outdoorsman, sent him on his way and stayed alone, to be met later by the sweep bakkie at about 11pm. It still had to go back for another two riders in the opposite direction. Instead of enduring a nine hour journey through the bush on the back of a bakkie, he opted to stay put and be picked up on the way back.

He ended up spending a long, cold night (the thermometer on his watch showed zero degrees) under a tree with his space blanket.

Eventually, he was told by a passing cop by that he couldn't sleep there so he joined some local workers at a small petrol stop and slept on the concrete floor there – not much of an upgrade! He's plenty tough and although he looked tired when I saw him the next day after he'd been picked up at 10am, he fixed his bike and went on to join the rally again to race the last couple of days. He clearly hadn't had his fill of adventure yet!

Donovan van der Langenberg, having finished two previous Amageza rallies, was a seasoned Malle Moto rider who rode fast and navigated well. However, he ran into some problems on Day Three, when an unclear section of the roadbook saw him take a turn – along with several other riders – that ended up costing him hours and several hundred kilometres as he tried to find petrol in rural Botswana to get through the stage. He persevered and rolled in to the bivouac very late that night, but still in the race.

This meant that he started at the back the next morning and as if the previous day's luck wasn't bad enough, his bike died right on the start line. He worked out that it was the fuel injector and got it cleared, but it was still leaking and seemed to be missing an O-ring. By now, most teams had left and he was desperately running around trying to get some sort of small O-ring. He managed to get something close enough and after two long hours and some grease, he got the injector in and had the bike running.

He set off two hours behind in the field, but he was not about to quit. He's a true rally racer and was in it till the end. Over the last few days he also dealt with a massive dent in his front rim that nearly ended his race, but ultimately he went on to the end and received his finisher's trophy. I never saw him without a smile on his face, despite the many challenges – true Malle Moto spirit.

Now for me. I had a slow start. I packed way too much gear to take with me on the bike on the first couple of days, which made the handling terrible in the thick river bed sand, so I really battled that first day to get into the racing groove. I had decided to carry a lot in terms of spares and tools, knowing how important the finish was for my progression towards my ultimate goal. The deep, camouflaged holes that the locals had dug for water in the wide sandy river bed added to the dangers. GG Alcock, a fellow racer, described them as being 'as deep as a grave ready to welcome you in with just the sand needing to be pushed back, once you were inside'. My strategy was to focus on the long game – and long it certainly was. I got back every day, except one, in the dark. I had a 20-litre long-range tank on my fuel injected KTM 450, but because of all the sand I found myself constantly trying to ration fuel.

This really hit home in Botswana on the second day, when I ran out of petrol alone in the dark African bush several kilometres from the bivouac. Once the light on my bike went out, I realised how in 'the middle of nowhere' I really was. I started walking, pushing my bike in the silence with a small compact headlamp lighting up a circle the size of a dinner plate about a metre ahead of my front wheel. As I walked, all I could hear was my motocross boots creaking and the sound of the bike's tyres on the sand road, accompanied by occasional rustling and movement from the thick bush around me. I turned to look but I couldn't see a thing, my pathetic little torch only catching a faint shadow moving now and again in the dim moonlight. I knew it was probably the odd cow or donkey often found wandering all over Botswana, but my imagination begged to differ. I've told my kids a hundred times not to be scared of the dark and there I was, trying to take my own advice, alone at night in the pitch black Botswana bush. I made sure I carried a proper torch every day after that.

I walked alone, pushing the empty bike, for about half an hour, until another rider came along. We tipped his bike over and managed to fill up the collapsed 1-litre Liqui-Fruit box that I carried for such emergencies with petrol. I poured the life-giving fluid into my bike. It was enough to get me in the last few kilometres and I arrived late that night in the sandy bivouac filled with thorn trees. I still needed to service my bike and change the tyres ready for the next day of racing and it would be after midnight before I got to sleep in my pop-up tent nestled between the thorn trees. I was still in the race and that's all that mattered.

The next morning was only the start of Day 3 but many of the competitors were already out of the race. The remaining riders looked a lot worse for wear as they emerged from their tents red-eyed, limping and still dirty from the day before. I'm sure Meredith wouldn't have found me particularly attractive that morning either and on top of everything, a problem with a catheter in the night left me with urine soaked tracksuit pants. It was now six years since I broke my back and yet I was still dealing with bladder problems.

At home I went to the bathroom and used a catheter once or twice each night, washing the silicone tube in the sink and putting it back into the sterilised solution. Out in the bush in a one-man tent was more of a challenge. Other times I had got up and dressed and walked the hundred-odd metres to the portable toilets and had done the same with a head torch and a bottle of water. It took for ever and left me wide awake when I returned to my tent. I needed a better plan and there wasn't exactly a handbook called 'How to race through the Botswana bush while dealing with a spinal cord injury'. I had found some disposable self-catheter tubes at the urology hospital in Pretoria and so each night in my tent I would tuck an old empty 500ml plastic cold drink bottle between my legs and drain my bladder into it with the disposable tube. Then I would push the catheter tube into the bottle, close the top, and voilà! All done, easy game. I had even brought black carrier bags so I could put the bottles in them and throw them away in the morning without anyone noticing.

The main challenge was that on a multiple day race my legs really took a hammering and they'd often spasm when I woke up at night and tried to use them. Apparently holding a half-filled bottle between them was too much to ask. The footage would have been a YouTube hit of me trying to hold on to my man parts with one hand and the other hand grabbing a half-filled bottle of urine while my legs did the Riverdance like Michael Flatley. The black carrier bag that next morning would contain my tracksuit pants along with the half-filled bottle. There was no time to wash and dry them and no ways I wanted to put the pants back in my steel trunk for the next four days. That morning I headed right out to the shower truck and stood under cold water trickling even more slowly than I could pee. The race wasn't for sissies and nor was my injury.

On Day 3 the roadbook required some guessing in parts and I made a few navigational errors and rode my fair share of extra kilometres. Some riders fared worse than me, only getting in before sunrise the next day. The route that day was a true test of skill and endurance as the sandy track wove tightly between the thorn trees. They ripped at every part of you, tearing jackets, gloves and boots alike. It wasn't uncommon to have to stop from time to time to pull a long white thorn out of a knuckle or forearm. The constant twisting made it difficult to get speed and ride on top of the sand that seemed to suck your tyres in the moment you let off the gas.

Now and again I saw a track where a rider hadn't made a turn and ploughed through a thorn bush. I chuckled when I saw it, think-ing of the wide-eyed cursing and blood-curdling shouts that would have accompanied it when it happened. I made the same mistake myself a few times and had the torn up nose, arms and neck as battle scars to prove it. Even if you stayed on the track the whole time, the thorny limbs hung ready to catch you like a poacher's snare. After many winding kilometres and long, straight as an arrow, cut lines that seemed never-ending I rolled into the bivouac that night, once again after dark. I knew that in order to finish I needed to be strict with my bike maintenance each night, no matter how late I came in. I got busy doing an oil change along with a new oil filter, a new air filter, tensioned and lubed my chain and gave the whole bike a once over as I would do every night.

Day 4 passed with similar terrain and challenges, the occasional salt pan offering a welcome break from the thick sand onslaught. That day I also came across a rider who had hit a mound in the track at high speed and had taken a massive fall. He had been unconscious and had some serious injuries. Seeing his bloodied face through his helmet was a stark reminder of the risks we were all taking. Others riders had stopped before me and I stayed with them until the ambulance arrived. I helped carry the rider into the ambulance. His name was Walter Terblanche. I didn't know him at the time, but our paths would cross again.

At riders' briefing late that night at the end of Day 4 we had been warned about the possibility of lions in the area, but I paid little attention. I figured that if I could drive around the Kruger National Park for three days and not see any, what were my chances now? I rode the next day and stopped several times to rest or drain my bladder and never saw a lion. That evening when I saw the photos from the photographers it turned out that just minutes before the first riders came through, they had come across a small pride, right next to the track! I can assure you, if I had seen them I would not have needed a catheter!

Along with cows, goats and chickens, wild animals posed a serious risk to riders. A rider had already gone out after breaking his shoulder in a collision at night with a kudu. Thomas Eich, who would go on to win the rally, also had a close shave with a hyena on Day 5, whilst racing down a wide sandy track just outside the Kgalagadi Transfrontier Park. The front guys ran a big risk, crossing the terrain first, often at dawn. We all knew the dangers, but the adventure far outweighed the risks. We were racing through the wilds of Botswana while some other unfortunate guy was sitting behind his desk dying slowly in the death trap we call the modern world.

My biggest challenge with regard to the bike, along with most of the other riders, was the speed at which I was wearing out my tyres and mousses. Mousses were essential in making sure we didn't get punctures going through the thorny Botswana bushveld. The front tyres were fine, but I had gone through several rears by the end of Day 5. The fast tracks and tar liaisons just ate up the aggressive tread and the excessive heat softened the mousses. I fitted my last back tyre on my bike at the end of Day 5 hoping it would last the final two days.

The end of Day 5 was an evening I will remember for as long as I live. The bivouac was on the Hakskeen Pan, a completely flat, dry mud and salt pan in the Kalahari Desert in the Northern Cape. The pan covered an area of approximately 140km². It was a place where much speed testing was done and was currently being prepped for an attempt on the world land speed record. This was the only day that I arrived before dark. The Malle Moto truck was held up at the Middleputs border post quite far behind us, so although most riders had changed out of their riding gear, the Malle Moto guys were still kitted up. In the end, this worked out really well, because the rally photographers asked us to sit on our bikes for an impromptu photo shoot as the sun went down across the pan behind us. I felt a little silly but did my best 'blue steel' pose, trying to look like a hardened rally racer sitting on my bike, hoping my facial hair didn't look too patchy. They then asked if one of us would do some wheelies in front of the sunset ... Well, let's just say they didn't have to ask twice! I wheelied back and forth across the pan in front of the sunset as the photographers snapped away.

Life was great, that night on the pan. I was still in the race, the bike was running well and the setting was incredible. The stars were unbelievable, the Milky Way shone brighter than I had seen in many years – it was truly amazing. As I lay there that night looking up at the stars, I was reminded of hiking the Fish River Canyon in Namibia years before my accident. I was in my early twenties back then, and the beauty of the stars in that dry region had left a lasting impression on me. I could never do a seven-day hike through a canyon like that now with my disability, but I could ride my dirt bike to these remote places and share the same sky. I thought of Meredith and my girls back home; I had so much to be grateful for! I was racing well, my bike and body fulfilling all that had been required of them each day. But the next day things were going to change – big time!

Day 6 was the penultimate day of the rally. The route started off with us racing across the vast, dry pan with a few instructions in the roadbook to navigate through the gates in the fences that divided up the pan. They sent us off two at a time with a minute's gap between each set. I lined up at the start next to another rider and the marshal informed us the starting line was in the wrong place, so we needed to zero our ICO at the first gate. By this, he meant to check at that first gate that the ICO should read about 2.25 kilometres to match the first instruction on the roadbook. I understood him to mean zero it to zero and start counting from there. This small confusion meant that after that gate, my ICO was out by just over two kilometres. As I raced across the pan, the 'triple caution' fence I was expecting at the 6.5 kilometre mark suddenly appeared two kilometres earlier. It was only a few minutes after dawn and visibility was low with the dust from the riders ahead hanging in the air. The moment I saw the fence appear through the haze, I braked as hard as I could. My back wheel lifted and my front forks compressed, pushing my front wheel hard into the surface, desperately trying to shed as much speed as possible before the imminent impact.

At the last moment I ducked behind the navigation tower and rode into the wires, still at pace, ripping the fence stakes out of the ground to the left and right of me, until the strands broke. (The organisers later told me I ripped out a total of 60 metres.) My bike and I cartwheeled across the flat pan and I came to a stop about 10 metres from my bike, encircled by the dust cloud and once again completely winded. I rolled over and onto all fours in the dirt, desperately trying to catch my breath. Peter How, who had picked up my bike at the Amageza Rally back in 2013 when I crashed, stopped to check on me. He once again picked up my bike, asked me a couple of questions to check me for concussion and after I gave him the OK, he was off. I was really sore but fortunately without serious injury. It seemed that I was getting better at crashing.

Many of the other riders came flying at full speed through the spot where the fence had been. I waved to as many of them as I could to slow them down, afraid they might get entangled in the circles of wire and metal rods strewn about. After the last rider had gone, I was alone, hurting and frustrated. The start was barely out of sight and I would need to cover about 750 harsh African kilometres that day. I needed to finish this race – my Dakar dream was riding on it. Quitting was simply not an option; I needed to make a plan.

So I got busy fixing and making my bike as rideable as possible. I loosened the triple clamps holding the front suspension and straightened the forks as best I could. My front headlight brackets were broken off and the front mudguard was also broken. My hand guard shields and side shrouds were torn from their mounts. I pulled out my duct tape and cable ties and got it all more or less back together. I lost about an hour in total but, once sorted, I was on my way. The bars were still a bit skew, but I was worried that I would miss the 2pm cut-off for the second racing special later that day, so I just raced on with everything the way it was.

Shortly after that, I came across two of my mates, Dave Griffin and Gerry van der Byl from the Omega RAD racing team. Gerry, on his first Amageza, had been riding well, but with less than two days left had taken a big hit after a high speed crash over a rough, hard packed section and he had been unconscious for a long time. The medical chopper was on its way and Dave was sitting next to Gerry holding his teammate's head as still as possible. It became very real all of a sudden, and I realised I had been very lucky to escape the fence incident without serious injury. The chopper came into sight and Dave said that he had it sorted, so off I went.

I was chasing the clock for most of the day, I had to make the 2pm cut-off to enter the second racing section, or my race would be over. I made it with just minutes to spare. Relieved to still be in the race, I headed out on the fast hard dirt track. Then just a few kilometres in, I felt the back of my bike fish tail all over the place. I pulled off to the side of the dirt track in a cloud of dust to inspect the back tyre and couldn't believe my eyes. My back tyre was a complete mess! There was a hole the size of a fist where the rubber was entirely gone, as well as another hole measuring about 6x4cm. The mousse had completely melted to a sticky goo and had been flicked out under the back mudguard, leaving what was left of the tyre carcass almost totally empty. I was utterly gutted! With about 230 kilometres still to go, mostly on single track with plenty of rocks, river beds and thick sand, this was a race ender for sure!

'NO, NO, NO!' I thought. 'This cannot end here, not after all these kilometres and surviving the fence! I'm not going out now! Think Joey, think!' I muttered out loud.

Because of the problems earlier in the day and the time I had lost there were only a handful of riders behind me. Dave was the first to stop, he saw my predicament and handed me his spare rear tube after I told him I was going to make a plan and ride through the night, if necessary at 10kph, but that I was not going to press my tracker for recovery. He said he respected my tenacity, but he definitely thought I was crazy. He was right, but I badly needed this finish. After he left, I noticed he had been carrying his tube on the bike and over the last five and a half days, it had rubbed right through in several places and was totally unusable. Could this get any worse?

There were only two more groups of guys to come through. Ian Henderson, one of the Team 525 guys, gave me a small bicycle hand pump and a fist full of cable ties. Then finally two of the nicest guys in the rally, 'Malle Moto' Gerrit and Claude Deyzel, stopped as they always do. Gerrit had another tube taped up and stashed behind his headlight. He gave it to me without any hesitation and they both offered to help, but I knew I was in for a long night so I sent them on their way. I had my bike lying on its side in the soft sand with the back wheel out and the tyre off the rim at this point.

Before Claude left, he suggested possibly using the elbow guard out of my racing jacket to try to close the gaping hole in the ruined tyre, so I shoved the elbow guard into the tyre carcass. I had my folded paper map of Botswana in its plastic sleeve and my flat 1-litre Liqui-Fruit carton which I used to cover the other large hole. I then slit open the inside of Dave's damaged tube with my Leatherman and wrapped it around the outside of the good tube, put it all inside the tyre and then back on to the rim. I inflated the tube with the tiny pump that was supposed to pump in both directions, but this one – typical of the luck I was experiencing that day – only worked in one direction. My shoulder was burning and my heart rate climbing until I nearly puked trying to get enough air into the tube, only to realise that now the other tube was leaking as well. Seriously! This cannot be happening!

All the other riders had long gone by now and this whole episode from when I first stopped had taken up nearly three hours. I was stone last and the sun was heading rapidly for the horizon. I decided to put the wheel back on the bike, cable-tie it to the rim and strap it around the big hole with a strap I had with me. Then I rode off slowly, sitting high up on the petrol tank in an attempt to keep as much of my weight off the back wheel as possible.

Several kilometres later, I saw an old bakkie heading towards me in the distance. I stopped before he reached me to replace some of the cable ties. A guy in a khaki shirt pulled up his white single-cab bakkie next to me in a cloud of dust. There was a lady in the front seat and his workers on the back. He asked if I needed help and I explained my predicament. As just about any South African farmer would, he offered to help me with a lift back to the main road or into town where I could be picked up. I thanked him but explained that I needed to go about 228 kilometres through the Richtersveld in the opposite direction.

He looked at me and I could tell he thought I had been in the sun too long or had perhaps hit my head a bit hard. The only suggestion he had for me was that there was a split in the road several kilometres ahead and if I took the right split about 10 kilometres down there was a farm where they had a motorbike and might be able to help me with another tyre. I thanked him again and we headed off in opposite directions.

I rode with my body perched forward again, my legs under the bars of the bike, stopping twice more to replace some of the cable ties in an attempt to keep the tyre on the rim. I eventually got to the split in the road, switched off my bike and sat there in the gravel track, considering the pros and cons of each option.

According to my roadbook, the track I was supposed to take was to the left. If I headed right towards the farm it meant an extra 20 kilometres of riding and then still taking a chance whether they might have the right size tyre and at least a patch kit for the tube. My rim could also totally fail before I got there, leaving me stranded on the wrong track and in a far worse predicament. If I went left I would be on the correct track but the odds of me making the 220-odd kilometres seemed near impossible.

I was also running out of water so I knew the decision was vital, the race and possibly my life rested on it. I decided to head left on the race route, based mainly on the fact that I would be where I should be if I didn't make it, giving me the best chance of recovery. I pushed on, looking at the time on my GPS – it was about 6pm, which gave me about 12 hours before my start time at 6am the following morning.

The rules of rally dictated that as long as I was in before my start time the next day, and provided I passed a short medical test, I could continue and still be in the race. I worked out that with the 12 hours left to cover 220 kilometres I just needed to keep an average speed of about 20kph. But my tyre was getting worse by the minute, the sun was setting and things were looking hopeless. I decided I would just keep riding as long as I could and then walk until I was time barred and picked up by the recovery vehicle. I saw some wire lying next to the track and stopped to put in in my bag, as I was sure it would come in handy to hold the tyre on later that night when my cable ties ran out. I kept thinking about what I would do as the tyre deteriorated through the night. I thought about wiring strips of tyre rubber to the rim once the tyre came apart, maybe even my racing shirt and then my jacket to make the rim last longer. No doubt my dedication would really be tested by the time I needed to use my pants. I pictured myself racing into the bivouac at 5am the following morning, freezing cold, with blue nipples, wearing nothing but my jocks and boots, sparks flying from the rim against the rocky track, remnants of KTM orange riding gear held on by bits of wire.

I rode on with the sun to my right, only just above the mountains, for about another 20 kilometres. I held my fingers up at arm's length, measuring the gap between the sun and the horizon as I rode, knowing that each finger represented about 15 minutes of daylight, until I had less than a finger.

Suddenly, up ahead I saw two riders coming towards me. I hadn't seen anyone for a couple of hours, let alone another rider. We all stopped as we met up. Mark, on his CRF450X Honda, had blown his engine and was being towed back to the tar road for recovery by his team mate Terrance on his KTM. They still had about 40 kilometres to go, but they knew I still had a chance of finishing and was leading the Malle Moto class, so without hesitation they offered me the back tyre off the Honda. I couldn't believe it; they were out of the race already, but this meant that they would be stuck there in the middle of the Richtersveld, possibly for the whole night.

We then realised that if they were going to stick together anyway, they could give me the entire back wheel from the working KTM, saving me the time and effort of swapping the tyres off the rims. Terrance, without a moment's pause, said, 'Take it!' They held the rear of his bike up while I took the wheel off and then he helped me fit it on to my bike. They insisted that I couldn't help them fit my wheel onto Terrance's bike for him to try to limp out on. Mark asked if I had any water and I told them I had run out a while ago. Luckily they had some water and insisted that I fill my empty hydration pack from one of theirs.

With cheers and slaps on the back, they sent me on my way, full of encouragement. I couldn't believe what these guys had just done for me! Although both of them were out of the race by then, by giving me their wheel these two remarkable guys faced the possibility of a cold night stranded in the veld, but they had given me a fighting chance of finishing the race. They didn't realise it then, but it was a moment in time that two selfless guys pushed my Dakar dream a little closer.

I left them on the side of the sandy track in the vast, arid Northern Cape near the Namibian border and raced off in the half-light with about 200 kilometres still to cover. I rode those kilometres like a motocross track – flat out. The vast black rocky mountains began to turn to shadows against the starry night. There were great grassy flower-covered plains with rocky outcrops as well as vistas of gold grass, delicate purple flower carpets and yellow, white and orange Namaqua daisies. But they were lost on me as the night closed in turning the area into a dark foreboding wilderness.

I raced on all alone through the night, my headlight in the broken mounts jiggling around like a fat kid chasing the ice cream truck. The kilometres at night always took longer but I pushed on as they slowly ticked by. I fought my bike through the dry river beds and up and down the rocky climbs. The water from Mark and Terrance couldn't have tasted sweeter as I persevered in the darkness. Nearing the end of the stage I struggled to follow the track in the darkness until I saw a light flashing up ahead. Andy Ross, a marshal, had spotted my light and was flashing his light to bring me in.

I arrived at the bivouac late that night. I could scarcely believe that I had finished the stage and nor could any of the riders who had seen me earlier that day, especially those who had heard about my tyre. The support from the other racers was nothing short of amazing. The Team 525 guys and Omega RAD teams congratulated me like one of their own. The Subtech Ryder team dropped everything and helped me out with a tyre and mousse for the last day, as well as a pair of elbow guards.

I found Terrance and Mark, who had managed to hook up with their team and had been brought back to the bivouac. I thanked them again and returned the wheel, now with a little less tread after my late night racing. That night was not over yet, I was up until 1am fixing the crash damage from earlier, changing the oil and air filter, fitting the new back wheel and any other prepping my bike still needed from its tough day of riding. I then set up my tent and climbed inside, exhausted but with a fat grin about the once in a lifetime day I had somehow got through.

On the final day of the rally I was up at 4am, the same as almost every other day. After only three hours' sleep, I was sore, full of bruises from the crash and feeling rough. That last day was all about survival, I just had to cross that finish line, 850 kilometres away in Kimberley. The day was long and fast, reaching speeds of over 150kph on the fast gravel roads. My eyes were heavy and my body was cramping and weak but my body doesn't make the rules. My mind was going to the finish and my body just had to keep up.

I sucked up the pain and fatigue and put in a solid, safe ride. I stopped to help Dave fit a rear tube after he had a puncture; luckily he had grabbed a new tube for the day after giving me his the day before. And I helped Simon Schimmel from The Netherlands nurse in a collapsed rear mousse. So after that final long day, I got to bring it home. I finished strong and collected my hard earned finisher's trophy and, on top of that, I won the Malle Moto class. Only 42 of the 85 starters crossed the finish line that day. Later that night I would also be awarded the 'Amadoda Yamadoda' meaning 'man amongst men' trophy for my late night efforts. Seven days and 5000 kilometres later, although exhausted and sore, I had made friendships and memories that would last me a lifetime!

I drove back to Johannesburg with one thing on my mind.

Dakar!

Chapter 14

ALL IN

The Amageza Rally had ended on 5 September 2015 and I knew the time had come to commit and choose the year I would race Dakar. A dream only really becomes a goal once it gets a date. I still had a way to go physically, but I felt the 15 months to the 2017 Dakar – to be held at the beginning of January – was long enough to prepare, yet short enough to force me to stay focused.

Almost every biker who throws his leg over an off-road motor-cycle dreams of racing in the Dakar Rally. There may be many reasons why a rider doesn't enter the Dakar, but in my opinion there are two main reasons that prevent them from being there. The first is not being physically capable in terms of age, skill, fitness, resolve and ability. The second is not having the financial means. I had neither of these sorted.

Physically, riders needed to be able to race a 180-kilogram rally bike in all conditions – rocky climbs, soft dunes, mud, high speed gravel, off camber shale, river crossings and steep loose switchbacks, to mention a few. They needed to be able to ride this terrain for between 14 and 22 hours a day for two weeks straight on just a few hours' sleep at night. While racing in these conditions they still needed to be mentally alert, navigating the correct route through the rugged terrain, often at high altitudes that peaked at about 5000 metres.

It wasn't the kind of thing they could train for by just going to gym. They would need to train by doing long multiple day trips to inhospitable places to simulate some of the conditions they would experience. Gym work and cross training would have its place too with many hours spent mountain biking, running and weight lifting. Even though every single rider who started the race would be phys-ically prepared, the reality was that usually close to half would not make the finish line.

Financially, the amounts needed are insane. The entry fee at the time was about R240 000 – and that was just the beginning. Riders needed flights, accommodation before and after the race, a team truck to carry spares and their mechanic, the mechanic's entry fee, new tyres and mousses for each day – the list was endless. In total, the two-week race alone would cost about R1.1 million and that's without the cost of the R550 000 rally bike! Then there were the costs of qualifying in another international rally and all the bike costs and maintenance while training for it. The amounts were colossal! It was easy to see why it was out of reach for so many riders.

I had a broken body and didn't have the money either, which made the whole dream way beyond my reach in both areas, but that was what made it so compelling. In my mind it was on, but I needed a full buy-in from Meredith and my daughters. The racing I had done up to that point was on the odd Saturday and the occasional over-night trips once or twice a year. This goal, however, would require massive sacrifices from the whole family. I would need to race a lot more and it would involve long training rides which meant being away from home for many days at a time.

Then there were the financial implications. Even as a passionate, diehard Dakar fan, I struggled to justify the insane costs – not just to compete, but to qualify for the race as well. Also, there was no guarantee that the whole dream might end after only one day, as it does for many riders every year. The cost is the same, but there is no reward. I wasn't sure I would be able to handle not finishing. As if all that wasn't enough, I ran the risk of injury – possibly being paralysed again – and as much as I didn't want to think about it, I might even die out there. I could only imagine the heat I would face from many people if I returned badly injured, or the heartache and challenges Meredith and our children would face if I didn't make it back alive.

The risks were insane and, much as I wanted to, there was simply no logical way to explain why this was a good idea. All I knew was that in some crazy way it made perfect sense in my head. I'm no psychologist, but perhaps having another chance at life after my spinal cord injury made me want to live more and take more risks. I had realised that life was short and could be snatched away at any time. I didn't want to let this once in a lifetime opportunity slip away as had happened with other smaller things in the past.

I remembered passing up an opportunity when I was in my early twenties to hike the Otter Trail – a five-day hike along the Garden Route shoreline – because the company I worked for was a bit busy at the time. Later, I looked back and saw it as a time when I sold a little bit of my soul. I turned down a 4x4 trip through Botswana about a year later for the same reason. No memories were made – and I no longer worked for that company. I chose to conform instead of following my heart. I had taken the safe, reasonable route, but it just felt wrong. Since the accident, I had tried to do things based more on what I felt was right and not on what I'd been told was right, or what others told me was expected of me. It's not always an easy thing to do.

Meredith knows me better than anyone and she understands the way my mind works (or perhaps doesn't work!). To her, the idea of racing the Dakar Rally was simply quite insane. But the beauty of our marriage is that even though she hated the idea, she knew it was important to me and so that made it important to her. That being said, it was still not going to be easy for her to agree to back me in this crazy adventure. She was there the day I broke my back and heard me tell the paramedics that I couldn't feel my legs. She had dealt with the outcome of that fateful day, living with a husband with serious disabilities and taking on many responsibilities that had been mine before. She had pushed my wheelchair and changed my soiled nappies. She had helped me use catheters at 2 o'clock in the morning and slept in chairs at my side in hospitals. She was also there the day I hit the cow in Pongola and dealt with all of that too.

I don't need to tell you that she had every right to draw the line and say, 'no more'. But she had also seen how my Dakar dream had motivated me and the excitement I felt watching it each year. She knew what it would mean to me to line up on that start line, shoulder to shoulder with the top riders in the world, after once lying paralysed in a hospital bed with all my life's dreams shattered.

The day I told her I wanted to put a definite date on my Dakar dream, she cried out of fear of how it might end. It broke my heart to see her so upset and I thought that perhaps I should just give up on the dream, because it simply wasn't worth it. The Dakar Rally at times seemed to me as though it was all that mattered, but at the end of the day it was just a two-week bike race.

I'm a husband married to my dream girl and a dad to four amazing daughters. People I wanted to spend for ever with. I knew my family was far more important to me than any race, no matter how big it was. I didn't mention it again. I thought about what I was asking and how selfish it was. I needed to get my head around moving on and finding a more realistic dream. I didn't realise it at the time, but Meredith kept thinking about it too and took a few days to work it over in her mind.

She came to me and said, 'I'm in one hundred per cent, but you have to promise me you won't die on this race!'

Deep down we both knew it was a promise I couldn't really make, but the promise was made none the less. It was all systems go to try to get an entry to the Dakar!

We spoke to the girls together, explaining the implications of how Dad would need to be away a lot for the next year, spending would be cut back and clothes would need to last. There had to be a lot of belt tightening and sacrifices made in terms of both time and spending. The girls were on board, excited although still concerned. They knew the reputation the rally had for serious injury and deaths.

I had some serious planning to do. First, I needed to make sure my entry would be accepted by the ASO, which meant I needed to have completed an international rally. I had originally looked at the Australian Safari Rally but that was now no longer running. Then I looked at the Abu Dhabi Rally and considered that because it would be held early in the year, right in time to add it to my entry which needed to be submitted by June 2016.

Then the ASO bought the Merzouga Rally in Morocco and announced that any rider who competed and finished in the pro class would be accepted to race the Dakar. That would be my ticket to the Dakar start line. It was scheduled for May and the dates worked out perfectly. I needed to put a budget together for the race and figure out how to ship my bike over there, so I fired off some emails to the organisers as well as several rally teams.

Originally I thought that about R100 000 should cover all my costs. It turned out later that I wasn't even close. After mails going back and forth, I realised that renting a bike from a European team was the way to go. The cost was similar to taking your own bike, but took only a fraction of the time and effort. The KTM 450 EXC enduro bike I raced with at home would also have needed extensive modifications to meet the strict requirements set by the organisers. After a lot of organising I signed up with the French based Nomade Racing Team and would be racing on a rented KTM 450 Rally Replica, the ultimate rally machine. The rally was due to start on 22 May 2016, but I had a lot to do before then.

My main source of income was my small business, Lex Pools, a swimming pool shop that specialised in pool heating and saltwater chlorinators. It was a company that I had started when I was 23 and had built up over the last 17 years. I would be lying if I said it was my passion, but I loved going to work each day wearing shorts and being in the outdoors. As the company grew over the years, I found myself stuck in an office more, still dealing with the usual daily challenges, but now caged behind a desk almost all day. It was sapping my will to live, but it paid the bills and with four children I needed to soldier on.

The last couple of months of 2015 I was swamped at work. I hardly got to ride and my stress levels were running high. By the time January rolled around, I knew I needed to make some changes. As most people who have built up their own businesses over many years can relate to, it was difficult to step away from the helm and free up my time. My brother Mike is nine years younger than me and had at that point been working with me for a number of years. I had started to edge away and he began to take on more responsibility. This allowed me to ride a lot more from early 2016 and my training was under way for the Merzouga Rally.

The Merzouga Rally may not have been the Dakar but in itself it was a massive undertaking. It was to be held over six days racing some of the original Dakar tracks and would cross the mighty Sahara dunes on the border of Algeria and continue through the rocky Atlas Mountains. It was a long, difficult race with many starters not crossing the finish line each year. I needed to be fully prepared to have any chance of finishing.

I was in the gym each morning before 6am. This time it was not the usual hang out with your buddies and chuck a few dumb-bells around. Not being able to run or play other sports I used the Orbitrek, rowing machine and swimming pool for cardio training. I also did weight training to help me to be able to pick up the rally bike because I was sure I would drop it on a few occasions. I worked my legs in the weight section too; they didn't really seem to get stronger but their endurance seemed to increase before they went into spasm. When my leg muscles are pushed hard I can't feel the burn, they just suddenly fail or go into spasm, which in a way made it easier to work them hard. There was also the downside when a skinny girl got off the leg press before me and I had to lower the weight before I could budge it!

I rode my enduro bike twice a week, once on Saturday with my mates and once during the week, generally on my own. It was a risk to ride alone for two main reasons. The first was that if you crashed and were injured, you could lie alone for hours before being discovered. This was even worse in remote areas so, to stack the odds in my favour, I always carried a full medical kit with me, a GPS and cellphone. The second big risk was being attacked. The places where I could ride around Johannesburg varied from the rocky koppies at De Wildt, to the canal roads near Brits, to the large sandy mine dumps near Maraisburg. All of these places offer great training, but they are littered with informal settlements and violent crime. A rider was shot a few years before, just for the bag he was carrying.

The mine dumps are infamous because of the violent and desperate Zama-Zamas – the gangs who illegally mine the old shafts and rework the dumps for the little gold they still hold. Most of them were friendly towards us bikers who they had seen riding over the years, but others locked in turf wars against rival groups were armed and didn't take kindly to anyone on their illegal claim. It was not uncommon to come across crime scenes from the night before which included anything from stolen cables stripped for their copper, all the way to dead bodies.

As dirt bikers, we were better off being on our powerful machines. It was the mountain bikers who took the biggest risk. When I rode alone, I carried my Glock 42 – one bullet up – stashed under my rally jacket. Not being able to run if knocked off my bike, I played the different scenarios in my mind. The reality was that if something were to happen, the gun probably wouldn't be enough to save me, but it made me feel a little safer. I remained cautious and gave any groups I passed a wide berth.

Over the years of riding, I had had my fair share of exposure to crime on the trails and had some close calls too. Once when I was riding at the front with a group of mates at De Wildt I nearly had my head taken off on a fast track that had a wire strung at head height across it. I saw it just a split second before it caught me and just managed to dip my head. It caught me across the helmet, taking the paint off and leaving deep gouges in the fibreglass. Somehow I managed to stay on the bike and the wire snapped as I came to a stop. I could see movement in the thick bush, but didn't hang around long enough to find out if it was children playing a sick joke or something far more sinister.

On another early morning, in a different, even more remote area of De Wildt, we came across a double-cab bakkie that had clearly been hijacked. The hijackers had lost control during the night on the dirt road and rolled the vehicle. There was no one with the car when we got there at first light, but the blood splattered throughout the vehicle and on the ground spoke volumes. A gun lay in the grass near the vehicle, seemingly dropped in the apparent mayhem and darkness, and a trail of blood led off into the bush. Judging by the sheer volume of blood, one of them was sure not to have got too far.

On a few occasions when we returned to our cars after riding we found that one of them had been stolen or broken into. Then there was the petty theft whenever you stopped to buy cold drinks or fill up with petrol – often little hands and small items.

One particular time when we were riding at Maraisburg we saw two men running through the veld. A third man was shouting at them from the direction which they had come from. We didn't pay too much attention at first, as shouting and fighting on a weekend wasn't uncommon. The man from behind came running up to us, telling us that they had stolen from him and his young daughter at knifepoint and now they were getting away.

There were six of us that day and four of us decided to take on the chase. One of the attackers had disappeared, but we found and chased the other who was running with the long blade in his hand. The area was rutted and steep, making it quicker on foot; but as it opened up, we closed the gap. In a desperate attempt to evade capture, the man dropped the knife and ran into a thick muddy marsh about 100 metres wide. With my dodgy legs, I knew riding through the marsh wouldn't end well and rode around, cutting off his escape route on the other side. Neal and Andre du Preez ploughed right on into the swamp. I will never forget the scene: the guy running towards me through the swamp with Andre and Neal chasing him, the roar of their engines and the thick mud from their back tyres spraying high into the air. It was like a scene from an action movie!

Neal was always up for a fight back then, and let's just say that the resistance the criminal offered was welcomed. Andre was well over six feet and weighed more than 100 kilograms, so once he left his mark the ruckus very quickly came to a halt. They dragged the guy out of the swamp, where a small crowd from the settlement had now gathered to see what the fuss was about. The victim had caught up by now and was throwing punches at the muddy criminal, who turned to Neal to be his protector. With animated gestures, the victim told the crowd what had happened, showing them the knife he had collected along the way. The crowd insisted that we give them our 'prisoner' – they would inform the police. Being vastly outnumbered, we agreed. I'm pretty sure the police were never called, but from the sounds of screaming as we left I think it's safe to say that justice was served that day … Africa style.

Any rider who has ridden these areas for a few years had these kinds of stories to tell. It wasn't all bad though. Most riding areas were near townships which, although poor, were filled with cheerful faces and waving children. For the most part, the bikers were considerate while riding through the settlements, not creating dust that could waft through the clean clothes on the washing lines and watching out for the goats and chickens. The bikers would roll through slowly, waving back and high-fiving the children on the side of the gravel streets. Sometimes we would stop to give them an energy bar or a packet of nuts to split between three of them (that quickly became 20). Feeling particularly generous, some riders stopped at the she-beens and supported the locals by buying beer. You could guarantee that they would always be accosted by the one guy who, at ten in the morning, had already had too much. He would shake your hand and linger, still holding on, calling you his friend, while relating a long, sad, barely understandable story, ending with the reason why he was your brother and that you should buy him a beer. You knew his eyes would always be bloodshot and that he would have a number of missing teeth that made his tongue look as though it's in jail. Africa can be a beautiful place.

My training continued as the Merzouga Rally drew nearer. I hadn't made my intentions public yet. As silly as it was, I guess I was worried about what people might think. With the falling South African rand and other unforeseen expenses, the bill to race in Morocco had climbed to more than double what I had originally thought it would be. I was going to need some help and some good advice. My first thought was to call Gary Franks. He had been a mate for many years and was emotionally invested in my journey to recovery. As the editor of *Enduro World* magazine and the organiser of a race series, he knew the industry well. I ended up going round to his house where I shared my goal with him. He's not a big fan of the fast flat-out racing, preferring the safer, more technical enduro style, but he knew my physical challenges affected me less the faster I could ride.

I'm sure he was surprised when I told him about my lofty goal, but he didn't show it. He was full of encouragement and said I should put it all out there – my injury, my recovery and everything in between. He said it was a story that would inspire many people dealing with their own difficulties. I didn't like the idea of that, it felt too pre-tentious, as though I had to make out that I was some kind of hero that people should look up to. It was also really embarrassing! I used catheters and had limited bowel control, and I didn't want everyone to find out about that.

Gary was serious, though, he had no doubt that I would go all the way to the Dakar finish line and also that my story needed to be shared. He was certain that if I shared my story people would support me all the way. I left his house feeling motivated, but unsure about 'putting it all out there'.

At home later that night, Meredith and I discussed what we should do and she pointed out that if I really wanted this dream to become a reality, I needed to be 'all in'. There would be no space for half measures and holding back. It was what it was and whether people knew or not wouldn't change my reality. We decided that night that we would put it all out there and I started to write my story.

Next I met Darryl Curtis, who was the ASO representative for the Dakar in southern Africa and two-time Dakar finisher himself. He was also a multiple national enduro and off-road champion. I had attended his Dakar workshop the year before, which was designed to help riders understand the requirements needed to reach the start line. This time I met him to discuss how I should go about marketing myself and we brainstormed ways to raise funds for my goal.

I had always assumed that it was easy for the top national riders to get sponsorship and that people would just come to them. After hearing what Darryl went through himself to get to the start of Dakar, I realised that the truth was quite different. He explained the ins-and-outs of sponsorship and how you needed to offer something that was of value in return for funds. Simply offering to put their sticker on your bike didn't hack it. I explained to Darryl about my injury and partial recovery and he, like Gary, was also adamant that I should put it out there. I needed to get it on social media and in the bike magazines. Basically, I needed to market myself and it would be a lot more difficult than I thought.

In the lead-up to Merzouga in May, I entered the Amageza Baja for further training – a shorter two-day race with a short prologue the day before to establish the starting order. It was held in Port Nolloth in the Northern Cape, near the Namibian border. I drove there over two days, stopping overnight in Upington where I met Geoff Patterson and his dad William. They were also on the way to the Baja. Geoff was racing his first roadbook event and his dad was pit crew. We chatted about our shared passion for rally racing and we were both chomping at the bit, ready to get on that start line.

The first night I arrived in Port Nolloth I slept in my tent right on the edge of the beach. I had been offered a spot in one of the chalets, but I preferred the tent. Besides, I was going to do the Dakar and needed to toughen up. The next day the pits opened and I set up with my teammates from the Subtech Ryder team. They were a good bunch of guys (and Sam, the only girl) and even better riders! I was my own pit crew and prepped my own bike each night. The race was challenging and great training, helping to improve my fitness and navigation skills.

I also got to equal the debt I owed Peter How – the guy who had picked up my bike when I had crashed twice before on the Amageza. Halfway through the first full day of racing he came up behind a side by side car that seemed to move over to let him pass. As he committed to pass, the driver hit a hump in the sand that threw him back into the track. Peter went down hard and was lights out. Greg Raaff was with him and by the time I arrived he had woken up but hadn't a clue where he was. We both stayed with him. I rode up a nearby dune to get signal and called the organisers, while Greg stood over him to shield him from the hot sun. Another teammate of ours, Toti, a big guy from Iceland, joined us and took turns with Greg standing over Peter; his shadow offered a lot more coverage than Greg's.

It would take over two hours before he was evacuated and we stayed with him the whole time. Peter went on to make a full recovery; like me, he's not perfect but he's the same as he was before the crash. We ended up winning the team category that weekend. I rode smoothly and had no major problems. For me, it was important to finish uninjured with Morocco coming up just a few weeks later. After the injuries I'd had in the past, I felt that I should have a board put up – like they do in large factories – showing the number of days 'injury free'. Alex, the race organiser, knew about my Dakar goal and announced it at prize-giving after the race.

'No turning back now,' I thought.

On the way back from the Baja, I got a call from Darryl who said that he had a KTM 450 Rally Replica that he was selling and asked if I would be interested. Those bikes are near impossible to buy because they only make a few each year. I was interested for sure, but it was a heap load of money that I simply didn't have lying between the cushions of the couch, so I asked him to keep it for me until I got home. The morning after arriving home Meredith and I went to Darryl's place. The bike was used, but it looked brand new. The carbon fibre tower and orange trellis frame had me drooling from the get go!

A Dakar rally bike is like no other bike. It holds 33 litres of fuel split between three tanks, compared with the ten or so litres of an average dirt bike. Then there is the navigation tower that stands above the handlebars like a cockpit with the roadbook holder and ICOs. The bashplate under the bike had a tank that held three litres of drinking water for emergency use, water that had saved many a

Dakar rider's life over the years. The engine was built to perform and last in the harshest environments and the gearing was set up for high speed racing. But all of that was nothing to the way it sounded! The deep throaty grunt from the large Akropovic exhaust just made you want to twist the throttle and go racing!

To Meredith, it was just another motorbike, but for me it was the Holy Grail! There was only one other in South Africa at the time and it wasn't for sale. We discussed it and decided on a price that was fair. I knew I needed to buy the bike, but it was a big financial commitment. A lot less than a brand new one, but still a lot of money at nearly half a million rand! I had the option of building up a rally bike from an enduro bike which would work out cheaper, but it would not be as reliable and any spares I didn't take myself to the Dakar bivouacs would be near impossible to find. The KTM factory truck only stocked spares for the factory rally bike at Dakar and that could mean the difference between finishing or not. I had, at best, one chance to race the Dakar and I needed to give myself the best possible chance of finishing. This was one area that I couldn't afford to scrimp on. Meredith and I discussed it briefly and then I made the transfer out of our access bond. For years we had put extra money into the bond, hoping to pay it off one day and now that was just about all gone in a flash. The sacrifices suddenly became a lot more real.

MEREDITH:

I was so relieved to have Joey back safe and in one piece from the Baja that to be completely honest I wasn't really paying attention to him talking about a bike that he wanted to go and have a 'look' at.

We have an unspoken tradition that the day after Joey gets back from time away riding we spend together and so we went out for breakfast that next day. Afterwards I went with him to 'look' at the rally bike. I knew we were coming home with the bike when I saw him smuggle the tie-downs into his bakkie just before we left. I sat through the lesson I was given on rally bikes and why this one was such a good deal. He laid out his case, explaining why it would be the right decision to buy it now so that his proper training could begin. I don't know who Joey thought he was kidding, we both knew he had already decided to buy this bike. This is how Joey often operates, jumping in with both feet, whereas I'm more of a dip a toe in and test the waters kind of girl. I don't know much about bikes, but I could tell it was a huge deal when I saw Joey's eyes light up, just looking at the bike.

While Joey took the bike for a short test ride I asked Darryl if he really thought Joey could finish Dakar. He replied, 'There's no doubt in my mind that he will finish.' I think my heart stopped right there and then. Darryl saying this with such confidence made me cold. I know Joey can do it, without a shadow of a doubt, and I've been telling anyone who will listen that he can. I'm Joey's biggest fan and I know he can do anything, but having Darryl confirm that he could do it, someone who'd finished the Dakar twice before, suddenly made this dream very real. I was quiet during the ride home, Darryl's words repeating over and over in my head. I looked in the side mirror at this massive rally bike strapped to the back of the bakkie and it all sank in. This was really happening.

At Gary's insistence, I finished writing my story for him to publish in the May edition of *Enduro World* magazine. He had also organised an interview with 2Wheels TV which was about to air. I decided to open a Facebook page, 'From Para to Dakar', and I officially launched my Dakar campaign on 3 May, 2016. I had come up with the name myself while riding and dreaming of the Dakar. The Dakar back in the 1980s had been called the *Paris to Dakar* and I felt the name just worked. The *Enduro World* magazine was published and the 2Wheels programme aired on 10 May. A few friends asked how they could donate or get involved, but it didn't feel right accepting money from friends when I didn't even have an entry yet, so I told them to wait until I had qualified, after which it would be all systems go.

A couple of days later, I sat in front of my computer at work going through the stuff I still needed for Morocco. I had a couple of pairs of goggles, but they were worn and scratched. Two new pairs would be just what I needed for the Merzouga Rally. I was also desperate for a new set of boots, as my old ones were worn through on the left sole, but then this rally was just to qualify for Dakar and it had already become a bit of a 'runaway budget'.

Darryl invited Franziska Brandl and Riaan Neveling from KTM South Africa over to his company Bandit Signs, based next door, to give me an opportunity to share my story with them. I felt awkward trying to market myself and it was way out of my comfort zone. KTM sponsor all the top racers around the world in almost every bike discipline and there I was, an average rider in my forties, with gammy legs, explaining how I wanted to race the toughest off-road race in the world. I could hear myself telling them my plans and was aware how unbelievable it sounded.

During the conversation, we discovered that Riaan was racing the day I was paralysed nine years before. I could tell that they both understood my vision. Then Franziska asked what I needed and I told her gingerly, 'Just a pair of boots.' 'Would Alpinestar Tech 10s be fine?' she asked. Now I've been through many pairs of boots over the years, but Tech 10s were top of the range and quite simply out of my budget. So to be asked if they would be 'fine' was quite an experience.

'Er, yes, that would be great!' I responded, maybe a little too eagerly.

They took down my size and it was a done deal. My first official sponsor – a pair of orange and white KTM branded Alpinestar Tech 10s! After I left Darryl's office I called Meredith to tell her. I think she had to tell me to slow down so she could understand what I was saying. In the big scheme of things, it was just a pair of boots, but it was the boost I needed and gave me a massive injection of confidence. About ten days later, Riaan called me to come and pick up my boots that had finally arrived. Little did I know that they had a surprise waiting for me: a huge KTM Ogio kitbag, packed full of riding kit. I might be at the back of the race in Morocco, but I was going to be stylin'!

I decided to contact Mark Henderson from Henderson Racing Products and ask if he would be keen to sponsor me for the goggles I needed. Although I had a huge boost from KTM, I still felt very awkward asking for sponsors but, as Meredith had said, I needed to be 'all in'! So in line with the whole theme of the dream, I thought 'Stuff it, fortune favours the brave, let's do this!'

I sent Mark a message with a link to my Facebook page and figured I had nothing to lose. It wasn't long before he called me back and he was dead keen to get involved! I drove round to his warehouse and he walked me through all the products they imported. Man, that was a lot of cool stuff! Then he asked me the million dollar question: 'So what do you still need?' I ended up walking out of there with three sets of X-brand goggles, with spare lenses, and a small mountain of EVS kit, as well as some factory Cycra hand guards – all fully sponsored!

Mark told me that he had heard about me from Errol Dalton many years ago when I broke my back at the race in Heidelberg, so he already knew that part of my history. When he heard about my goal to get to Dakar, he wanted to be on board and part of the dream. It was a long shot, but he was on board.

The last sponsor I got before I left for Morocco was Raceworx KTM, my local KTM dealer. I had originally thought that I would race in a rally jacket, but the forecast daytime temperatures were in the high 30s and low 40s. I needed some motocross shirts instead. Herman le Grange, the dealer principal, was happy to help and gave me a bunch of riding shirts. That completed everything I needed to race in and I was ready with all my kit.

Physically, I was still dealing with a number of challenges as a result of the spinal cord injury. I was walking well and often people didn't notice that I had a problem, but I couldn't run or jump, apart from a dodgy looking sort of fast jog, sometimes ending on the ground in a cloud of dust. I could feel touch, but I still couldn't feel hot, cold or any kind of pain sensation below my chest. Once, while wearing shorts, I burnt the inside of my calf on the exhaust of my KTM 690 and only realised what I had done because of the smell of burning flesh!

Also, I didn't sweat below my injury, so overheating was a concern, especially now that I was heading to a race in the Sahara Desert. My legs also went into spasm whenever they were fatigued or my adrenalin was pumping. Those were two things that were no doubt going to happen many times at Merzouga and Dakar. And I still needed to self-catheter several times a day, something that was a major challenge in a rally racing environment. Trying to keep things clean and sterile was an issue under normal conditions and the last thing I could afford would be a urinary tract infection. I still dealt with constant neurological pain, pins and needles in my feet and my skin constantly feeling sunburnt. My elbow, where my triceps had been reattached with a titanium anchor, also flared up every now and again and was painful after a heavy day of riding.

The limitations played heavily on my mind and I became concerned. What if I fell in the desert and couldn't push the bike off me? Not being able to sweat below my chest meant my body's cooling system only half worked, something that was sure to be a challenge in the 40-plus temperatures I would be facing. It was not going to be easy for anyone to finish in Morocco, but I knew that it could be fatal for my body. But it was too late to worry about that now, I was officially 'all in'!

Chapter 15

THE MIGHTY SAHARA

Merzouga Rally, Morocco, North Africa

It sounded extreme and mysterious. It was also one of the countries the original Dakar Rally had raced through in the 1980s. I was stoked about the opportunity to race there and add my name to those who had endured those same Sahara dunes years before. There were a few days till the start when suddenly all the excitement and hype turned into nerves and a general feeling of 'What have I got myself into? What have I forgotten? Can I actually pull this off?'

Up to that point, it had all been about flights, medical tests, international licences, transfers, booking tracking devices, hotels, service packages and bike rentals. Now all that was about to turn into soft dunes, rocky mountains, hot gravel tracks, roadbooks, CAP headings and triple cautions. It was time to produce the goods! In order to achieve my main goal of racing in the Dakar Rally come January, I needed to finish the pro class to ensure my entry would be accepted. It had also cost a lot of money to get me there, money that could perhaps have been spent on far more sensible things. A lot was riding on this race and I felt the pressure.

The day arrived and my brother-in-law David drove me to the OR Tambo International Airport. It was there that I met up with Vincent Crosbie. We had met the previous year and spoken briefly at a fuel stop on the Amageza Rally. Vincent had raced in Morocco the year before in the Libya Rally, but had been forced to retire with a broken hand. In an attempt to continue, he had ridden several hundred kilometres with it taped up and in severe pain, but finally he had to throw in the towel.

Vincent was from Botswana and his goal was to become the first Motswana to finish the Dakar Rally. He was about 25 years old, fit and a top national rider who had won many of the national races he entered in his native Botswana. He didn't have the cash to do it, but he was determined to get there somehow and had been running his fund-raising and publicity campaign for more than a year already. Vincent had grown up riding bikes with his dad until he was 12 when his dad sadly passed away from pancreatic cancer at the young age of 45. He spent much of his high school career in boarding school in South Africa, returning to Botswana during the long weekends and holidays. But Vincent is a true Motswana in every way. Despite being a white guy with English as his first language, he spoke the Setswana language like a local. When going through Botswana during the Amageza, he was often surrounded by locals, the surprise on their faces obvious as he jabbered away. He loved his country and was a great ambassador, always speaking highly of his homeland.

Vincent and I had both purchased a racing package, including bike hire, from the French team Nomade Racing run by Manu Braga – a passionate racer himself – and his partner Angelique. We flew out to Frankfurt, where we had a layover of several hours, and then flew on to Marrakesh. We arrived in hot, dry Marrakesh to find our car pick-up wasn't there yet. Vince and I sorted out our phones with local SIM cards and managed to get hold of the drivers and a couple of hours later we were on the road. And thus started the scariest drive I'd been on in a long time.

We were picked up by Yusuf and Mohammed in an old beat-up Toyota Prado, the kind where one of the doors opens only from the outside. If you wound down one of the windows, it wouldn't go back up again and it took three turns of the key and a firm kick to fire up the engine. We climbed in, needing to slam the door twice to close it and embarked on our 600-kilometre, nine-hour drive to Merzouga.

Yusuf was driving and clearly had aspirations of being a WRC driver one day. The small issue of other drivers using the road was not going to stand in the way of his glorious destiny. Mohammed, for all I knew, was there just to operate the radio and fill the empty seat, jabbering away in Arabic on his cellphone most of the time. The radio blared away, working perfectly in contrast to the vehicle, with local tunes and the odd pop song which we recognised. It made me laugh that they couldn't speak English, but knew all the words to the pop songs. The road was really tight and narrow, winding its way on hundred-year-old tracks through the Atlas Mountains, often with only a small 30 centimetre high rock wall barrier separating us from some sheer drop-offs that fell hundreds of metres. The rusty shells of vehicles which we sometimes spotted at the bottom testified to the danger.

Yusuf was driving flat out, passing on solid line blind corners, missing oncoming trucks and buses by millimetres and driving so close to the back of other cars that I could read the washing instructions on the drivers' shirts! The poor guys on scooters, wearing their traditional dress and sandals, scurried to get out of his way. There we were, two Dakar hopefuls who had raced bikes at eye-watering speeds in hostile terrain, now suddenly sitting in the back seat with our fingers pressing deep into the foam, smelling like urine, wide eyed, and scared for our lives. It was insane!

I felt seriously carsick and the high altitude and lack of sleep probably didn't help either. I went a nice shade of light green and we had to pull over twice because I was close to vomiting. But, fighting it back, I managed to keep the cookies in the jar. By no small miracle we arrived, thankful to be alive, at the hotel in pitch-black darkness at 1am. The 30 hours of expected travel ended up being closer to 35 and I had had only about an hour and a half's sleep in the last 45 hours … and the rally hadn't even started yet!

Yusuf and Mohammed helped us to offload our kitbags and we stumbled out, red-eyed but relieved, into the small hotel foyer. Even in the faintly lit, quiet reception, we could see it was a beautiful, traditional building with rugs and hammered brass showpieces – although at the time we didn't care. We were shown to our room and hit the sack. Within minutes, exhausted and amazed still to be alive after the journey of a lifetime, we were out cold.

The next morning we woke up in an incredibly beautiful Moroccan hotel right on the edge of the mighty Sahara Desert. The golden dunes were right outside the door and they were massive. Camels gathered around a small well and fed on a pile of hay, overseen by their nomadic looking herder. We could see some of the riders testing their bikes in the distance, but we took it easy as our team and bikes were arriving only later that evening. We walked a few metres towards the dunes where we met a couple of locals selling fossils. I found them interesting, but we weren't there for souvenirs.

Walter Terblanche, another South African rider from Cape Town who I thought I hadn't met before, saw us and came walking over. Later I discovered he was the rider I had helped to load into the ambulance on the Amageza Rally the previous year. He was there with his team, BAS trucks/van der Velden Racing from Holland. Although it was the first time we had met officially, standing on a small dune on the edge of the Sahara, we hit it off right away and the three of us chatted together like old buddies.

We followed Walter back to his team's truck, already set up with a number of shiny KTM rally bikes lined up and ready to race. For a couple of hours we sat around the wooden pit table on benches in the sand, shaded from the North African sun under the branded pit awning and talking about rally racing, our lives and why the Dakar needs to come to our incredible southern African landscape. Bart van der Velden was the team manager and he generously handed out some much needed cool drinks and made some sandwiches for us. We were both impressed by the slick operation they ran and they seemed well prepared. To top it off, they were good guys following their passion. Their team had a great truck rig, complete with a small room with bunks for the riders, fridge, washing machine, toilet, and all sorts of extras. Those guys were the real deal!

After a while we all had a swim to cool off from the 40 degree heat and took a moment to chill out in anticipation of the madness soon to follow. The teams slowly started arriving as the day closed, setting up their massive trucks and pit awnings. Things were getting exciting! The Nomade team arrived just before dusk and I got the first glimpse of my race bike. A full-on race bred, carbon fibre, fire breathing KTM 450 Rally Replica. The undisputed king of dirt bikes! On the front tower was a sticker with a small South African flag that read 'Joey Evans O+' – a little intimidating to say the least. We often joked that they needed to know our blood group so they knew who to donate our organs to if we died.

'Let's hope they won't need that info,' I thought.

The next day was taken up with registration and scrutineering; it was a big undertaking and the organisers were very strict. Scrutineering is done at all races where they check all your paperwork, medical information and bike. Generally it's a pretty simple operation but at the big rallies you were given a book in which you would have to get each section stamped before being allowed a position on the start. I moved through the small hall without air conditioning, sweating and hoping I had all the paperwork I needed. We moved from one table to the next, getting all the clearance stamps and training classes on the ERTF GPS system, as well as the safety tracking system that was mounted on our bikes. The organisers would know exactly where we were at all times, as well as the speed at which we were travelling.

I hadn't raced with this system before so I paid special attention. There have been many racers over the years who didn't finish the

Dakar, or other rallies for that matter, simply because they did not properly understand the rules or navigation equipment. It took several hours to complete and it was a lot to take in. Finally with all the stamps in my little entry book, I was awarded my entry number – 54.

The following day was the first of six race days. Each evening we were given the roadbook showing us the route for the following day, along with a code that we would enter into the GPS to show us the waypoints once we came into range. That first day was relatively easy, giving us a mixed terrain loop of about 45 kilometres to get the hang of the roadbook and navigation equipment. I came across a dead camel about halfway through and thought 'damn, how tough is this race!' That evening we had the first racing special, a short loop through the desert dunes – more like a motocross race – to determine the starting order for the next day. I ended up about mid-pack, which suited my plans perfectly. Then there was a riders' briefing, collecting and marking of our roadbooks, filling our hydration packs and, eventually, trying to get some sleep. My mind was running wild with so much to absorb and learn from the past two days – and I loved it!

We woke before dawn the next day and kitted up in our riding kit, feeling like gladiators about to enter the Colosseum. They weren't about to let us off lightly and the first real stage was super tough! There were lots of dunes and the navigation was on a whole new level to racing back in South Africa. They seldom sent you on paths or tracks like those I had raced before. The majority were just a compass heading and a distance.

Naturally, you can't ride as the crow flies, so you end up zigzagging through obstacles like dunes, dongas, washouts, deep ruts and rocky outcrops, so your distance odometer was constantly out as well. I really had to be on my game, constantly adjusting my distance to match the roadbook. My plan was obviously to finish this race, thus earning my place on the Dakar start line. But this was also my only chance to familiarise myself with the way the route was set up and learn how to navigate well – a skill that would be vital come South America in January. I made sure I rode a little slower and focused on perfect navigation, ensuring I didn't waste time riding unnecessary kilometres or receive any time penalties for missed waypoints.

From the moment we walked out of the hotel room, the morning heat hit us and it just intensified for the rest of the day. From following the Dakar for many years, I knew the fatal results of dehydration and heatstroke. I made sure I had plenty to drink before the start and drank often from my hydration pack while I was riding. I was cruising through my water and ended up drinking my full three-litre hydration pack by the 60-kilometre mark, with the next chance of a refill only at the 120-kilometre checkpoint.

I pushed through the now 45 degree heat for about another 10 kilometres when I came across a rider who had crashed hard in the rocks, he needed air evacuation and there were two choppers already on the scene. I stopped, recognising Marc Coma, a five times Dakar winner himself and now the sporting director for the race, at the scene. I asked him for some water and he gave me another three litres out of the chopper, pouring it into my hydration pack as I held it open. That carried me through to the next checkpoint. In total that day I drank nearly 12 litres!

That day we would cover 201 kilometres which didn't seem far on paper but the terrain ensured that we earned every kilometre. The morning terrain was made up mainly of hard packed rocky trails and dry river beds, but as the day wore on we entered some really big dunes and I struggled in the midday sun. It was so difficult to read them with the sun directly above us. There were no shadows, the dunes were all identical in colour and the reflecting sun just seemed to merge them all together. There was no telling when it was up, down or off camber. I couldn't even judge my speed! It was like being snow-blind.

I misjudged the crescent while climbing one dune and went over the top airborne, landing on the other side several metres down the soft slope. The sand was super soft, the front wheel just vanished and I went over the bars. I hit my head and it rang my bell good and proper! I took a few minutes to compose myself, my helmet and gloves full of sand combined with sweat, and after a fight almost to the death I managed to get the bike up out of the sand and carried on. I had to pick the bike up a number of times in the dunes and it really drained me. I knew it was something I needed to work on big time.

I felt out of my depth with my dodgy legs on the big rally bike in the soft dunes and I probably was, but it was too late to turn back now. I just had to learn on the job and get through each kilometre one dune at a time. Cresting the dunes was very difficult and I needed to get the timing just right. Some were what they called 'broken' dunes, where one side is almost a sheer drop. You couldn't just ride over the top or you would find yourself a bit like the cartoon character Wile E Coyote, treading air with a 20-metre drop below you. If you went too slowly, your wheels would sink into the soft sand and even if you were just half a metre from the top, it was impossible to get up. You would have to drag the bike around, go back down and give it another attempt. Once I dropped it just as I got over the top of a dune. A rider behind me came over the blind rise and went right over my bike. It was easy to see how quickly you can get injured in these conditions. I was just glad it wasn't some crazy Russian in a six-ton truck!

The theory was to 'surf' the dunes. Instead of riding straight up them, you would ride up at an angle and along the ridge for a few metres, looking over the dune, before committing to going down the other side. This way you knew how steep it was and could choose your line. As soon as you committed, you got on the gas hard, shooting a wave of sand off the crest behind you and accelerating as you descended to make sure your front wheel didn't dig in and send you over the bars. It had all sounded simple when it was explained to me, but putting it into practice was a different story.

I stopped twice that day and helped riders who had run out of fuel. I had plenty and no one else was stopping. It cost me a bit of time and a few positions but I wasn't fussed. It helped me stay out of the crazy red mist and focus on what I was here for – the finish! As the day passed, the kilometres ticked by and I found myself crossing the finish line for the day, relieved that it was over.

The provisional results of the day's racing came out and I was 84th, but then they posted the penalties for missing waypoints and I'd moved up to 70th out of about 120 riders. I was happy with that, but I had battled with the big rally bike in the dunes and still felt out of my depth. I could hear the voice of doubt creeping in and it took a lot to shut it up, stay positive and focus on the goal. To finish that stage made it a good day, but even with many lessons learned I knew there were still more. I realised I needed to raise my game big time if Dakar was to be a reality. I needed to master the dunes. The organisers knew this would be the case for many riders and ran classes with Marc Coma each night, training us in the various skills of cross country rally racing. The experience was invaluable and, as bikers, it felt a bit as though we were seated at the feet of our sensei, training in the path of the warrior.

My conservative strategy had been working well, as I hit every waypoint that day despite being passed by many riders. Already 11 riders were out of about 120 starters, five of them with serious injuries, including one guy on our Nomade team who had broken his shoulder and needed air evacuation. Suddenly all the safety checks and tracking classes made sense – this was the real deal!

The second day's stage would be 341 kilometres long and started with a 30-kilometre dune section. I was starting to get the hang of the dunes by now and thankfully I was dropping the bike a lot less. The trick was to stand up, get hard on the gas and ride them with purpose. I started hitting them at an angle looking over the top briefly before committing, then going over with the throttle wide open, keeping the front wheel light down the face as I had been taught. Riding the dunes was more difficult than racing on a thick sandy motocross track and it just sapped your energy. I would ride hard for a couple of kilometres, stop on top of a dune for a few seconds to catch my breath and shake my arms out a couple of times and go again. This worked well and I made fewer mistakes and used less energy not having constantly to pick my bike up.

On that day, I came across a rider who I later learned was John Comoglio from France, one of the guys I had given petrol to the previous day. He was sitting on his bike in the middle of the dunes and he was in a bad way. He was vomiting and hadn't even been able to get his helmet off in time; it wasn't pretty with the vomit dripping from his mouth guard. I stayed with him for a minute to make sure he was OK. When he gave me the thumbs up I was off again. As a matter of interest, he went on to finish the whole rally – these guys are tough! (I've been told you should eat strawberry yoghurt if you're vomiting; it doesn't stop you throwing up, but it does make it taste better.)

The day was long and there were plenty of dry river beds and smaller dunes; some were hard and others were as soft as powder. It was easy to tell how hard they were by the width of the tracks going up them. The wider the tracks, the softer the dune. I hit one that didn't have any tracks going up it, expecting to ride right over. However, my entire front wheel just disappeared into the side of it and I did a perfect scorpion. I think I even had boot scuff marks on the back of my helmet. I was lying in the sand a couple of metres ahead of my bike, my bike was standing perfectly upright with sand up to the top of the wheels.

A while back I would have started digging, but Marc had explained to us how to get a buried bike out the sand. I started the bike and standing next to it and twisting slowly on the throttle, I pulled it towards me while pulling upwards on the bars. The bike climbed up onto the sand and I was on my way. While getting the bike out,

I noticed my race number was coming off on the right hand side. My rear tank had a crack and was leaking petrol. On the rally bike you can select which tanks to draw petrol from and I only ran the back tank from then on, to keep the petrol level below the crack. I managed to nurse the bike through the day to the finish, arriving in 62nd place and I moved another day closer to the finish and, more importantly, closer to my Dakar goal.

Day 3 was 464 kilometres and the start of the marathon stage. That meant two days of racing without your team or mechanical support and sleeping in a remote location. To top things off, my team didn't have a spare rear tank, so my mechanic had to make a plan and fix it with putty and duct tape. I could carry about eight litres before it reached the hole and I had another 14 in the front, so I thought I would be OK. I think we both knew the patch wouldn't last, but it was the best of a bad situation.

That morning I was feeling rough, my back was sore from fighting the bike through the soft sand. Riding in the multiple tracks of the riders ahead of me, the bike would tug left and right and it was a constant battle to keep it upright. It was very difficult to eat breakfast that morning. It was just before 5am and I knew I had to get it down my throat as I would need the energy, so I fought each mouthful down. Then, at first light, I was racing again.

There were lots of broken dunes that day and riding them was both difficult and physically taxing. That day I was introduced to camel grass which would become my next nemesis. These were thousands of mounds all about a metre or so high with a tuft of grass on the top. The spacing between them varied and some were steeper than others. Some you could ride over and others you had to go around. Riding through them was torture on my body. The constant up and down made my legs feel like shock absorbers. They struggled to maintain my weight and kept failing and going into spasm. I felt frustrated as riders passed me in that terrain because I was forced to sit down and ride more slowly till my legs recovered.

Walter had a big crash that morning. His bike was a bit smashed up and he was a little the worse for wear himself. But he was in survival mode, so we hooked up and rode together for most of the day. At one point while I was alone, my GPS lit up with the arrow leading to the next waypoint and I followed it down a canyon until I was about 200 metres away, only to realise that it was just over the canyon wall in the next one. I was tired and the thought of heading back out through the broken dunes again, now having to go up their steep side to get there, was the last thing I wanted to do. I looked at the steep rocky wall and figured that with a decent run-up, I could get up it and take advantage of the short cut to the waypoint which would save me time and energy.

I started a run-up but pulled out at the last second. What was I thinking? I would be taking a massive risk and if I was just a metre short climbing up the rock face, my bike would fall all the way back down and be destroyed, effectively ending my race. So I put on my big boy pants and rode back through the broken dunes and to the next canyon. Once I got there I realised that even if I had made it up the other side, it was a sheer cliff and I would have ended up there on the canyon wall with no way down. A big lesson learned – do not take unnecessary risks!

The weather was incredibly hot, with the mercury hitting 45 degrees and the wind blowing a massive sandstorm that felt like a hairdryer in your face. It seemed the faster you rode the hotter you got. I stopped at each checkpoint and wet my legs and shirt with water in an attempt to make up for my inability to sweat. Visibility was down to just a few metres, which meant it was like navigating in the dark. There were already a couple of riders who had been airlifted out with serious injuries and by the time I got to checkpoint three of four, the race section had been neutralised. We still had to ride the route but were no longer racing against the clock. It was something rally organisers did in the interests of the safety of the riders. The sandstorm was making it impossible for the helicopters to fly. The riders before checkpoint two were sent on the road to the marathon bivouac, but from checkpoint three onwards we had to ride out the whole stage and the rest of the liaison.

In retrospect, it worked out well as I got more navigation training and it pushed me physically. The area was barren of almost all vegetation; the rock and sand landscape couldn't be less inviting. We followed the route on the roadbook as best we could in the dark sandstorm, picking up the invisible waypoints hidden in the unforgiving valleys. Many riders had become disorientated and were coming from various directions but by riding slowly I had managed to keep my bearings and hit every waypoint till the end of the special.

After that I still needed to ride the liaison. I had a terrible nosebleed at the start of the liaison that just wouldn't stop no matter what I did – I think my body was just too hot. I told Walter to go off without me as I could tell it was going to take a while to get under control. After trying to stop it for more than 25 minutes and pouring water over my head in an attempt to cool down, I decided just to ride with my face plugged up with blood soaked tissue.

The final climb up to the marathon bivouac was insane! A small track zigzagged its way up a sheer rock face in the Atlas Mountains – it was like something from those 'world's most dangerous roads' programmes. I had ridden some pretty hairy tracks over the years but this one was in another league. I tiptoed around loose, rocky, hairpin bends, with drop-offs that fell straight down for literally hundreds of metres.

Reaching the top, we were rewarded with a view I will remember for ever. It felt as though I could see the whole of Morocco! A few kilometres later I arrived at the marathon bivouac. It was spectacular – a massive Bedouin tented camp with ornate red carpets covering the floors and gaps between the tents. This was truly a once in a life-time experience. What a location! It felt incredible to be there – the kind of place that just feeds your soul.

I dumped my stuff in a tent, pulled out my satellite phone, walked about a hundred metres from the camp and called Meredith, wanting to share the moment. It was great to hear her voice sounding positive and full of encouragement. I wished she could have been there with me. We spoke for a while, but I had a lot to do, so I soon got about preparing my bike. I filled up the petrol and lubed the chain, then I swapped my air filter, putting the old filter in my marathon bag to be transported back the next day. I noticed all the top pros were just throwing theirs away. Back home they cost about R600 each and we would wash them and use them many times over. 'Stuff that!' I thought, thinking of my tight Dakar budget, as I collected about four of them out of the bin and added them to my marathon bag, ignoring the looks from the factory riders. Then I was off to supper. I had finished 35th that day, mainly because I navigated well, so once again I took my time to mark and note all the changes in my roadbook. I took a quick shower and was off to bed by about 11pm, warm and comfortable, high up in the spectacular mountains of Morocco.

The next morning I woke up, surprised to find an extra rider in the tent who had arrived sometime during the night. He was practically still in his full riding kit. He had obviously just stumbled in and gone to sleep. No doubt he had a few stories to tell when he got home. It was 4.30am and time to get up, and I once again forced some break-fast down. I kitted up and was ready to go with 15 minutes to spare before my start time. I just had to load my roadbook onto the bike ... but it was nowhere to be found!

I searched everywhere. I'd spent well over an hour on it the previous night. I checked my jacket pockets and bags, lifted up the mattress and turned everything inside out. Every bin was packed full of roadbooks from the day before, so it would have been impossible to find if it had been accidentally thrown away. Eventually I accepted the fact that it was gone and rushed to the organisers to beg for a new one. They issued me with another, but there were more than 20 changes that had to be made. I changed as many as I could in the remaining minutes, shoved it in my bag and just managed to make my departure time. Once I had started, I rode a couple of hundred metres and pulled over, taking the time to make the important changes from the photos I had taken on my phone of the competitors' noticeboard and loaded it all onto the bike. No time for highlighters today.

The day was 311 kilometres and a good one for me. Knowing that my roadbook wasn't marked up properly, I think I focused a lot more on the navigation. I hit every waypoint again in a section where guys were criss-crossing all over trying to get on the right track. Camel grass and I became better friends, but fesh-fesh and I are not friends and still have some issues to sort out. Fesh-fesh is super fine sand, similar to cement powder or talc. You rode *through* it as opposed to *on* it, and it disguised the underlying ruts and bumps in the track. If you fell over, it would get into everything – including your goggles. It would also puff up into the air, making it near impossible to see when following another rider. But like every other rider, I had no choice but to battle on through it all.

The day went on and I came into a checkpoint early in the afternoon where we needed to refuel. I asked the guy to add only two litres in the back tank to keep it away from the leak, but no doubt the language barrier intervened because I soon realised that he had filled it right to the top. The patch on my tank seemed to be holding, so I just rode on. However, a couple of kilometres later I could smell petrol and my leg kept going into spasm the way it does when there is pain on the skin. Then my leg started hurting dreadfully. I stopped and saw that my leg was completely soaked in petrol, right down into my boot and so was my whole seat. It was just trickling out of the side of the tank now. I let it run out a bit on the side and then carried on, making sure to stand the whole time.

I pushed on to be met by several steep rocky climbs towards the end of the day which were similar to those I had ridden before in Lesotho. Fortunately, I worked my way through them without any major incidents. There had been several more injuries over the last couple of days. A guy from the UK to whom I had been chatting just the night before broke his pelvis in a big crash on one of the rocky sections. I got through the day, although by the end my leg was pretty raw and stained black from the colour bleeding out of my riding pants. But I was relieved to have that day in the bag. I was in safely and another day was ticked off.

During the race, we sometimes passed though villages and rural areas. Something that really struck me that day was how the people lived so simply, working their small patches of land, transporting their crops on small donkeys and living in small houses, but somehow always content with what they had. It certainly seemed a better way to live when I compared it with the crazy-paced lives we lived back home, constantly chasing and never finding the time just to enjoy it all.

The last day finally arrived. All I had to do was finish and I could be on that Dakar start line in January. That day was about 90 kilometres of liaison and a special that was basically a crazy mass start with 75 kilometres flat out through the big dunes. If you want to feel adrenalin, then line up shoulder to shoulder with 70 guys facing the Sahara Desert and stare at a 30 second board, one dune in, waiting for the flare to go off. It was awesome!

The flare went off and the mayhem began. Just before the start, an older rider from Austria said to me, 'You could die out there today, not much to gain and everything to lose.' He was right. I kept to the right of the main pack, but still saw some nasty spills, with one Polaris side by side vehicle (SSV) having a big crash, no doubt writing the vehicle off. A number of guys threw away a finish on that last day. I didn't intend being one of them.

I had my best day in the dunes that day, riding with confidence. I would like to say I never dropped the bike, but it did happen about five or six times. There was one section where I was behind an SSV for several kilometres and it was some of the best riding I've done in my life. He was doing a good pace and I sat about ten metres behind him following him through the dunes. As he crested each dune, I looked at his roof and could see if the dune was flat or dropped off on the other side. This made the terrain much easier to ride and I loved it.

Well, that was until one dune that had a nasty kink on the face going up. I was behind the SSV and we both got a bit of air, landing flat on the face of the dune halfway up, robbing us both of our momentum. We both came to a stop before the crest at the top and then he started coming down, sliding backwards straight towards me.

I was stationary and upright in the sand, still facing the top, I dived off to the side, shouting for him to stop but he couldn't hear me above the sound of the engines. He rode over my wheels and got his front wheel tangled between mine, with my bike half under his vehicle.

Unable to communicate because of the language barrier, we used a lot of sign language to move back, a little at a time, while I dragged the bike out from under the car. Miraculously there was no damage to the bike which had sunk into the soft sand. After a big heave-ho, the bike was up and I was off again, this time riding solo.

The relief of racing those final few hundred metres towards the finishers' podium was tangible. I would finish 39th out of only 58 finishers. I rode up the podium ramp, stopping next to Marc Coma and Xavier Gavory who awarded me my finisher's medal. It was a fossil with the Merzouga Rally engraved into its shiny face.

It was worth a lot more to me than the ones for sale from the guy at the hotel. Vincent, who had finished well ahead of me, was there too and joined me in my celebrations. This was our ticket to Dakar! I had goosebumps the size of sand dunes.

Chapter 16

JUNE 2016 – 7 MONTHS TO DAKAR

After I arrived back from Morocco I filled out my Dakar entry and sent it in, along with the hefty deposit. I knew that the chances of having my entry accepted were almost certain, but I was still concerned that they might exclude me for medical reasons. It would be six weeks before I knew for sure. .

After finishing in Morocco the time was right to market myself and get my name out there to have some publicity to offer any prospective sponsors. It still wasn't easy and at the back of my mind I was worried about what I was setting myself up for. The more publicity and the more people who knew, the harder I felt it would be to face everyone if I didn't get to the finish at Dakar. I was worried that I wouldn't be able to deliver the goods after building up all the hype. I would rather just have gone there, unknown, without any pressure, and just ride my own race under the radar. The catch-22 was that I needed to market it all and build the hype in order to get enough sponsorship to get there in the first place.

Just as when I was back in the hospital, I had to get over it and get on with what I needed to do, so I jumped at every opportunity to be interviewed and to share my story. I was offered the chance to be interviewed by Adriaan Groenewald on The Leadership Platform for CliffCentral. It was my first radio interview and was done live, so I was pretty nervous, but it worked out well and was aired on 6 June. The hosts loved the story and were really supportive, which helped to boost my confidence and encouraged me to keep chasing publicity opportunities wherever possible.

Each day was a constant battle of priorities. I had two goals with regard to Dakar.

The first was to get to the start. In order to do this I had to punt my story, organise a website, post stuff on social media, approach possible sponsors, think up and execute fund-raisers, organise my support team for the race, book flights – the list was never-ending.

My second goal was to get to the finish. For this I needed to train in the gym, ride my bike at the MX track, go on multiple day trips, race, eat right, improve my navigation skills – again the list just went on and on.

Both goals were equally important, because I needed both to achieve my dream. Some days I would have a great training ride, cranking through a bunch of laps at the motocross track, but didn't get any closer with my fund-raising. Other days I spent behind a computer and on the phone ticking off admin task after admin task, but I didn't get any fitter or closer to the finish. Add to that all the normal daily pressures of being a husband, father, business owner, brother, son, and friend. It was a constant messy juggle of priorities and I never once felt that I was getting it right during the entire build-up to Dakar.

Meredith and I had been stressing about the mammoth fund-raising task that lay ahead. The R1.1 million price tag, just for the race, hung over us like a dark cloud. The rally bike and the race in Morocco had drained our savings and we still had to pay for the training, trips, tyres, maintenance and racing that needed to be done leading up to Dakar. We could – at a stretch – cover those costs, but we needed to raise the R1.1 million for my time at the Dakar and we had just over six months in which to do it. The task seemed completely impossible. It was a ridiculous amount of cash, but I had overcome bigger obstacles along this journey and at the end of the day, it was only money. (Yep, but still a big fat stinking pile of it.)

We had brainstormed ways we could raise the money in a short period of time. Our list included selling a kidney and child trafficking. When we were faced with some ethical questions, we started to put other plans in place and were getting organised, but I didn't expect the huge boost I was about to get.

On 4 June we attended the joint birthday party of my good friend Mark and his wife Lianie Campbell at their home in Hartbeespoort. Greg Raaff, a 2012 Dakar Rally finisher, was there too with his partner Angela, whose slim, feminine figure hid a ball-breaking divorce lawyer who would shop anyone under the table and wasn't afraid to speak her mind.

Meredith and I loved it! She was like a breath of fresh air in a stuffy, overly PC world. We chatted throughout the night, mostly about the race, the discussion no doubt equally enjoyed by the ladies. At one point Greg and I were in Mark's garage admiring his rare KTM rally replica. It was just the two of us and Greg, who never liked to make a big deal of things, casually said that he was keen to help me reach my dream and wanted to donate R100 000! I couldn't believe it! He said he wanted his company Subtech's logo on the bike, but we both knew it had nothing to do with sponsorship. He was passionate about racing and believed in my dream. Greg was a guy who spoke with actions rather than words. He didn't want to make a big deal of it and said I should just keep it to myself. I did at first, but that might have changed now that it's in the book. (Sorry Greg!) Much like the meeting I had with KTM before Morocco, it had me fired up with confidence and renewed motivation. His gesture that night had a huge effect on my outlook and brought my Dakar dream a whole lot closer.

Morocco had been really tough and I realised that physically I still had a long way to go before Dakar. I remembered that one of the French riders in Morocco, who had done the Dakar, warned me not to be lulled into a false sense of security, thinking that Dakar was like this. In Morocco, we stayed in hotels and the first bike left at 6am – two hours later than the Dakar start time. I had struggled through those dunes, but 'this is a holiday compared to Dakar', he warned. I knew I needed a lot more sand training on the big rally bike, so when the opportunity came to join my Subtech Ryder teammates in Mozambique, I knew I needed to go.

I had only been back from Morocco for a couple of weeks when I had to leave for Mozambique. It was a tough ask for the family, but they were amazing and willing to do whatever it took and made every effort to make it easy for me. Mark and I travelled together in my double-cab bakkie and, with our bikes loaded on the back, we slipped out of Joburg in the early hours of the morning. It was much like what I had done many times before, heading out for an adventure, leaving the city sleeping before they had to face another day at the office. I had the bills to pay, just the same as them, but I had learned – perhaps the hard way – not to pass up an adventure when it's put before you.

Mark had been a commercial diver for many years, mainly working offshore all over the world. We chatted the whole way and I found his career and life experiences incredibly interesting. He was married now with two beautiful little daughters and so the travelling for him had now lost its initial appeal. A few years back, before the children arrived, he and his wife Lianie had followed the Dakar Rally as spectators through South America, each on their own motorbike. Mark was well over six feet tall and built like a house, so you could easily picture him roughing it through South America. Lianie, on the other hand – being a delicate, petite lady with blonde hair and perfect make-up – was harder to envision on that kind of expedition. Meeting her for the first time, you would never have believed she'd done that! Over the next few years, I discovered that behind the pretty exterior there was a 'skrik-vir-niks' tough girl. I remember once going to their house and finding her amidst the noise of power tools, fitting her own kitchen cupboards because 'the contractors are just stuffing it up!' If she ever decided to race the Dakar, I wouldn't bet against her.

Mark and I arrived in Pongola, Northern KwaZulu-Natal, where we met up with the other riders from Durban and where we would leave the bakkie. We kitted up and set off with Dallie from Pongola following in his 4x4 as back-up. Roger Kane-Berman led us with the route mapped out on his GPS. Roger ran a BMW bike dealership at the time, but raced with his KTM rally replica. He was a top racer, but far too pretty to be taken seriously as a biker. He had long curly blond locks of hair, while the rest of us 'real' men had shaved heads (mainly to disguise our receding hairlines). Mark was riding his older KTM rally replica that was bigger and heavier than the KTM 500 EXC that I was on. Although he was a good rider, he struggled to find his groove that day in the thick sandy river beds. We ended up swapping bikes for a bit, and stayed that way for the rest of the trip. He was styling on my lighter 500 and I loved the training I was getting on the big rally bike.

We rode much of the sandy routes used for the Pongola 500, also making use of the dry river beds. We rode past the place where Greg had fallen only a couple months before, landing on a tree sapling that had been cut at 45 degrees. It had gone up into his helmet and tore open his face. He was fine after a few stitches, but if it had happened to Roger's face, it would have been a huge loss. We continued winding our way up towards the border. We stopped next to Lake Sibayi just metres from the water's edge. There was a pod of hippos right there in the water, probably 15 metres from us. The other guys didn't seem too concerned and it dawned on me that if the hippos decided to attack they didn't have to outrun the hippos, they only had to outrun me! It wouldn't be too difficult for them; I decided to stay on the bike, just in case. I hadn't been to Mozambique before, so for me it was quite exciting crossing the border into a new African country. We rode well into the dark on a crazy dirt road, struggling to see through the dust, and spent the night in Catembe.

The next morning we boarded the ferry to cross the Umbuluzi River into the capital of Maputo. Mark and I swapped back to our own bikes for this part of the ride as, with my dodgy legs, I was not keen to push his heavier bike up and down the ferry ramps. It was a typical African scene with all sorts of bags, packages and live chickens being packed into every nook and cranny. Some serious Tetris skills were used to fit all the cars, bikes and people on board. 'Always space for one more' seemed to be the motto. I had heard about ferry disasters in the past and now it didn't surprise me how the death tolls would always be so high.

Once, when I was in my early teens, we hiked through the Soutpansberg Mountains, up near the border with Zimbabwe. There had been a lot of fires in the plantations that year and many of the trees had been felled and left floating in a dam, making the water pitch black from the charred bark. We passed the dam just before the overnight stop and a group of us boys walked back to explore. It was a weekend and no forestry workers were around. On the bank we found a raft made of a flat wooden base with steel oil drums lashed underneath for buoyancy. There was a metal railing running around the edge.

As teenage boys – and for the sake of adventure – we decided it would be a good idea to 'borrow' it and take it out for a spin on the dam. We paddled in the black water fighting our way through the logs. The raft rocked and we laughed as we rocked it more, increasing the height with each sway, until we reached the point of no return and the raft suddenly flipped upside down. I was trapped underneath it, submerged with my leg between the railing and a sunken log. I fought the near overwhelming urge to panic and just focused on staying calm, knowing that panicking would only sap my oxygen supply more quickly. I managed to free my leg only to find myself under the upturned raft that now formed a cage with several of the other guys out the water and back on top of it. I could feel the sunken logs and branches all around and under me in the thick black water where there was zero visibility. I needed air desperately and somehow managed to find my way around the railing, through the logs and branches to reach the surface. I'm sure the whole ordeal lasted only for about 30 seconds, but it had felt like an eternity to me. On the ferry now, many years later, I made sure I stayed on the deck just in case things went a bit pear shaped.

We arrived safely on the Maputo side and edged through the crowd with our bikes, passing locals selling all sorts of curious things. Greg had been caught up at work but was determined not to miss the trip and had flown to Maputo to meet us. His bike had been brought up on the back of Dallie's bakkie. We set off along the main street next to the shore, unable to resist the urge to wheelie. Dallie and Greg had been this way many times before and warned us to keep the front wheel down, because with the police on this side of the border, we were more likely to sit in jail for a few days than get a fine.

We headed to Beline along the thick sandy tracks and even got to ride a short way along the beach. It was a beautiful country despite the signs of the years of civil war still apparent with occasional bullet holes visible on some buildings. Others had been completely destroyed. The riding terrain was endless and simply incredible. I battled at first to manhandle the big rally bike around the thick winding sandy trails, but I improved as the trip went on. Often when we stopped, I would do my signature fall-over with the bike on top of me, unable to hold the bike up once it started to tip. The guys offered to lift it up each time, but I needed to do it myself. There would be no good Samaritans at Dakar.

During the day I asked Greg and Roger for riding tips and each night I fired questions at Greg. He had finished the Dakar back in 2012 and was a valuable source of information and advice. I liked his approach; he was strict about routine and keeping to the rules you set for yourself, like not riding blind in the dust and keeping yourself hydrated.

He had seen first-hand what cruelty Dakar was capable of. On the first day of his Dakar race, they started the riders two at a time on the first racing special. He lined up next to Jorge Boero, a top Argentinian rider racing in his home country. They chatted before the start, both looking forward to a good race. Greg commented on what a nice guy he was. He was a faster rider than Greg and took off climbing through the riding field ahead. Greg later reached the paramedics in that special who were attending to a fallen rider. It turned out to be Jorge who had crashed on that stage and died as a result of his injuries. Greg told me how hard it had hit him and he was just about ready to pack it all in right then and there. He had questioned his own reasons for being there and the risks he was taking. He warned me that there would be times when I would need to dig deeper than

I had ever done before. It was not going to be fun, guys like us don't 'enjoy' Dakar, we simply survive it.

I decided not to share that story with Meredith.

Chapter 17

JULY 2016
– 6 MONTHS TO DAKAR

July started off with a meeting on the first day that would lift my Dakar campaign to a whole new level. I met with Riaan from KTM SA and he introduced me to Simon Morton, Grant Scott and Dave Cilliers from the online biking magazine *ZA Bikers*. We met at a restaurant and I shared my history and Dakar dream with them. They were completely on board from that first meeting and we went around the table with ideas of how to tackle the fund-raising. For a while I had had the idea of putting the names of any individual who donated to the fund onto my Dakar bike. The guys loved the idea, but my ability to find these people was very limited. Dave was certain that the biking community would get behind me, and if we could get a few hundred guys to donate a little bit we would be a whole lot closer to the target. It was a lot of money, but I could see that they all believed that if we worked together, we could somehow pull this off.

Simon was practical and suggested that we needed a good website and to make the donation process as easy as possible. The ideas came pouring out, with everyone adding to and building off one another's ideas. They offered to make a promotional video at their cost to boost the whole campaign.

Riders were always trying to raise money for one thing or another and I was worried that people would just dismiss my campaign as some pie in the sky dream and not want to get on board. We decided that we would need some riders and guys from the industry to add credibility to the video. Riaan would be great from KTM's side to show how they were supporting me. Louwrens Mahoney, a multiple national champion and Roof of Africa winner, would be perfect, as he won the race the day I broke my back and visited me several times while I was in hospital and rehab. He had witnessed my story first-hand and been full of encouragement for many years. I asked him if he would speak on the video and he agreed straightaway. Next, we needed a Dakar finisher to round off the idea that my goal was possible and the obvious choice was Darryl. He also agreed without a moment's hesitation. Darryl knew my history and his constant belief in me the whole way leading up to Dakar was a massive boost to my confidence. The rest was organised by the *ZA Bikers* guys over the next couple of weeks and the date for the recording was set to take place in August.

I had been riding a lot and training daily in the gym, so my fitness was coming along nicely, but I was still struggling with my elbow. The doctor had used a titanium anchor to reattach my triceps and with all the training I was now doing it was constantly painful. I saw the orthopaedic surgeon and he confirmed it was tendonitis. I couldn't afford to rest it completely, so my physio Sharne and I managed it as best as we could. Fitness was a challenge, because I was unable to run or play most sports. One of the things that worked well for cardio was swimming.

Swimming had felt very awkward since my spinal cord injury. Before the injury I could swim well, but that had changed and even now I can't get my legs to move at the same time as my arms. It's like when you try to rub your stomach in a circular motion while patting your head at the same time. Early on in my rehabilitation process, the pool was brilliant as it gave me a chance to move my legs without gravity weighing them down.

But there was a lesson I learned the hard way the first time I swam at home, shortly after leaving the hospital. It took a while to get me into the pool. First, I had to get out of the wheelchair and onto the paving and then pick up my legs and place them over the edge and into the water. Finally, I had to try to lower myself into the pool without scraping my back on the edge of the pool. I couldn't feel the temperature of the water until the water level reached to just below my chest. I floated around back and forth, using my arms to propel me. After a while I sat on the step with the water level around my chest only to notice blood in the water around my toes. I couldn't feel pain below my injury, so I didn't notice that my feet had been dragging on the marble plaster floor of the pool, slowly sanding away the skin on the top of my toes.

After that incident, I always wore shoes to swim at home. Getting out the pool presented another set of challenges. I had to be aware of the hot paving around the pool, because I was unable to feel it burning the bottom of my feet or legs. The girls jumped in the pool and swam, as they always had, practising the backflips that I had taught them just months before. But now I found myself begging them to stop – I just couldn't handle it. I hadn't given it a second thought before, but now it seemed too dangerous. I could picture one of my little girls diving backwards and catching her head on the edge of the pool and breaking her neck, ending up quadriplegic or worse. It just made me feel physically sick. I had a glimpse of what my mother must have gone through watching her four sons do their 'stunts' in the garden. Her fretting and concern back then – which had seemed so petty as a child – suddenly made perfect sense to me.

*

As the years went on I really enjoyed swimming at home and it came to be an opportunity to play with my daughters because I could move much more easily in the pool. We raced each other, and unlike the times when I would let them win, now I was going flat out and still being beaten. I would make sure I talked it up before we raced, about how I was going to whip them and they weren't to cry when they lost, making sure their win was that much sweeter. I would then blame my loss on the pool cleaner pipes that were in the way or misunderstanding the number of laps. We would end up wrestling, four against one, while Meredith urged them to take it easy on me. All of this was the opposite of how it had been before my accident.

About three years after the accident, my girls entered the open water swim at Sun City. Kayla, the oldest, was confident and looking forward to it. My second oldest Jenna, who was nine at the time, was a bit nervous about swimming alone, so I foolishly offered to do the 600-metre swim with her and nearly died in the process. She had only swum in pools before, so the dark water and the reeds brushing against her legs had her feeling really nervous as we walked into the water. I held her hand and encouraged her.

We started swimming and I did breaststroke with my arms, my legs dragging in the water behind me, keeping my head above the water and talking her through it the whole time. After about the first hundred metres she was doing well and off she went. She could swim like a fish and soon left me in her wake. By now I was pretty spent from the breaststroke and the constant talking, with 500 metres still to go. I put my head down and continued with freestyle – well, my top half at least. By the time I reached the halfway buoy I could taste

147

blood and I could see a light opening up where my granddad stood ready to welcome me to the other side.

The serious swimmers called this a fun swim.

'Fun swim my arlie!' I thought. 'This is suicide!'

Those guys were going to be dredging the bottom looking for my body tomorrow. An elderly lady swam past doing breaststroke, and pointed out that I was swimming off course. All I wanted to do was grab on to her and save the life that was slipping away from me. There were rescue boats around and lifeguards on Sups, but I have a rule about quitting. It doesn't happen. Death before DNF, was my motto but never before had that seemed like the actual choice I was making. More elderly ladies and toddlers swam past me, my gasps for breath and wide panicked eyes no doubt scaring the children.

By no small miracle (and after a very long time) I made it near enough to the shore for my feet to touch the ground under the water. The sweet, sweet solid ground. The water level tapered to waist height and I tried to stand up, but sucking in air in my near death state made the world just spin around me. I crouched in the water for a moment, not wanting to pass out, trying to regain my composure. I'm sure that to the people standing at the finish I looked like some creepy guy taking a last pee before exiting the water.

Once I had recovered enough to walk, I exited triumphantly and joined the back of a long queue to receive my finisher's medal. Jenna and the other small children had their medals and their costumes were already bone dry. I could see Meredith in the background telling the marshal to call off the search party she had asked for. I mumbled something about swimming around for 20 minutes looking for Jenna, not knowing that she had gone ahead and then I quickly changed the subject, desperately trying to talk while panting for breath. I had an image to project, er, I mean, protect.

*

July continued and I had two mates step up to help me out with my website, free of charge. Adrian van Rooyen organised the registering and hosting of the website and put the whole thing together. Werner van Greunen sorted out the payment portal for people who wanted to add their names on the bike. I added in my whole journey up to that point and the website 'fromparatodakar.co.za' went live.

Slowly the first donations started to trickle in. The first one was from a friend of my wife's, Becki Mitchell. Meredith hadn't seen Becki since junior school back in England! Then family and close friends started to donate. With each small amount, the total started to climb. Adrian added a thermometer to the website where people could track progress, hoping it would encourage others as they saw it climb.

There are hundreds of reasons why riders don't finish the Dakar each year. Some are avoidable and some are not. The finishing rate is normally only around 60 per cent – and even lower for first time riders. For me, being a first time rider with a disability and on the wrong side of forty, the chances of finishing were looking pretty slim on paper. But then again, I had been given a 10 per cent chance of walking again, so I wasn't about to let the odds bother me. What I did decide to do was to eliminate as many possibilities for failure as I could before I got there.

I made an effort to call and speak to some of the previous South African Dakar riders to get some advice. Brett Cummings, a two time finisher from Witbank, had given me some good advice on a rally a couple years earlier where we pitted together, and now I certainly needed all the help I could get. I called Brian Baragwanath, who had finished third in the Quad category, and he was a wealth of informa-tion, as were Ted Barbier, Iain Stevenson and Kobus Potgieter. Darryl and Greg had been feeding me information for a while at that stage, so I felt that I had good idea of what I was in for, as well as quite a few 'tricks of the trade'.

I had been given advice such as making sure you put your rain-coat on before you got wet – especially at altitude – and carrying spare warmer gloves as well as a neoprene facemask. I should make sure to put sunblock and lip ice on several times a day because the speeds and dry air would suck the moisture out of my face, leaving my lips cracked and face raw within the first few days. They also recommended two sets of goggles, making sure one had a clear lens for night riding, and gave a lot of advice about hydration, navigation, nutrition, which tools to carry and the importance of pacing myself. It was all really valuable advice and I absorbed as much as I could, making notes to give myself the best possible chance of crossing that finish line in January.

Apart from the finances and training, there was a whole bunch of medical challenges to deal with too, one of them being my bladder. I still needed to self-catheter several times a day, which on its own is no issue, but I had developed another problem on top of that. As soon as my bladder was full, I started to leak when bouncing around on the bike. It only happened when I was riding, but naturally it was frustrating and very embarrassing. If I took muscle relaxants to help with my back on the multi-day races, it made it even worse! I had even used absorbent pads so that I could still ride.

I'll never forget the day I first bought them. I stood in a long queue at the pharmacy, eyeing out the different counters I might be called to and hoping like crazy that I would get the quiet, older guy at the far end. No such luck. I was called to the counter directly in front of the queue. In a hushed tone I asked what the different solutions were for men dealing with this issue. I was sure it was something guys with prostate cancer, older guys or people with other injuries also had to deal with on a daily basis. It was a common problem and there turned out to be a whole range of options.

A large female assistant loudly barked out info on the different products, including their various sizes and the amount of liquid they could hold. She may as well have asked me over a megaphone about the frequency and volume. I was dying! All I could think was, 'Would you mind using your inside voice and could you call them something other than pads?' She held the different samples up like trophies and I could feel the eyes of the other people in the queue burning into the back of my head. I wanted to snatch them out her hand and put them down on the counter. The only thing that could have made the situation worse would have been if she had tried to fit one into my jocks right there! I tried to smile at the whole situation, thinking that one day I would look back and laugh about it. I should have ended the conversation with, 'Thanks, I'm sure this will work well for my granddad!' Instead I took the packet and, like a scolded child with my eyes fixed on the floor, I walked back past the queue.

I needed a better plan for Dakar and on 27 July I went to see a urologist at Wilgeheuwel Hospital, and explained my predicament. He was a fantastic doctor and made it easy to speak openly about the challenges I was dealing with. I had thought about racing with an indwelling catheter, attached to a bag or even a pipe and valve I could just stop and open. He said the indwelling was not a great idea and could possibly lead to even more complications. He had a better plan. He helped me out with some better disposable catheters and put me on some medication that worked well and stopped the leaking. It was one less thing to worry about.

Then finally, on 21 July 2016, I received an email that turned out to be simultaneously the most exciting and the scariest email of my life:

Subject: Motorbike and Quad selection for the Dakar 2017

Dear Joey,

First and foremost, we would like to thank you for registering for the 2017 edition of the Dakar. Like each year, we have carried out selections from the many applications that we have received.

Because you participated in the Afriquia Merzouga Rally 2016 and you raced the entire route without penalty, you confirmed your level and proved you have the requested technical, physical and mental abilities.

Therefore, we are pleased to confirm your registration for the Dakar 2017.

At that moment, sitting alone looking at the screen, it all became very real. I was going to be a full-on Dakar bike competitor! Something I had wanted, dreamed about and worked towards for years was suddenly right there within my reach. My chest felt as though it would explode. I smiled from ear to ear and let out a childish giggle that would have put all four of my girls to shame!

I read on. The letter covered all the entry requirements with regard to finances and dates for payments. It was now only a little over five months to the start, which was set for 2 January in Asuncion, Paraguay.

'Oh crap, what have I done?' raced through my mind.

Would my dream turn into a nightmare?

Chapter 18

AUGUST 2016 – 5 MONTHS TO DAKAR

August was a crazy month with a lot going on. It was going to be tough on the family with all the travelling, so we needed to make sure we still had some kind of balance. A while ago, Meredith and I had decided to have date nights with our daughters, one on one. We made sure it took priority over anything else. One month would be Meredith's turn and one night of each week she would have an evening out with each daughter. The following month was my turn, and so on. It worked well and I looked forward to the dates and the fun we would have. We laughed while I listened to stories about school, teachers and friends.

As a dad of teenagers, my primary function was to embarrass them at the mall. The impact of my singing or dancing varied according to their age. Kayla and Jenna – the oldest two – walked away, pretending they didn't know me. Tyra just laughed and Shawna, the youngest, joined me. I saw it as revenge for when they were very young and threw tantrums at the tills when I didn't buy them the sweet they wanted. On date night, no cellphones were allowed and they got the fast food of their choice, normally ending with an ice cream when Tyra would argue over the number of scoops. She generally got her way.

We would always look for new opportunities to spend more time together as a family, so when the Pongola 500 came up again from 5-7 August, we made sure we went together. It was a perfect training ride and we got to spend time together too.

We arrived in Pongola and as a result of the aggressive cow that viciously attacked me a couple years before, I dealt with the nick-name 'Cowboy' like a man. My buddy Thomas Eich, whose company Omega Fibreglass had manufactured my bike's carbon fibre bashplate, made sure to wrap it in a black and white cowhide vinyl decal, complete with a picture of a cowboy.

The 500-kilometre ride was fantastic as usual and on the Saturday night after the ride, we sat on the benches with the family, surrounded by mates. Gary Rowley, Ludwig Buchner, Warren Strong and Bruce Will all chatted about the ride and some of our individual racing goals. Gary, who had grandchildren of his own, had a way with children and he had my girls laughing and chatting with him like old buddies. It was cool to watch!

Dallie and Maryanne handed out the various fun prizes and I received one for not killing any livestock that year. Then Dallie asked me to share my story with everyone there. I told them about my spinal cord injury, racing in Morocco, and my build-up towards Dakar. I also spoke a bit about the challenges I had faced and the massive amount of help I had received. Everyone clapped and it felt great to be surrounded by such support.

If you speak to any biker, regardless of what bike or discipline they ride, they will tell you that a brotherhood exists among them. You can't really explain it in words, but you can certainly feel it. I had felt it many times in my life and I definitely felt it that night. Dallie was not done yet, though. As I was about to sit down, he grabbed me by the arm and asked me to stand there a little longer. The emcee then asked who would like to donate towards my goal and help me to reach my dream. It was quiet for a couple of seconds and I felt awkward once again, put on the spot and feeling like a bit of a beggar. Then a hand went up near the back. It was Ludwig! 'I'll give R1 000,' he called out. He kicked it off and then the floodgates opened! One hand after another shot up and amounts were called out.

Maryanne grabbed a piece of paper and scribbled as fast as she could, taking down all the names and amounts, desperately trying to keep up with outpouring of support. Gary put his hand up and donated R5 000! I looked at Meredith through the crowd, her mouth was open and tears were flowing down her face. She had felt the care and generosity of individual bikers over the years, but to see it all happening live, right there in front of her eyes, was incredibly special. One individual, Gary Prentis, a one-legged helicopter pilot, donated R25 000 and also won the auction of a weekend away, kindly donated by Jozini Tiger Lodge. However, he donated the weekend right back to Maryanne's parents, Margaret and 'Chookie' – a beautiful older couple, the kind you look at and hope to be like one day. Her dad had just celebrated his 83rd birthday and they had been married for

54 years! I made an effort to personally thank as many of them as I could. The support was beyond anything I could have hoped for.

As the dust settled, I sat back down with my family and my daughters feeling absolutely astounded. They had never seen anything like it before and I felt proud to be part of that community. In a matter of minutes that night, R62 000 was raised and my thermometer jumped up. Since then, we have spoken about that night as a family many times and the unbelievable way we all felt.

I needed a logo for my campaign, something for people to recognise and it needed to really look good on the T-shirts and caps we were going to sell. Bevan offered to help and we went back and forth with a ton of designs. Some just sucked and others were the wrong shape or didn't feel right. I sent the different ideas to mates, receiving mixed reactions, until one day it all just clicked. Bevan nailed it spot on! Everyone loved it and on 11 August we had ourselves a rocking logo. I got hold of Clinton Achadinha from Al's embroidery soon afterwards and we started getting the caps and shirts made. As I'm sure my daughters will tell you, I'm way too old to pull off the flat billed caps, so initially I ordered a hundred fitted curved peak caps, but needed to order a second hundred within about a month. I bravely ordered 200 T-shirts in a range of sizes. I knew I wouldn't make a ton of money out of the sales, but it all slowly helped my thermometer rise and, as a bonus, increased awareness.

It was National Women's Day on 9 August, so I decided to let the girls enjoy their day and I headed out to a big farm in Bronkhorstspruit to do the filming for the *ZA Bikers* promo. Louwrens Mahoney was out there, busy marking out the track for the off-road race coming up that weekend. It worked out perfectly because we could do the interview with him there and get the riding footage we needed at the same time.

Tebz Lechela was the camera guy, as well as editor, and had the near impossible task of making me look fast. He's pretty well known in the Joburg supermoto circles for reasons I can't really share with you for fear of being arrested. Let's just say if you see a black guy with tattoos standing on the seat of his bike and flying down the street on the back wheel, I might just know his name. At first, it felt weird being filmed, but I got into it and the day was a blast. Zoon Cronje, an extreme sports photographer, pitched up about halfway through our shoot to film some stuff for the upcoming race. He had heard about my story and offered to help, free of charge, taking some cool pics and pulling out his serious camera drone that had Tebz drooling!

The weather played along and the day worked out perfectly. Over the next few days, we got the interview footage in the workshop at KTM that we needed from Riaan and Darryl. I was dying to see the end result, but Tebz first needed to work his magic.

I'd ridden enduro bikes for years by now, but believe it or not I had never ridden an adventure bike. Enduro bikes are much lighter, normally going up to an engine size of about 500cc. They are often referred to as 'plastics', usually weighing about 90-110 kilograms and are perfectly suited to the worst terrain Mother Nature has to offer.

Adventure bikes, on the other hand, are designed more for longer distances and comparatively easier gravel tracks and off-road trails. They usually had 800-1300cc engines and often weighed over 200 kilograms. My good friend Francois du Toit from Raceworx KTM invited me to join him and a couple of mates on an adventure trip to Memel and back on 21 and 22 August. He had a KTM 1190 adventure bike from the shop that I could use and it sounded like fun. I was in, but I had one big concern. At times I still struggled to keep the enduro bike upright when I stopped and this bike was nearly double the weight. I went along on the trip, but often had to throw my leg over before coming to a stop, standing next to the bike as it stopped to ensure I didn't land up in a heap under it. We were joined by John Meijer and Heiner Meyer, both experienced adventure riders, and the weekend was a lot of fun. I had shared my story and Dakar plans with them and John had a great idea.

He was keen to help me with my Dakar campaign and, as luck would have it, he also needed a motivational speaker for his management training session coming up in a few weeks. We made a deal and I agreed to be their speaker. I had never done anything like that before and enlisted my brother-in-law David to help me with a PowerPoint presentation. I took my rally bike with me as my 'show and tell' item and shared my story with them. It went off well and John was really appreciative, even upping the fee agreed for the talk. I had really enjoyed doing it and I even thought about the possibility of doing it as a career one day, but it was way too early for those thoughts. I had bitten off more than I could chew already: I had to survive Dakar and get that finisher's medal first!

Walter, whose entry to Dakar had also been accepted, invited me to join him in Swaziland for a few days to train together. Early in the morning of 25 August I headed out there and spent three days with him and Mike Johannes, riding the gravel tracks and sandy dry river beds. We racked up hundreds of kilometres and it was good fun hanging out and getting to know them better. We sat around the braai at night and Walter and I compared our Dakar preparations and spoke about the kit we were using and our plans leading up to the big race. We had the same dream and were equally excited and nervous about how the race in January would unfold.

After leaving Swaziland, I made a stopover in Pongola for a day, where Bruce Terblanche took me on a ride of their local trails along the hills of the Swaziland border. It was a beautiful area and the riding was unbelievable. There were steep rocky hills with cattle tracks that wound their way through the mountains. We rode for hours on the trails, passing through rural villages where we stopped for the occasional cold drink at some rundown dusty spaza shop. As a city guy, I was envious of the perfect riding terrain he had right on his doorstep. We rode late into the afternoon, after which I loaded my bike onto my bakkie and drove the five-hour journey back home late into the night.

My training had been going well and I was riding a lot, but I needed to get my body as strong as possible before January. Sharne recommended that I see Derek Archer, a top trainer who had coached many professional athletes. Now it's not right to use my name and 'professional athlete' in the same sentence, but he agreed to help me prepare as best as I could. I could tell he had the same 'death before DNF' attitude as I had and he loved the challenge I had taken on. I liked his approach, first giving me a full evaluation and working out my areas of weakness. I had been right-handed before the spinal cord injury and it had been my stronger side. However, after my injury my left side had made a better recovery. The way I moved favoured my right side and was causing me a lot of pain, which added to my fatigue. Derek gave me training routines to help me strengthen my core and balance my efforts better. I also saw Jenny Meyer, a dietitian who worked not far from Derek. She had me stand on the scale and I heard it creak under my weight. She pulled out the big calculator to work out my body fat percentage, the results of which I can't share with you. Let's just say I'm built for comfort! A few days later I saw her again and she gave me my eating plan and some practical advice. I was on track for January! My friends, sugar and carbs, would see less of me for a while.

I had worked on my own bikes over the years, but just the basic stuff. Heading towards Dakar I knew that I would need to know my bike inside out and be able to diagnose and solve any mechanical issues that might happen during the race. I spent many evenings with my mechanic Mike Grove at Raceworx KTM going through the bike and equipping myself with the knowledge I would need.

On the fund-raising side, August had been really quiet. There had been a few people adding their names to the bike, but we were nowhere near where we needed to be and time was flying by. Although I was worried about reaching the target, I was fully committed and determined to be on that start line no matter what. I called my bank and enquired about extending my bond. I had all the forms ready and made sure I would be able to sort it all out in time, just in case. I now knew I was stepping dangerously close to the edge of insanity, ready possibly to lose my house over a bike race. I had a little over four months to go and I decided I would reach the financial target, whatever it took.

Paul, Brian and Jason van Aswegen were brothers with whom I was good mates and we had ridden together many times. I had helped to teach them to ride early on, but they had long since become better enduro riders than I was. I had confided my Dakar dream to them early on and Paul had told me how he would love to help when the time came. Well, the time had come and I needed the help now more than ever. It was difficult calling companies for financial backing, but to call a buddy was even worse. It took me a few days to build up the courage, but I had to do it and there was no time like the present. I made the call and I honestly don't know why I had stressed so much about it. Paul made it easy and said he would speak to his partners at Kwikbuild Cement and Summit Trucking and get back to me. A couple of days later he called and was in for R50 000. I was ecstatic! I made sure I added his logos on to the bike with their names, and my thermometer climbed a little higher.

As always, life continued but with every step forward there always seemed to be a step back. The month ended with a painter touching up paint at my house falling off the roof and landing in the pool with a freshly opened 20-litre paint tin. He was fine but the pool paving and my patio were covered in paint, as were the windows, and the pool looked as though it was filled with milkshake.

All I could do was laugh. It reminded me of those photos of small kids who have been left alone too long and got into the kitchen cupboards. The pool needed to be drained and we spent the evening scrubbing paint off everything. It was all part of the crazy roller coaster of challenges and successes I faced chasing my dream.

Chapter 19

SEPTEMBER 2016 – 4 MONTHS TO DAKAR

The *ZA Bikers* guys called and I met with them, as well as with Tebz, to watch the first edit of the video. A few changes were made and on 7 September the video *Let's get Joey to Dakar* was released. *ZA Bikers* put it on their website and they posted it all over social media – putting some money into it to ensure a wider reach. I made sure I shared it on my Facebook accounts and it quickly got more than 20000 views. The response was fantastic! Lots of guys I had met and ridden with over the years called and messaged me to wish me luck and offer their support. We saw a boost in the donations on the website and my money thermometer crept a little higher.

Vincent from Botswana also had his Dakar entry accepted and had been training and fund-raising, much the same as I had been. We had spoken many times since Morocco and he had invited me to come up to Botswana for one of the national off-road races. On 8 September I made the five-hour journey across the border to his home, a small-holding on the outskirts of Gaborone. On arrival, I was welcomed by Vincent, his girlfriend Angelique and his group of mates. They made me feel part of the group right away with a welcome braai and the familiar routine of the guys working on their dirt bikes late into the night.

The next morning I awoke to a beautiful Botswana sunrise and Vincent and I loaded our enduro bikes onto his bakkie which Angelique and his mate Heine were going to drive for the three and a half hour trip to the race in Serowe. In order to get maximum training distance in, Vincent and I were riding there off-road, through the bush. I rode my KTM rally bike and he rode his Yamaha XT 660. We rode all day through the thick sand, with thorn bushes whipping at our arms, and couldn't have been happier. We spotted the occasional game and passed through some remote villages, our path occasionally being blocked by a barbed wire fence which we found our way around. We rode just over 430 kilometres that day, arriving in Serowe at dusk.

The next morning was race day and I lined up at the start at a track lined with spectators. The Botswana people in general have a love of motorsport, with the country being host to the famous Desert 1000, going back many years. A race like this brought out hundreds of fans. I rode well and felt great for the entire 200-kilometre route, with my lap times getting better lap after lap, showing my fitness was up to the task. Vince won the race overall and I finished high up the rankings too which boosted my confidence. That, and finishing injury free, made the race a total success.

The next day we rode back to Gaborone on a similar off-road route through the bush, covering another 430-odd kilometres which made it three days of back to back riding. The trip was well worthwhile and, apart from the great training I had managed to work in, I had developed some friendships that were sure to last a lifetime. I loaded up the next morning and headed back home across the border. After three good days of riding, I had to focus again on getting to the start line of Dakar with my fund-raising campaign.

I had a call from Power FM and went through for a live interview on 15 September. It was still a bit nerve-racking, but I was starting to get the hang of it. At least by now I knew I had to wear the head-phones! I had also been invited by The Bike Show to be a guest on their programme that was being recorded on 21 September at Rim and Rubber, a bike-themed restaurant and bar in Greenside. Riaan from KTM gave me some KTM shirts and asked me to wear one on the show. It may sound silly but for a guy like me to be asked by KTM to wear their shirt was pretty damn cool! I had made the big leagues! (I considered not even doing the Dakar in light of my huge, new-found media pull …) The reality was quite different. I'm sure Riaan had heard about my poor dress sense from my daughters and didn't want me to make a fool of myself on national TV. I took my rally bike with me and we parked it on the set. Riaan and Fred Fensham from Husqvarna came along to support me and the show went off really well. The interview was done in front of about 30 guys in the venue and they were really supportive, wishing me luck and pledging to donate.

On 22 September Darryl, through his partnership with Mauritz Meiring, had the company Bandit Graphics, offered to do all the sticker kits for my practice bike and my race bike at Dakar. The cost of graphics can add up quickly and with all the names I was adding it was going to be a lot of design work. Mauritz and I spent many hours behind his computer designing the graphics to fit the growing number of logos and names as I got more people on board.

My thermometer had been creeping up slowly, but time was running out way faster than I had anticipated. Each week a few people would add their names on the bike and now they started to be names I didn't recognise. Meredith took on the task of organising all the names of people who donated, matching their payments in the bank account and making sure the names were on the list for the decals. Often after a quiet week, we felt the thermometer would no longer climb. But every now and then I got a generous unexpected donation, providing us with the boost we needed – just like one I received on the 25th.

A friend of mine named Craig Kurten had shared my story with his work colleagues at Avior Capital Markets and they generously donated R20 000. Other mates' names popped up on the list, some of whom I hadn't seen for more than 20 years. Old buddies I had done missionary work with in the early 1990s, friends from school days, friends of friends who had heard my story, guys I had ridden and raced with over the years, and even teachers from my children's schools. Many of these people had witnessed the journey first-hand, while others knew me but had no idea of the physical challenges and struggle my family and I had been through.

Then one day I got a call from Judy Hardy which turned out to be a massive boost for my campaign, as well as helping me on a personal level. Judy and her husband Mark worked part time as adventure bike riding instructors at ADA, a training facility near Hartbeespoort Dam. They were not wealthy people by any means, but they were touched by my story and were determined to help in some way. Some people had given me money, others gave their time. Both were appreciated, but time is often harder to give.

Judy and Mark offered to run an adventure bike training day to help raise funds. We decided to meet up one weekend and I went through to ADA with my family. Judy was fantastic with my girls and they clicked right away. She was like a big sister who wasn't afraid of anything. She had organised a big workhorse type quad bike for them to ride on to let them explore the property while we chatted. I struggled to focus because all the feelings I had in the pool watching my girls do backflips came rushing back. I was constantly looking for them to make sure they were still OK. Judy picked up on my anxiety and reassured me. Then she said something that I really needed to hear. I don't remember the exact words she used, but she basically said that I mustn't pass my fears on to my children. They needed to experience life with all its ups and downs and although risks should be calculated, they were a vital part of growing up and tasting the full flavour life had to offer. It had never been explained that way to me before and it made perfect sense. Since that day, I have had a different outlook and I'm slowly (ever so slowly) changing.

We spoke about the skills day and Mark had some great ideas to make it even bigger and better. We bounced ideas back and forth and before we knew it, we had some pretty huge plans. We scheduled the day for 29 October and had a lot of work to do before then. My daughters arrived back on the quad with dusty faces and smiling from ear to ear. They couldn't stop talking about the adventure they had just had, as I stood sheepishly next to Judy who was beaming with pride.

Chapter 20

OCTOBER 2016
– 3 MONTHS
TO DAKAR

October arrived while I was riding the Quads 4 Quads event, a charity ride for bikes, quads and side by sides from Johannesburg to Durban, mainly on dirt roads and gravel tracks, with the occasional more technical bits thrown in here and there. It covers a total distance of 1000 kilometres over four days. A portion of the entry fee goes to the Quad Para Association of South Africa (QASA) which assists people with spinal cord injuries.

I had originally heard about the annual ride back in 2007 from my physio Melanie, while I was lying in hospital. Being a cause close to my heart, I had wanted to do it many times over the last nine years, but it had just never worked out. I needed to ride as much distance this year as possible and I loved the organisation it supported, so I made a plan to squeeze it in. I paid my entry fee and was on the start line at Carnival City on 29 September.

Most guys have buddies who ride in backup vehicles carrying their stuff, but I was on my own. The organiser Glen Foley offered to put my kitbag and tent in his vehicle, so that worked out well and I rode the four days down to Durban along with a ton of other guys and girls.

On one of the nights along the way, Glen asked me to briefly share my story with the guys. I shared my journey more as an inspirational message about overcoming challenges, making sure never to mention anything about my fund-raising. This event was about QASA and they helped a lot of people who were way more deserving of help than I was and I didn't want to water that down in any way. After four days of riding I arrived in Durban having made a bunch of friends along the way.

The finish was at Cane Cutters, a backpacking type venue, and everyone sat around the rustic wooden tables eating supper and having a few drinks. I grabbed a plate and saw a gap at one of the tables.

'Howzit, okes? Can I sit here?' I asked.

'Ja, pull in, boet,' was the reply in typically welcoming biker fashion.

I sat down with two guys whose names I later found out were Philip Nixon and Martin Cornelius. They were from the East Rand, the same area where I had grown up. We spoke for ages and even discovered that Martin's brother-in-law, Grant Gooch, and I were friends and had worked together at the same company for a while, many years ago. We spoke about the ride and I discovered that they rode it nearly every year. Philip asked about my Dakar plans and how I was going to afford it. I told him about the fund-raising we were doing and how we would be putting the names of all the people who had donated anything on the bike. It didn't matter about the amount: ten bucks, a hundred bucks, a thousand bucks, I would put all the names on the bike.

'I'll give you a hundred,' he said. I thanked him and told him about the website with the details. 'Great, yeah,' he replied. 'I'll give you R100 000.'

Obviously this caught me a little off guard. 'Er, what? ONE HUNDRED THOUSAND?' I said.

'Yes, that's what I said,' he answered, totally straight faced, as if asking me to pass the salt. I wondered if he had been celebrating the finish of the ride with a few too many drinks. I looked at Martin, who nodded as if to confirm that Philip was a man of his word. He gave me his card and told me to send him my banking details and that was it. We carried on chatting as though nothing had happened, but in my head I couldn't believe it. Was this for real? Only time would tell ...

Leaving the other riders still sleeping and enjoying their well-earned finish, I climbed on to my rally bike the next morning just before 5am and rolled out in the dark – and in the pouring coastal rain. I rode back through the sugar cane fields in the slippery black mud that we had crossed the day before. I followed the route we had covered the last four days – this time in reverse – making my way back solo towards Johannesburg.

That day I rode 950 kilometres, changing the route a bit near the end and arriving home dirty, wet and freezing cold just before 11pm. Meredith, fighting her repulsion at my smelly and sorry looking state, welcomed me home with a big hug in the dark on the front driveway of our home. I had also broken one of my front teeth again eating something along the way. I had spent 18 hours on the bike that day, the kind of hours I knew were waiting for me in South America come January. However, there would be no warm welcome each night. Just a couple of hours' sleep and then I would need to do it all again. Repeating the cycle every day for two weeks.

The next morning I told Meredith about Philip and the donation. It all seemed too good to be true but I sent him the banking details as he had requested, cautiously allowing myself to believe it would come through. A week later nothing had come in and I started to lose hope.

I really didn't want to because I thought it might be really awkward, but I decided to give him a call and follow up. I introduced myself, unsure if he would recall the conversation from the ride, but he was switched on. He explained he had received my banking details but had had an urgent overseas commitment and had only just arrived back. He said the money would be transferred that day and, true to his word, the deposit was made a few hours later. Meredith and I were excited beyond belief and also completely shocked. We couldn't believe his generosity. I added his 'PD Nixon Containers' company logo to my decals and my thermometer shot up nicely. The Quads 4 Quads had been a ride where I was giving back, but thanks to Philip it turned out to give a huge boost to my Dakar dream.

The next couple of days were tough, as I got really sick with a urinary tract infection. Unfortunately, it was something that happened from time to time with having to use catheters. I hadn't had an infection for more than a year, so I had been doing well, but travelling and camping always increased the risk. Being stressed about all the plans and physically worn out from all the training and riding didn't help either. I didn't have time to sit around and feel sorry for myself. I knew there was a real possibility it could happen at Dakar. If it did, I would not be quitting, so I got my antibiotics and got on with what needed doing.

I had a couple more interviews that month. The first was for the online publication *This is my Jo'burg* and at about the same time I had another one with Dan Lombard from *Game On* magazine. Dan is an incredible guy who broke his neck at rugby practice in high school, damaging his spinal cord and leaving him permanently paralysed from the neck down. He is only 26 now but, with the help of his buddy Lunga Ndzinisa, he doesn't let being a quadriplegic hold him back, working as both journalist and editor for the magazine. He is still very passionate about sports – particularly rugby, where he covers the game at every level. Dan and Lunga don't let the disability slow them down.

A few days later I met with Clinton Pienaar from *Superbike Magazine*, who had also covered my story, and the team from Ride for a Reason. The latter organised many rides to raise funds for charities, their favourites being ones that cared for animals. They had heard my story and were keen to organise a ride to help me, for which I was really grateful. We decided on a ride where the guys on street bikes would ride from Johannesburg out to ADA at Harties on the same day we had our fund-raiser with Mark and Judy. They took care of every detail and I didn't have to lift a finger. It was another moment when people gave freely of their time, expecting nothing in return.

On 13 September I headed out to the Natal Dual Bike Adventure (NDBA). The organisers, Rika de Bruyn, Treffon Smith and Mark Taylor, had invited me to join them to share my story in the evening. They kindly paid for my accommodation and I put together the presentation, complete with photos of my journey up to the point of qualifying to race the Dakar. Troy Barwell was the emcee that night and I've never had such an introduction in all my life. If you've watched the movie *A Knight's Tale* you'll remember the introductions given by his sidekick before each joust. It was something along those lines! He stopped short of calling me 'the protector of Italian virginity'! The guys loved it and I received a standing ovation after the talk. It was a night to be remembered. Then, as had happened at the Pongola evening, Troy auctioned off a Top Box that had been donated by Bruce McDonald from 3DX for my fund. Troy worked his magic and many of the guys started donating. This time it was Rika scribbling away, trying to keep up with all the names. We raised a total of R34 500 that night, getting me that bit closer to the start. Moments like those, where guys pulled together to help me, had me close to tears on many occasions. I'm a hard-core biker and I never cry, but I did consider it.

I left straight from the NBDA to join the Subtech Ryder team in Pongola again for a couple of days of training. Trying to keep up with Roger and Greg was never a good idea, and on the last day I took a fall on a fast, compacted, sandy section going through some S-bends. I escaped with a few bruises, roasties and a slightly damaged ego. It was always a challenge to ride long and hard, and still avoid injury. Walter had had a bad fall in Swaziland not long after I had ridden with him.

He went down hard, shattering his collarbone and needing an operation. With not enough time for it to heal completely he would have to race Dakar with the plate and screws still in place.

About 18 months earlier I had been so frustrated with my repaired teeth constantly breaking that I decided to sort out a more permanent solution. I had seen a specialist and the best option was to get titanium implants – but the costs were huge. The maxillofacial surgeon was brilliant and his wife, who worked with him, helped me out with some discounted fees to make it easier on my pocket. We started with the bottom jaw, removing the worst teeth one at a time, replacing them with titanium inserts. Then I was handed over to the prosthodontist who did the crowns. I spent many hours training with my helmet squeezed over a swollen face, stitches in my mouth and high on painkillers. Eventually, my bottom jaw was complete and I decided to leave it that way because of cash flow problems and the pain it would entail. I would wait until Dakar was over before I carried on with the upper jaw.

I had more help from Matt and Claudia at MSR, a bike shop near Kyalami. Along with Andy from the Adventure Academy, they organised a one-day outride supported by a bunch of adventure riders to raise a bit more for the fund. They all contributed themselves as well and they managed to raise a further R6 500.

The 25th was the annual Dakar workshop that Darryl planned, where he spoke about what it takes to get there and how to be prepared. Rob Howie, an experienced Dakar navigator from the Toyota team, spoke about the challenges they had faced. He was very helpful and I spoke to him afterwards, picking up some valuable tips. Darryl had asked me to talk for a few minutes about my road to Dakar. It was tough to fit a nine-year journey into a couple of minutes but it went off OK. Once again, I left with renewed motivation. I needed it, as I still had a long way to go with my fund-raising.

It was just two months and a couple days to go and we had raised a total of R470 000 at that point. It was a ton of money but we were not even halfway yet. It had taken us just over four months to get that far and a lot of donations had come from friends. Now we had to make up the balance in less than half the time – things were looking bleak.

My good mate Tristam rallied a bunch of our mutual mates together and they donated another large sum of money that week. Every couple of days I felt really stressed about the money but each time someone else would step up and help. I really started to believe we might just pull this off. I had the fund-raiser with ADA coming up in a few days and needed to pull out all the stops.

The fund-raiser was on 29 October and Judy had come up with the name 'Dream Makers Day'. It summed it up pretty well. The day had grown to include an enduro track that consisted of three different loops on the neighbouring farm owned by Wayne Leigh, who had been kind enough to let us ride there. Brett Stevens and Jason Faulkes, who had sponsored me with some DC kit, knew the farm well and we rode together with a couple of other guys to work out some good routes. The farm not only had a fair bit of wildlife, but it also had amazing riding terrain with rocky koppies, winding paths, off camber trails and shady river beds. The event was just a few weeks before the Roof of Africa enduro, so we wanted to make sure the route was tough enough to attract the guys who were training for it.

It took a long time to mark it all out and I found myself alone there one morning, tying bits of orange KTM tape to trees and bushes marking some of the route. There was no cellphone signal in the valleys, but when I got to one of the mountain tops my phone lit up with a bunch of messages. Everyone was messaging to tell me that John Robbie on 702 was trying to get hold of me for a live interview. The signal was terrible and I ended up standing on top of a big anthill at the top of the mountain to get my phone to work. I called the number and they said they would call me back in a few minutes when they were ready to go on air.

I didn't want to miss the call, so for the next 15 minutes I stood on top of the anthill, pointing my phone in different directions, trying to get the best signal. It reminded me of my dad doing the same with the TV aerial when I was a kid. We sat in front of the screen shouting 'stop, just there' as he balanced the bunny ear aerial at arm's length on the top of the curtain rail. About 15 minutes later, my phone rang and they put me live on air, still balancing on the anthill. The interview went well and by no small miracle the tracks were mostly marked by the time the day arrived – with some of the final markers being added by Brett and his mates on the morning of the ride.

I was feeling really stressed leading up to the event; I really wanted it to be a success. We tried to make the day as big as possible and we had a huge amount of support from many people, all offering to help out in so many ways. Judy and Mark had gone all out, working for days before pulling favours from everyone they knew. Some were marshals on the different tracks, others were score keepers. Others made food and sold drinks. Meredith and her sister Verity did all the registrations. Family and friends all pulled together, helping wherever there was a need. My daughters helped in the running of the day too, all wearing their 'From Para to Dakar' T-shirts, customised with the standard 'Team Evans' embroidered on the sleeve. They sold our branded T-shirts and caps, made candy floss and sold ice creams. Chris 'Monkie' Muller played live music with his band and organised a few other bands to make sure we had live music the whole day. Charaine van Jaarsveld ran the bar and walked around with a bucket asking guys to fill it with donations. We had a slip 'n slide and jumping castle as well as a paintball shooting range. The street guys rode through from Joburg and *Superbike* magazine and *ZA Bikers* covered the whole event, posting it in the magazine and online. Dave from RAD KTM had sent out mails and messages promoting the event, making sure we filled the enduro track, and the guys from Raceworx KTM sponsored the skills track.

The feedback we received from the enduro riders was very positive, despite a few nasty falls and the 35 degree heat that day. Mike from Raceworx did the mandatory burnout with his R1 street bike on the dirt track. Troy emceed the prize-giving, building me up once again to far more than I could ever live up to. (If I could, I would have won the Dakar!) More than 15 companies sponsored prizes or events that day and it was a huge success. So many individuals helped – I wish I could name them all. All that time and money was donated towards my Dakar dream and no one accepted any payment for any of the services they provided.

Later that night – after what had been a very long day since most of us had been up since 4am – Judy gathered us all around a big table after everyone had left and emptied out the bucket of donations and the day's takings. Mark, Judy, Meredith, our girls and I sorted the notes into piles before counting it up. We then put aside the costs we had incurred for the drinks and food and carefully worked out the profit. We had made a total profit of about R61 000 that day, all because of two people who wanted to help, but didn't have much money to give. They gave so much more than money, along with a life lesson that I will never forget. Don't ever tell me that as an individual you don't have the power to make a difference!

October bowed out on the 31st with a live interview on 5FM with DJ Fresh, as the 'Monday Motivator'. It was done over the phone and the line wasn't great, but it was cool to be on a big national station.

Chapter 21

NOVEMBER 2016 – 2 MONTHS TO DAKAR

A couple of days into November and with just less than two months till Dakar, we hit the halfway mark of R550 000 on the fund-raising thermometer. I was starting to sweat bullets and found myself on Google looking up ways to sell my body parts to the Far East. I didn't want to face the possibility of not reaching our target, but it would take a small miracle to get there.

I was leaving for the 2016 Amageza Rally in a few days and I was physically and mentally worn out. On 2 November, I woke up feeling really sick and noticed I had a couple of sores on my right cheek. The entire right side of my face was painful to the touch and I assumed it must have been some kind of spider bite. I went off to see our family doctor, and with all the symptoms considered, it seemed just that. She gave me a course of antibiotics and we both figured I'd be sorted in a day or two. It was the fourth course of antibiotics I'd been on that year, twice for my teeth, then for the UTI and now this.

When I woke up the next day, I felt even worse and couldn't handle anything touching the entire right side of my head – it was so painful. The marks on my face had started to blister and I was leaving for the Amageza in 48 hours where I would be wearing a helmet for the next six days. It wasn't looking good. I figured I had the meds and just needed to suck it up, so like a typical guy I didn't call the doc that day. The following day, I was worse still, so I gave up my foolish approach and went back to the doctor. She did some more tests and it turned out that I actually had shingles. She got me on the right meds immediately and asked if I was under any stress at the time. That would be a big fat yes! As a doctor she recommended I took it easy, but she knew me better than that. She had seen me for many years and had been through a lot with my family and me. We both knew

I wasn't going to miss the race. She knew about my Dakar plans and was almost as excited about it as I was, even making sure her name was on the bike. She made it clear she did not recommend I do the Amageza, but wished me luck and sent me on my way.

I still needed a bracket for my GPS to fit on to my rally bike, which I had not used for Amageza before. Steve and Angelique from Rost Engineering had offered to help me out with anything I needed a few weeks before and I decided to take them up on the offer. I drove there with my bike on the trailer, where Steve measured up the mounting area on my bike and they machined me a custom bracket on the CNC machine for the rally bike while I waited. It fitted perfectly, right off the bat, and bike-wise I was ready to go racing.

Neil Ringdahl and I left early the next morning, making the usual predawn exit out of town, and drove the eight and half hours to the start in Upington. We met up with Alex Ruprecht-Gersteroph at a guest house which he had paid for to help me save some cash. The three of us were riding Malle Moto along with about another ten guys, all of us good mates who looked out for one another. The Malle Moto guys had become a bit of a brotherhood over the past few years. It was only seven weeks till Dakar and I was still not well, so my objectives were pretty clear. I was there to train and improve my navigation and fitness and, most importantly, to return home uninjured. I decided to take it easy with the speed, staying safe, and I stopped to help anyone with problems, making the days longer, and in turn more difficult as preparation for the Dakar.

On the first day, Roger from Subtech Ryder was the first to test my helping theory. He had won the Baja earlier that year and was a top contender for the win. On a rocky climb, his front wheel had ricocheted off a loose rock and had gone over the edge. He was OK, but his bike had taken a big knock, breaking the oil cooler hose off the casing and losing a lot of his oil. He was alone with the bike on its side when I got there, trying to save as much oil as possible. The attachment was broken in such a way that it was impossible to reconnect. We tried all sorts of methods and eventually managed to block off the holes bypassing the oil filter. It took us a good hour in the Northern Cape's hot sun. We drained some oil from my bike to top his up and, feeling proud of ourselves and our ingenuity, we started riding again.

Within about a kilometre his bike engine seized in a sandy river bed and we were stuck with 200 kilometres still to go that day. I offered to tow him but he refused. The terrain was very technical, with steep rocky climbs, soft river beds and steep, loose descents. He didn't want to hold me up and in any event it would be near impossible to tow through that terrain. I told him I couldn't care about the standings and we might as well give it a go. We were in so remote an area that he really had only two choices: we either tried to tow or he spent the night there. We looked at each other knowing it was totally crazy, but decided to go for it.

When you tow another rider, usually you each stand with the tow rope under your boot, pinching it to the foot peg. If there's a problem you can lift your foot and the two of you are separated. The problem we faced was that the terrain was so rough that the rope just pulled out, so we needed to tie it on the foot rests between the bikes. To tow like that on the road would be risky and in this terrain it was simply insane. We put our lives in each other's hands. There are few guys I would trust to ride like that, but Roger was a skilled rider and I knew he wouldn't get me killed. For him to trust me was just stupid and really poor judgement on his part; I think he was a bit delirious at the time.

We rode on for several kilometres, my engine revving out in the thick sand and trying to keep the acceleration even and controlled up the rocky climbs. It was hair-raising, with whoops and cheering from both of us after each hectic climb. The first time we fell, he went down and I dragged his bike for a few metres not knowing he was no longer on it. The second time was just after a rise where the path split. I took the right and not being able to see the split past my bike, he went left. My bike pulled out from under me and we both went down on the rocks. We were both a bit bruised, but nothing serious, and we laughed at the comedy of the situation. On we rode for several hours, the sun was hot and we were burning calories by the ton. At one point where the track split again, we stopped. Roger was exhausted.

The area was very rough so I rode ahead to scout out the best route before we committed to a specific direction. I arrived back and we headed out again. Eventually, we made it through the worst terrain and rode through to the end of the day, arriving about four hours after the other riders. Greg was there, an engineer by trade and a bit of a guru on the KTM rally bike. He was impressed at first with our handy repair to the casing, using the back end of a spark plug.

'That's quite clever,' he commented. 'You remembered to take out the tube inside so the oil could flow through, right?'

Roger and I looked at each other sheepishly while Greg shook his head. We vowed never to speak of it again – well, at least not in front of Greg.

They had a spare motor and together they spent a few hours taking out the old one and fitting it into the bike. Roger was on the start line the next morning and went on through the next couple of thousand kilometres to cross the finish line five days later.

A few days later I came across Johan Jansen van Rensburg at the side of the track. He had his back wheel off and the tyre was badly damaged. He was originally running a tubeless system, but the large gash in his tyre made it impossible to repair. He was very well prepared and had tyre irons and a spare tube but he had already used the tube and it was now also damaged. He had his patches out and was making another plan.

One of the unspoken rules of racing is that you always help someone who is helping themselves. If you come across someone working on their bike and they need help, you stop and work with them. However, if someone has broken down and he's standing next to his bike telling you it's broken, but hasn't bothered to carry tools on him and is not even trying to fix it, you should wish him luck and carry on. Luckily for Johan, he was the first type. He was making a plan and told me to carry on. But I had been there before and I was more than happy to work alongside him. His tube was in a bad way and he really needed a new one. Rudi Neethling, one of the Malle Moto guys, had been waved on by Johan just a couple of minutes earlier, and I knew he had a tube. I rode off to catch up to him and asked if he would part with it. Without a moment's hesitation, he handed me the tube. I rode back to Johan and we fitted the tube. I shadowed him the rest of the day and we stopped twice more. Each time we found ourselves removing the back wheel and patching the tube again, as it had rubbed through on the inside of the damaged carcass. Johan is the kind of guy who would have made a plan on his own and finished. But together it was easier and he appreciated the help.

I came across Chris Opperman on the second last day. He had been running in second when he took a massive fall that really rang his bell. He had snapped his throttle cables in the crash and had tried to make a plan to fix it, but it was near impossible. When I got to him he had pressed his recovery button and was waiting to be collected, frustrated to be out the race. He had waved me on but I stopped to find out what the problem was. He showed me and I immediately told him to cancel the recovery, we would make a plan. I pulled open the storage in my bashplate where I had stashed a piece of cable with a few universal attachments. It took us a few attempts, but together we made a plan and got the bike working again. I thought he was going to kiss me, he was so stoked to be back in the race! He went on to finish the race and if I remember correctly, he even won the stage on the last day.

The final day was full of drama. Not long after the start, along with a couple of other riders, we came across Mark Kapnoudhis who had taken a massive fall on a particularly dangerous sharp rocky section. He was in a bad way and there was a lot of blood. He had broken his pelvis and had a deep laceration on his side that was on the brink of entering his abdomen. There was another deep cut on his arm and several other lacerations. The skin had been ripped off some of his finger tips and the webbing between two of his fingers was torn.

I called race headquarters for help on my satellite phone and an ambulance was dispatched, but it was going to take them a while to reach us. Claude and Gerrit, the same guys who had stopped with me the previous year when I blew out the rear mousse, were with me. Between the three of us, we cut off some of his kit and did our best to patch him up while we waited for the paramedics. It was an unusual situation. Mark, who was injured, was an orthopaedic surgeon. Claude, who was treating him, was a vet and he was being assisted by a pool guy – me! I think Mark was just grateful that Claude didn't put him down! The ambulance arrived and the medics took over and the three of us who were now right at the back, pushed on. We had lost over an hour and there was a cut-off that day which we needed to make to reach the finish.

We rode on but took a wrong fork in the river bed, which lost us even more time. Later that evening we heard that most of the guys had made the same wrong turn, with many of them riding over a seriously hectic rocky mountain to correct it instead of going back. Fortunately, we had chosen to go back, managed to find our error and corrected our route. A few kilometres later, I came across Rolf Basler, whose motor had completely seized and there was no way to fix it. I called it in to race headquarters on my satellite phone and they dispatched a team to collect him. While I was there making the call, my mate Ludwig who had broken down about 100 metres further on had walked over. Ludwig's head bearings had totally seized and his bars were completely locked and unable to turn. He was just about ready to give up. I wanted to help but I still needed to make the cut-off and ride the entire route and so I found myself torn between the two options. I told him to get back over to his bike and start making a plan. Then I rode over to him and grabbed my tools and together we started stripping the bars and triple clamps. Once we got the bars off and the headset stripped I really had to go, so I explained to him what he needed to do and that he should add some engine oil to help them move. Ludwig was more than capable and he was now fully committed to making a plan and getting to the finish. He sent me on my way.

With all the time I had spent in the sun, I had drunk all of the three litres of water in my hydration pack and I was dehydrating. Luckily I had filled the emergency three-litre water tank in the bashplate of my bike. I decided to stop and siphon it out into my hydration pack and added a couple of the rehydrate sachets I was carrying. The water was as hot as tea and tasted foul, but it kept me hydrated and that's what mattered.

I had spent a lot of time that morning helping the guys, but somehow managed to be the last rider through before the cut-off. We all thought that I would be the last one in that day, but long after I arrived, one final rider came limping home. It was Ludwig! He had managed to get the head bearings working by ingeniously using his lip ice to lube them up and had reassembled the bars without one of the bolts that he had accidentally dropped into the petrol tank. But it was working, so he had pushed for a while, until the back wheel bearings also completely collapsed. But he had gone too far to quit. He had used engine oil to make the wheel turn, adding it again and again as he rode on. He had faced numerous challenges that day trying to keep his bike going and refusing to quit. He basically dragged his bike across the finish line. It was a mammoth mental and physical achievement to finish that day and one he can be proud of for the rest of his life.

The race had been a success for me. I had achieved what I had set out to do. I finished the full distance, increased my navigation skills and upped my fitness once again. I placed far down in the final standings, but I was awarded the 'Amadoda Yamadoda' trophy for the second year in a row for the support I had given in helping other riders to the finish. It was a result I was more than proud of and I had once again made friends and memories I will hold on to for ever.

I had sold a few T-shirts and caps at the race and on the way back Neil and I stopped in at the Holfontein enduro that was held just west of Joburg. The race was run by Hein Kock, a good friend of mine.

He had generously pledged to donate a portion of each entry to my Dakar campaign and asked me to speak briefly at the prize-giving. It was a well-attended event and the racers loved my story. I sold some T-shirts and caps again and we added some more funds to the pot.

I picked up a few more opportunities to present motivational talks in November, one from Mouritz Hill at Cronimet Mining and another from Paul Wepener at Tiger Brands. I also spoke at MSR's send-off evening for their riders heading to the Roof of Africa. 'Death before DNF' was the message I left with them. The talks really helped to boost the funds and I loved doing them.

Towards the end of November, I got my Dakar race number. I was rider number 132. I liked it – I had been number 122 when I broke my back and now, ten years later, I was number 132 at the Dakar Rally. It worked out nicely. I'm not at all superstitious and proved it a couple of years before.

At the beginning of the Dakar in 2014, I mentioned to Meredith once again that it was my goal to compete. Her biggest fear was that I would die. To be honest, I had given her just cause to feel that way!

She had said, 'OK, that's fine. Let's see if any riders die this year, if one does it's a sign you shouldn't race.'

I just laughed, not wanting to base my future on such an uncertain outcome. The race went on and sadly one rider did die that year – Eric Palante, a biker from Belgium on his eleventh Dakar. What was strange for us was that his number was 122, the same number I had raced with for years. If she wanted a sign, that was certainly it. I kept quiet about it, but she did hear about the death. But to keep her mind at ease, I made sure to keep his number to myself.

I was ready to order my rally jackets with my Dakar number printed on them when I got a call from Dave Griffin at RAD KTM. He had helped me many times over the last few months with advice and ideas for fund-raising, as well as sponsoring prizes and attending all my fund-raisers. He offered to buy the advertising on the sleeves and arranged for Motul to buy the front. It was a fantastic offer and the cash pushed the mercury in my thermometer higher.

More sponsors came on board, including Zodiac, who were one of my company's suppliers, and Muelmed Clinic, where I had been treated after my accident. I met with many other possible sponsors, including a guy from a large company who promised to cover the outstanding funds in full, but he didn't return any of my calls after our meeting. It was difficult to know when to cut my losses and move on with sponsors. Some guys were in and deposited the cash right away, while others kept me hanging on for months and then made some excuse or just avoided me. I was cool if the guys weren't keen to get involved – things were tough, I got it – I just wished they had told me straight out.

Henderson Racing was one of the sponsors that didn't mess around. I went to meet Mark, walked through the warehouse, picked what I needed and walked out with a box full of stuff. KTM SA was the same with sponsoring my kit and spares; I made the list, it was approved by Franziska, parts were ordered and I collected them the following week. They really made it easy for me to focus on my fitness and riding.

It turned out to be more cost effective to sell my rally bike at home and buy a new one from the KTM factory in Austria which would be sent direct to my team in The Netherlands. That enabled me to use my rally bike at Amageza and was a lot less hassle than crating it up for shipping. Gerry van der Byl bought my bike after the Amageza and my new bike reached my team, and they promptly started to prep it. They sent me a picture after it arrived and I couldn't wait to race it. It was the same feeling I had on that Christmas morning so many years ago when I got that first second-hand bicycle.

I went for all the medical checks for my international racing licence, which included a few heart tests, and I got the required inoculations. I had a few more tooth problems, so found myself at the dentist again, and ended the month with a migraine that had me vomiting and passing out. Over the years I had suffered from migraines from time to time, but had been a lot better for the last year or two. I think the stress and physical challenges I had been through over the last few months were really catching up with me. My body was definitely feeling the strain!

Chapter 22

DECEMBER 2016 – 30 DAYS TO DAKAR

Meredith and I tried to spend as much time as possible together as a family in between all my fund-raising and training. It had been difficult to do this and the balance between race prep and family was certainly skewed the whole year, but we made it work as best as we could.

On 1 December, out of the blue, we decided to go to Sun City for the day as a family. The weather was perfect and it wasn't too crowded. We had always wanted to have our children close together so that when they were teenagers we could all do stuff together. This was one of those days. We went on all the slides and round the lazy river, where we ended up racing. I tipped the girls out of the tubes and they splashed Meredith, or tried to climb on her tube, accompanied by squeals of laughter.

Apart from my daughters' comments on my farmer's tan or man boobs (moobs), the day was going great. Just after lunch, we were in the wave pool competing with each other for who could ride the waves the furthest in to the beach. There were quite a few people in the pool and space was limited. I was goofing around, giving them the low-down on technique and strategy. I explained how you needed to create space around you first by splashing about and diving in all directions. I assertively demonstrated the complicated technique, receiving concerned looks from other confused swimmers as they backed away from me. My girls were hanging on each other, weak with laughter at this point, but my lesson continued as I rolled my shorts up for extra speed, exposing more pale white flesh.

Meredith buried her face in her hands unable to look directly at my 'magnificence'. The wave approached as I did my Michael Phelps inspired stretching, while breathing rapidly in and out like an

Olympic weightlifter just before a big lift. The perfect wave arrived and my arms spun like a propeller carving through the water ahead. My path was well clear of other swimmers thanks to my ingenious strategy and forethought. I rode the wave like a pro, with my arms stretched out ahead, my hands flat and on top of each other, and my head tucked in between my shoulders – I was streamlined, like a majestic dolphin.

I could feel the admiration radiating from the seasoned lifeguards and awestruck onlookers alike. The next thing I felt, however, was quite different. It was the large steel bars of the pool grate against my unprotected bald head at the end of the beach, where the water met the middle island. I stood up slowly, staggering. If it had been a cartoon, there would have been stars circling around my head. Two lifeguards were right there and grabbed hold of me, telling me I was injured.

'No, I'm fine,' I assured them. (Well, at least physically I was OK.) My ego and reputation as a world champion body surfer lay dead in the shallow water alongside me.

'No sir, you need to come with us,' they insisted, as blood began to run down my face. They escorted me to the medical centre and I left there a couple of hours later with stitches in my head.

We often laugh about that day. Those are the kind of days which, when strung together, make up a pretty damn awesome life.

I wasn't the only one injured that month. Shawna, my youngest, was sleeping at her best friend Caitlyn's house one night. They live on a rocky koppie and the two girls had walked barefoot through the garden late one evening. Something in the rocks had 'bitten' Shawna and she was in a lot of pain. I got the phone call and shot up there as quickly as I could. Naturally my first thought was that it could have been a snake. I had had a pet snake as a kid and knew most weren't venomous, but in typical parent fashion, I assumed the worst. By the time I got there they had found the culprit. Shawna was crying and her foot was red and sore, but we were relieved to find that she had been stung by a scorpion. The usual Google search followed to identify the species and we discovered that although the sting would be painful she would be fine. It was a minor incident, and in the end we decided that it didn't compare to my near-death experience at Sun City.

At the beginning of December the total money raised stood at just under R750 000. We were more than R350 000 short of the target. We had come a long way, but the time remaining seemed just way too short to close the gap. The final fund-raiser we had planned was a dinner at 'Social on Main' a trendy restaurant in Bryanston. A mate of mine, Bruce Beattie, owned the place and had given us a really good deal on a catered evening. He had already donated to my fund and also sponsored the sound and visual equipment we needed that night.

We called it a 'Dakar Evening' and I asked Darryl and Brian to share some of their Dakar experiences. They were both happy to help and did it free of charge. I also spoke about my journey to Dakar and the challenges I had faced. We charged R300 a head, which included a two-course meal.

At first, we were worried that we wouldn't get a big enough turnout, but on the night the place was packed. We held a raffle and my girls went table to table selling the tickets. I remember asking them halfway through how it was going, knowing that it wasn't easy asking people to buy raffle tickets. They were having a blast: 'It's easy Dad, everyone wants to buy one!' The prizes had been kindly donated by many of my sponsors. My daughters also manned the table at the door, selling T-shirts and caps. The support was incredible and the food was delicious. Franziska and Riaan from KTM had a big surprise up their sleeve that night. Not only had they already committed to covering the spares I would need and a ton of riding kit, but they presented me with a cheque for R50 000! I certainly never expected it after all they had already done. Darryl had known about it and told me later how keeping the secret had killed him the whole day. The cheque combined with the money we raised that night totalled R96 000 – way more than I had ever dreamed we would make.

Another mate, Giovanni Fantin, booked me for a motivational talk at his company Southern Implants, which was really cool. His guys all turned off the CNC machines and I wheeled the big KTM rally bike into the middle of the workshop. They pulled up their chairs while I told my story, and then fired questions at me. I could tell they would be watching come January. Those talks always ended on a cliffhanger – 'to be continued …' was how I ended the talk. They would get to watch how it ended 'live'.

We put it out all over social media that now was the last chance to get names on the bike because the decals needed to be printed. There was a final flurry of donations from individuals, many of them extremely generous and often from people that I knew didn't have much to spare. We topped the R1 million mark and there were only 10 days until I left!

I had all my riding kit, clothes, sleeping bag and medical stuff laid out in piles across my garage floor and I had checked all my lists several times to make sure I hadn't forgotten anything. I had different piles for stuff I would carry on the bike, stuff that would go in my jacket, stuff for before the start, and piles containing warm and cold weather riding gear and several pairs of goggles with different lenses for different riding conditions. It took me the whole day to make sure I had everything I needed and get it all packed. I wanted to get it done before Christmas, so that we could enjoy the festive time together as a family. It was a lot of stuff, including a set of spare wheels and Cycra handguards. I would be paying for excess baggage, for sure. I crammed everything into three large kitbags, sitting on them in an effort to get the zips to close.

A couple of days before Christmas Meredith and I spent the day together. We collected the finished bike decals from Darryl at Bandit Graphics and bought a South African flag for the podium. Mark Campbell came round and dropped off three hundred dollars and some Bolivian and Argentinian currency that he had left over from the time he had followed the Dakar through South America. He wanted nothing in return and gave me a bit of a pep talk for encouragement. I also had to exchange a ton of money to make sure that I had cash for petrol and to save me in case something went wrong and I needed to 'live off the land', as they say. Carrying a wad of US dollars could save your race. If you broke down in the middle of nowhere, a fistful of notes to a local farmer could get you a tyre, get some welding done or a lift into a local town. Alex RG, who had already donated to my campaign, traded me some dollars and between him and his sister Kristine they threw in several hundred more to help me out. I took a mixture of notes to make change easier.

Physically, I felt that I was ready. I had lost about 10 kilograms and now weighed 86 kilograms. I had been training in the gym five days a week, whenever I wasn't riding, for the whole year. I had ridden and raced every week and done a lot of multiple day trips. I knew I would need to dig deeper and push harder than I could train for, but I hoped I had done enough. I stopped riding my bike now because I didn't want to take any chances of picking up a new injury in the last couple of weeks. At our year-end function for my staff where we played paintball, I marshalled instead of participating. A rolled ankle or tripping and hurting a wrist could be a deal breaker for me. There was just too much at risk at this stage of the game!

Just before Christmas, with six days until I flew out, I got a call from Justin Lewis, a friend I had last seen 24 years ago back in Norkem Park High School. He had been following my journey on Facebook and asked how close I was to reaching my target. I still needed R66 250. He said he needed to make a few calls and would call me back and then hung up. Less than half an hour later, he called and said along with his business partner, Mark Qandil from the States, he would cover the balance and asked for my banking details. I couldn't believe it! Before the end of the day the money was in!

In the space of about six months we had raised the R1.1 million! Justin had found the last bit. I looked back at what it had taken to get there. There had been so many people who had donated, more than 320 names on my bike, and even more names in my heart of people who had helped and given of their time. Over 50 companies had donated both money and products, not to mention all the people who had attended and supported our fund-raising events. Above all, there were the sacrifices of time and money that Meredith and my daughters had made. I might be alone on the bike in a week's time, but if ever there was a team effort to get a rider to the finish, this was it.

Christmas morning arrived and it played out the same as every year. The night before we decided what time the girls were allowed to wake up. My vote was 7am, theirs was 3am, so we met halfway at the ungodly hour of 5am. On Christmas morning, they came running into our room. It was 5am, but their excitement had got them up earlier and they were now over the top. We have a gate in the passage separating their rooms from the lounge where the stash of presents lay under the tree. I had hidden the key to ensure that we all kept the rules of Christmas. Christmas is a huge deal for Meredith and she always made sure the choice of presents was perfect; we didn't ever water it down with the 'just give them money' option for the girls. She had done all the Christmas shopping – I could say that was because I needed to focus on training, but the truth is that's how it is every year!

'Where's the key?' the girls shouted, finding that it wasn't in the usual place next to the alarm pad. I had the key, but they needed to help me out of bed first. The covers were ripped off and they proceeded to try to drag me out of bed. I never resisted, but I made myself as heavy as possible. They pulled my legs out and yanked me up into a sitting position. The moment they moved away, I flopped back down onto my back.

'Come on, Dad, help us!' they screamed, weak with laughter themselves.

'I'm trying!' I insisted, trying to sound sincere.

Eventually, I was up and tried to walk slowly, with four sets of hands pushing me on. Once at the gate, I got 'the shakes' and was totally unable to get the key into the lock. My hand constantly missed the lock as the 'masses' crushed me against the gate, like fans at a football match. After some serious encouragement, the key was in but I wasn't about to surrender just yet. It was the wrong key, I explained to them – 'it's just not turning!' The looks I received at this stage told me that the game was over if I wanted to escape with my life, so I opened the gate and they ran through like greyhounds.

As usual, wrapping paper flew off like confetti as they ripped into their gifts. Once again, Meredith had nailed it. Everything was spot on! Right colours, right sizes, just like the one they had seen, all exactly what they had hoped for. Meredith even filled a stocking for me and I filled one for her. I wasn't a Christmas pro like Meredith, but this year I had done well. I had booked a weekend away at a game reserve for the two of us when I got back from Dakar. She loved it and my marriage was saved for another year!

Once the presents had been opened, we were off to church for the Christmas service. It was as festive as always, with the children talking about their gifts and the Christmas story and carol singing that Meredith always loved. As we were leaving the service, several people came up to Meredith and me – it was almost like they were saying their final goodbyes! There were a few hugs that lingered a bit too long and the odd 'you'd better make sure you come back alive' while grabbing my shoulders. They all meant well, but it wasn't helping Meredith's nerves. They looked at Meredith with sympathy – but then again, now that I think about it, that had been happening ever since she married me.

We had decided to spend the day as a family at home that year and did a 'Family MasterChef' dinner. It was something we had done a few times before, where the family split up into three teams of two. Each team was responsible for one course of the meal. It didn't matter what the others made that day, the important part was that Jenna and I were on dessert and were the clear winners. We made snowmen with scoops of vanilla ice cream, complete with facial features, arms and buttons. We both knew that we could easily launch a top-class restaurant with our combined skills set, but we put that aside for now. I had Dakar to focus on.

Finally, 27 December arrived and it was go time! It was a day Meredith and I had been both looking forward to and dreading at the same time. I was flying out of OR Tambo airport that evening. The normal challenges of life continued to poke fun at us, with a flat tyre on both my and Meredith's cars, which I quickly got fixed that morning. Then we went out for a family lunch and shared a few pizzas before heading back home to pick up the bags.

I knew that day would be particularly difficult and emotional for Meredith and the girls, so I had organised a surprise for them. I had bought 13 different gift bags – one for each day of the Dakar – and on all of them I wrote the day, the places of the bivouac, the length of the stage, what it would be like, the time difference and a short note. Then, I filled each bag with a gift for Meredith every day and gifts for the girls every second day. It had been crazy trying to find the gifts over the last few weeks and it hadn't been easy keeping it a secret, but I had pulled it off and they loved it!

Chapter 23

DAKAR GO TIME

The goodbyes at the airport weren't easy.

MEREDITH:

I'd been worrying about this day for approximately a year. I realised I was going to have to put on the show of a lifetime for our girls' sake and so I had my meltdown in the privacy of our bedroom about half an hour before we were due to leave for the airport. Joey hugged me until I calmed down and assured and promised me he would be extremely careful and come home alive to me and our girls.

Whenever Joey goes away I write him a love letter or card and buy him something for the plane/car trip and hide it in his luggage for him to find later. This time I asked family and friends to write down something I could give Joey to read on the plane to motivate him and keep him amped and I put it in his carry-on along with letters from myself and the girls.

I had hoped to have pulled myself together by the time my parents and Verity arrived with David and their boys, but my blotchy face gave away how I was feeling. I got the sympathetic head tilts from them which had the tears spilling down my cheeks again.

We travelled to the airport in convoy and while Joey checked in people started asking us about the 'From Para to Dakar' T-shirts we were all wearing. We had a lot of good luck wishes from complete strangers which added to the excitement building in all of us.

I couldn't have been prouder of Joey and he hadn't even left the airport yet!

The full BAS/Van der Velden Dakar racing team. Back:
Maikel Verkade, Walter Terblanche, Ronald ter Beek, Joey
Evans and Ibraheem Alrubain. Front: Mark Tielemans,
Bart van der Velden, Peter Verkade, Willem Jan Besaris
and Gwen Cuppen.
(Photo credit: Rallymaniacs)

Big smiles after just completing
the scrutineering at Dakar 2017
(Photo credit: Jose Mariodias /
fotop.com.br)

At the end of the first
Dakar special with Walter
Terblanche and Fernando
Sousa (behind the
cameraman)
(Photo credit: Rallymaniacs)

Cold and wet, climbing up into
Bolivia on Dakar Day 5
(Photo credit: Gustavo Epifanio /
fotop.com.br)

High altitude dune fields in Bolivia, Dakar Day 7   (*Photo credit: Gustavo Epifanio / fotop.com.br*)

Wide open racing down a sandy dry riverbed in Argentina, Dakar Day 10
(Photo credit: Victor Eleuterio / fotop.com.br)

Thick deeply rutted sandy riverbed on Day 11 in Argentina. The track is in its worst
condition when you're near the back.   (*Photo credit: Jose Mariodias / fotop.com.br*)

Only about an hour before the car rode over my bike on the penultimate Dakar stage in Argentina (Photo credit: Marcelo Machado / fotop.com.br)

My bike as it lay in the fesh-fesh full rutted track immediately fter the car had crushed it on the penultimate day at the Dakar. I still had about 660 kilometres to cover that day.

hysically broken along ith my crushed bike

The Dakar finisher's podium, a dream come true (Photo credit: Marcelo Machado / fotop.com.br)

At the Dakar finish with one hard earned medal, Buenos Aires, Argentina
(Photo credit: Andre Chaco / fotop.com.br)

Reunited at OR Tambo International Airport, the real finish
(Photo credit: Zoon Cronje Photography)

Team Evans hug, OR Tambo International
Airport
(Photo credit: Zoon Cronje Photography)

One very happy and relieved family, OR Tambo
International Airport, Johannesburg
(Photo credit: Lynn Franks)

It was soon time to say our goodbyes. Joey hugged my parents, David and Verity and our nephews Ethan, Adam and Nathan and then one by one he hugged our girls. I fought back the tears watching him whisper something into each of their ears and then it was my turn. I held on to him and closed my eyes. So much had happened in our lives up until this point and now that he was actually leaving, I didn't want to let go. Something I wasn't prepared for was Joey getting emotional, that's my job! Joey told me how much he loved me and said, 'We've got this.' In 19 years we've not once said 'goodbye' when he's left on a trip, no matter if it's just for a day or a couple of weeks; instead we say 'see you just now'. I started praying that the next three weeks would fly by and that I'd see him 'just now'.

I was experiencing a multitude of emotions; I was pumped for the racing and the opportunity to live my dream, but I worried about my family and all the possible outcomes the next three weeks might hold. Meredith had a good cry before we left and was strong now, but I felt the lump in my throat and really had to fight hard to hold back my feelings. I think it was in part because of the R1 600 I had to fork out for the extra bag! I kissed Meredith and the girls and gave them all a big hug before walking through the security entrance. Then there was the usual waving again and again as the railings zigzagged towards the X-ray machines. I took my belt off, emptied my pockets and walked through. The detector beeped as it always does, probably because of the hardware in my back, elbow and jaw. I had the usual complimentary massage and was then let through. My phone beeped; it was Meredith telling me that Francois and his wife Lindsey had just missed me. I could see them on the other side and we waved. And then, just like that, it was just me and this mammoth task that lay ahead. I sent Meredith a final text message telling her how much I loved her, thanking her for her support and promising yet again to come home in one piece.

There were several other Dakar participants on the flight. Darryl Curtis, who was involved with the KTM factory team, Gillian Dykes from Botswana as an official with the ASO, and Walter Terblanche, my teammate from Cape Town. Darryl was the only one with a business class seat and enjoyed stretching out his legs and smiling as I passed him on the way to cattle class. The flight was through the night and if I slept for an hour, it was a lot! I'm not great with the 'sleeping while travelling' thing. I remembered that Vincent in Morocco could sleep anywhere, anytime. I could do that when I was younger. (Maybe it has something to do with the worries of a family, house bonds and school fees?)

The plane landed in São Paulo, Brazil, the next morning and I checked all the messages on my phone. I had a ton of good luck messages and the first good night voice message from Meredith and my girls. They made one every day while I was away and they were the highlight of each day. Each one of them told me about their day and then there was the daily joke. It has always amazed me how they have grown up in the same home, yet each is so different in personality. We caught our connecting flight to Asunción, Paraguay; no turning back now.

Upon arrival, we were greeted by a band playing traditional music, complete with traditional dancers in long colourful dresses. People recognised the KTM bags Darryl, Walter and I were carrying and several people asked us if we were there for the Dakar. We organised some SIM cards and caught a taxi to the hotel in town. It was really hot and the air was thick and humid, similar to Durban in the summer. They had experienced a lot of rainfall, so we knew we were in for a fair bit of mud, at least in the first couple of days.

By chance, the KTM factory team were staying at the same hotel as Walter and me and we found ourselves a bit star-struck at breakfast, surrounded by our riding heroes. Darryl naturally knew them all well and introduced us to Toby Price, the current Dakar champion, as well as the other team riders: Sam Sunderland, Matthias Walkner and Laia Sanz. He told them about my injury and goal to finish and they all wished me well. It was very cool!

The next day our support team BAS trucks/Van der Velden Racing arrived in the vehicles driven up from Buenos Aires where the Dakar ship from France had docked. Our team had two vehicles, a big BAS truck and a 4x4 Mercedes Sprinter. A total of ten of us made up the team. The five riders were Walter Terblanche and me from South Africa, Maikel Verkade and Ronald Ter Beek from Holland and Ibraheem Alrubain from Kuwait. Bart van der Velden was the team manager and would also drive the big truck during the day. The mechanics were Gwen Cuppen, Mark Tielemans and Willem Jan Besaris, who would need to work on the bikes during the night and sleep on the truck during the day, while Peter Verkade would drive the Sprinter. Gwen was a seasoned Dakar mechanic and was assigned my bike. I liked him and we got on well right from the start.

Once they had the pits set up, we went about putting all the decals on the bike and fitting the handguards. Gwen and I fitted the decals together and I told him that all the names on the bike were people who had helped me raise the money to get there.

*

I also added six extra names in memory of people who had died. Kevin Gass and Rob Dickey both had a positive influence on me as a teenager; Rob had died in a car accident and Kevin sadly died from Lou Gehrig's disease. Both of them had loved motorbikes and I knew they would have been rooting for me. Then there was my friend Errol Dalton and Graeme Shellard, who I had never had the opportunity to meet, but was the brother of Tessa Shellard, a friend of mine and my children's swimming coach. He had been paralysed a few years earlier but was a fighter and had learned to live a full life in spite of his injury, only to be tragically murdered on his smallholding just months before Dakar. There was also my friend Mike Ceprnich's son, Matthew Ceprnich, who had tragically died in a road accident just months before.

The last name was Stephen Lategan. He was one of my best friends throughout high school. I could write a book on the stuff we had done together as kids growing up in Kempton Park. Stephen had taught me how to make chlorine bombs the 'safe' way. We put about half a cup of chlorine into an empty two-litre plastic Coke bottle, pinched it in the middle, folded it over and added about two tablespoons of brake fluid to the folded over area. This would allow you to get the lid on before the ingredients mixed. A quick shake and throw would result in the desired explosion and massive boom, complete with fireball. Once Stephen accidentally threw one, in the split second panic before it exploded, over the neighbour's precast wall where it landed directly under the circular washing line. I remember clearly how the clothes flapped upwards from the force as the chlorine burst through them.

Stephen and I used to roam the underground tunnels that connected all the rainwater drains along the streets. We lay flat on our skateboards, holding a candle while rolling slowly along the pitch black, narrow concrete tubes. They were full of spiders (the big ones got fried by our candles as we moved along). Our favourite pastime, along with another buddy called Peter Babcock, was to reach the drain next to the local shop where we would shoot passers-by with our 'fly katties'. They were made of coat hanger wire and elastic we got from the postman and we fired bits of soldering wire bent in a 'u' shape. People shouted and looked around as we sat quietly sniggering in the shadows inside the drain. Only once were we discovered, as we scrambled over each other to get out the drain box and back into the tube whilst being pelted with stones and half bricks.

Stephen also loved snakes and had a pet red-lipped herald. Once we needed to force-feed it, as it wasn't eating on its own, so along with another mate, Baymen Greenfield, we caught some tadpoles at the river to feed him. We mushed them up (gagging all the while) and got the stinky black goo into a syringe. We attached a rubber tube lubed with raw egg to the front of the syringe and we carefully pushed it slowly down the snake's throat. Once it was in, we pushed on the syringe plunger which seemed to block about halfway down. Using full strength, we pushed harder on the plunger and the pressure that built up resulted in the rubber tube being shot off the end, covering us in the black tadpole guts. It was disgusting and took a lot of washing to get the smell off our hands.

Stephen and I had lost contact since high school, but about a year before I had started with my Dakar preparations, I contacted him through Facebook and we had talked on the phone for ages as if we had seen each other just the week before. He had two kids and we laughed and spoke about our memories of high school. It was great to catch up with someone with whom I had so many shared memories. We tried to meet up, but the timing was always out. About a month after getting back in touch again, I learned that Stephen had taken his own life. I couldn't believe it. I will never know what he was feeling, or how he had come to that point. After experiencing overwhelming despair in hospital after my spinal cord injury, I felt I could in some small way understand, and I was filled with a deep sadness. It hurt thinking what he must have gone through and I just cried. I really miss my buddy Steve and I was proud to have his name on my bike.

*

I had been assigned two steel trunks on the truck for my stuff and I packed my kit into them. I had cut up a couple of cardboard boxes for partitions to separate different items and I had a few plastic bags for my dirty kit. I labelled my knee guards left and right, knowing from previous rallies that when you get really tired you need everything to be as simple as possible. I packed my jacket with my earplugs, sunblock, lip ice, passport, bike papers, driver's licence, money in several currencies, toilet paper, wet wipes, disposable catheters, medicine and first aid kit and then placed spare goggles and gloves in the big pocket at the back. With Bart and Gwen's help, I fitted all my tools and emergency bike spares onto my bike. I had two small bags which I had been given by Gary Franks that I filled with energy bars and some food and fitted onto the handlebars. I filled my USWE hydration pack and Gwen made sure the bashplate on my bike was filled with the emergency 3 litres of water which it was compulsory to carry.

I went through the registration and scrutineering – a considerable undertaking in itself, taking the entire day. We were each issued with a book requiring a ton of stamps from all the different stations. They checked all our entry paperwork, riding and international racing licences, checked that fees had been paid in full, took down next-of-kin information and checked we had done all the necessary medical examinations. We were also offered photo and video packages we could purchase.

After that, we still had to attend a couple of classes on the use of the tracking and emergency response equipment. All our hardware was then thoroughly checked: the bike, riding protection, emergency equipment, medical kits, survival supplies, emergency water carriers on the bike and our hydration packs. We were all constantly worried that we had forgotten something until the final check, after which our race numbers were issued and stuck on the bike. Only then were we officially added to the start list.

It was clear from the process that although the Dakar was notorious for deaths, it was not because of carelessness on the part of the organisers. They were strict and made every effort to keep it as safe as possible. I opted to take out extra medical insurance, just in case things went south. It was money I hoped I was wasting. The bikes were then placed in *parc firmé* until we collected them just before the start.

I called Meredith just before 7pm, but it was nearly midnight back home and we counted down to the New Year together. I wished each of my girls a happy New Year and promised Meredith I'd catch up on the kiss as soon as I was home. I would have loved to have had them there with me, but it was far too expensive and would have made everything even more complicated, so we decided to have our moment when I arrived home. I knew they would celebrate and be proud of me no matter what happened, but in my book anything short of a finish was not going to be good enough.

That night we were invited to a rookie introduction held at one of the fancy hotels for all the new riders and drivers. A lot of the guys were dressed up, but I had rushed straight from the pits and felt pretty self-conscious in my sweat-soaked T-shirt. Walter and I attended along with David Thomas from Cape Town and Vincent Crosbie. I also met Conrad Rautenbach from Zimbabwe for the first time; he was also competing in his first Dakar, but in the car category. He's a really good oke and we chatted for a while. He would go on, partnered with Rob Howie, to finish in the top ten and be the highest placed rookie driver in the car category. Fernando Sousa, my good friend and teammate in Morocco, was there, as was John Comoglio, with whom I had made friends after coming across him vomiting through his helmet in the middle of the desert during the Merzouga Rally. They had both also earned their place on the start line and had made plenty of sacrifices to be there. That night we were all a bit nervous about what lay ahead. We talked about our preparations and the excitement we all felt being on the edge of realising our colossal shared dream.

The next day it was off to riders' briefing before the start. I had been to many riders' briefings in my racing career and they were often held on the start line or under a gazebo or stretch tent. The organiser shouted or used a megaphone, although there might be a sound system if it was a big race. This briefing was very different! It was held in a massive theatre, where the competitors were packed into all of the four-storey levels, with many having to stand at the back. The stage had a huge screen on which the organisers covered the mayhem that would take place over the next couple of weeks. They also spoke about the protocol in the case of emergencies, as well as in survival situations. It did nothing to calm any of our nerves.

After riders' briefing, we walked down to the start and collected our bikes from the *parc firmé*. There were crowds everywhere, cheering and waving Paraguayan flags. We rode through streets lined with fans and it just wouldn't have been complete without a few wheelies. It probably wasn't the smartest thing to do, but I was at the freakin' Dakar and moments like those needed to be felt on the back wheel with the throttle open!

After riding through the crowds which were lined with crowd control rails, with my arm out, connecting with the outstretched hands, I arrived at the base of the official start ramp. There were a few guys ahead of me, so I switched off my engine and sat there on my bike looking at the ramp. This was it, more than ten years to get here. I had overcome more obstacles than I cared to remember. I had hundreds of people's names on my bike and many hundreds more had helped me over the years. It had been no small task to reach this point. The moment sank in and I looked down, my gloved hand across my face as I felt my eyes well up.

Then my name was called out over the loudspeaker and I rode up the ramp with my South African flag tied to my handlebars. I stopped on top, hoping my legs wouldn't spasm with all the adrenalin rushing through me and that I would be able to hold the bike up. I imagined me lying on the floor with the bike still between my legs, as had happened so many times before. But this time, I held it up – my legs must have realised the magnitude of the moment and played along. Xavier Gavroy was there with Mark Coma, who shook my hand firmly and told me to ride smart and make sure I reached that finish line. I gave him my word that I would see him on the finishing podium and I meant it.

I knew I was in for the test of my life, but it was death before DNF, and this boy doesn't die easily!

Chapter 24

STAGES 1 TO 4

STAGE 1

The start podium the previous day was more of a formality and was geared for the crowds in Asunción. Today was the day that nearly 150 bikers who had qualified to start would actually begin the real racing! Stage 1 was considered a fairly easy day in comparison with what lay ahead, but anything can happen at the Dakar and it generally did.

It started all wrong for me that morning. I didn't know that I had to switch off the organisation's GPS on my bike manually and through the night it had completely drained my battery. I pressed the start button and the bike remained completely silent. I felt a rush of panic run through me at the thought of going out before even reaching the first racing section. I fought it and remained calm, knowing that I needed to think straight. I finally figured out what had happened and took out from under my bike's seat the small set of jumper cables I had made up at home. Walter brought his bike over and we hooked them up together and pretty soon my bike roared to life. We both had a nervous laugh about what could have been and then I left the *parc firmé* and lined up at the start, making sure not to stall or switch the bike off. I noticed a few other riders had done the same thing; several bikes stood running, waiting for the start.

We started with a short liaison and just a couple of kilometres in I came across a bike on the side of the road with smoke coming from the engine. The rider was there with his teammate and they were working on it so I rode on, soon reaching the start of the first racing special. There was about 20 minutes until my start time and with the temperature already in the high thirties, I huddled under what little shade there was, trying to keep cool in my riding kit along with many of the other riders.

I heard someone call my name and looked over to see Jeanette Kok-Kritzinger, one of the journalists from South Africa with the Toyota team. We had spoken over the phone, but this was the first time we met in person. I think she was more excited than I was to be there, she was full of energy and encouragement and we did a quick interview that she recorded for the guys back home. I introduced her to Walter and she ended off offering a short prayer for our safety and left us upbeat and ready to race.

My start time arrived and I lined up behind my friend Fernando, who was scheduled to be set off about 30 seconds ahead of me. The track was lined with spectators for as far as I could see. They counted Fernando down and off he went. While still going fairly slowly, he must have caught the first corner at a tricky angle and he went down, his wheels sliding out the off camber flat rock. He was fine, but no doubt some choice words were going through his head! He quickly picked the bike up and was off. I was counted down and I tiptoed round the first corner, not exactly the racing start of flying dirt and revving I had pictured. I picked up the pace, riding at a fast but comfortable pace, not wanting to take any unnecessary risks. I passed a few guys and others passed me going flat out as though it was a single lap race. A couple of seconds on this first short 39-kilometre special could push you up several positions, but in my mind the risks far outweighed the possible reward. I chose to play the long game. The route was mainly a hard pack dirt track and with the recent rains it was full of washouts, ruts and gullies. Mud and pools of water sometimes filled the width of the trail. I rode on the edge of most of them, choosing just to get through each one without unnecessary risk. Most riders did the same but some hit them flat out to gain maximum time. Mostly the gamble paid off but there were one or two guys who crashed in the deeper pools and ended up drowning their bikes and putting themselves at the back of the pack. It was usually easy to spot the deeper pools of water and mud from the number of spectators. I have learned over years of racing that whenever you see a big group of spectators or a cameraman it means the track is about to get pretty gnarly!

After about an hour the finish of the special came into sight. I raced up, stopping next to the marshal who stamped my time card and then I pulled ahead and over to the side of the track. I had finished my first Dakar special and Walter arrived shortly behind me. News crews with cameras and microphones scurried around waiting for the first cars which were about to arrive. Walter and I were just minor details who barely formed part of the massive Dakar machine. We stood back, drinking from the supply of bottled water stacked at the finish and watched the top guys being interviewed. From a riding point of view it had been relatively easy, but ticking off the first special helped both of us get rid of the nerves. The day was still far from over.

We left together on the remaining 415-kilometre liaison that crossed the border into Argentina. I had done some long liaisons before on the Amageza Rally, but this was on another level. We had to ride under the speed limit, something bikers are not really used to doing. When you reached within five kilometres per hour of the speed limit, the siren on your bike would start to go off, beeping loudly every second. If you got within three kilometres per hour of the speed limit, the siren would beep constantly and it was piercing, even through the earplugs and over the sound of the bike. If you kept accelerating and breached the limit, you would get a time penalty and a fine in Euros. The time penalty didn't bother me, but I certainly couldn't afford the fines, so I paid special attention to my speed. It was a good system and ensured the riders kept the speed down through populated areas.

But it was mind-numbing on the open roads and I knew from previous cross country rallies that your wrists took strain holding the throttle open for hours on end. I had made a plan this time. I had seen a mate of mine, Andrew Johnstone, use a throttle control on the Amageza Rally, so I had made a makeshift plan on my bike. I took a piece of inner tube – like a large black elastic band – and put it around the throttle and over the hand guard. It kept the throttle open and I could rest my hand. Some guys didn't like it, because if you fell asleep on the bike, it meant almost certain death. I don't have much muscle on my butt since the accident and I knew that constant sitting on the liaisons would not do me much good. Although nothing says 'Dakar Finisher' more than a guy walking slowly, bow-legged and grimacing, I opted to avoid that particular battle scar. I had an 'airhawk' motor-cycle pillow that I inflated and sat on during the liaisons. It didn't look particularly 'cool' but I could have sold it for some serious cash to other riders later in the race.

We needed to stop for petrol along the liaison and were swamped by fans. I had been warned about the fans, but I couldn't have imagined this! The moment you stopped they were on top of you with constant requests of 'photo, photo!' nearly knocking you over and making it near impossible to get off the bike. I worried about some of the kids because the exhaust was so hot that if they touched it, it would take the skin right off. They all wanted a photo with you, no doubt for social media bragging rights. Babies and small children were shoved into our arms and placed on the bike as we tried to fill up with petrol and get going. I appreciated where they were coming from and did as many photos as I could and signed caps and T-shirts. I let some of the kids hold or wear my helmet in the photos and they loved it. I could spare the few minutes it took and it was kind of cool feeling like a rock star. It was all part of the race and I wanted to take the whole experience in, but at the same time I had a job to do and at some point you just had to say 'no more' and get going.

We arrived at the bivouac at Resistencia, Argentina, around 4pm before our service truck and I took the time to rehydrate and lie down in the shade while I waited. I knew from riding in the Northern Cape that the sweat from your body often evaporates as quickly as you produce it and you could easily end up dehydrated way before you realised it. Later that night, one of the riders collapsed midway through riders' briefing. The medics were on hand and he was taken care of, but if you didn't stay on top of your game it could happen so quickly.

Race Stage 1 was done. It was just a short introduction to what lay ahead but I could tick Day 1 off my list. It was more than I could have dreamed of achieving when I was lying in hospital all those years back, but it wasn't enough. I hadn't come all this way to make a valiant effort and do my best, I had come here to finish. Eleven more stages to go, whatever it took.

Darryl had kindly offered to help me get a report home each day. I found him at the KTM factory team pits and he did a short interview and voice recording that he sent back to *ZA Bikers* who would publish daily updates on their website. I then went about marking my roadbook, filling my hydration pack and restocking my jacket. I sent Meredith and the girls a message via WhatsApp and listened to my daily message from them before falling asleep in my bunk on the truck.

By the end of Day 1, two bikers were already out of the race.

STAGE 2

This would be the first real test of the rally. Riders would fall out for sure and I didn't want to be one of them.

The stage was a total of 803 kilometres and would end in San Miguel de Tucumán, Argentina. The first riders left at 4am and the sun came up rapidly as we rode. The sky was clear and the sun beat down as the mercury rose. The temperature that day rose to 43 degrees and the air was thick and humid. There had also been torrential rains in this area over the past few weeks, turning the dirt tracks into the now familiar large mud pits and deep puddles of water.

We arrived at the start of the special after already riding several hundred kilometres late in the morning and the marshals set us off down the track in twos. I lifted the front wheel as I rode through the mud and puddles, again carefully going around the deeper sections. The thought of going out played heavily on my mind and I found myself riding even more slowly. I passed a couple of guys who had taken heavy falls in the deep mud and they were covered in it, making them completely unrecognisable. It reminded me of the time that rally bike covered me in mud crossing the river in the Northern Cape on the Amageza a few years back.

I rode on and found myself spinning the back wheel and falling at low speed on the slick surface. I fell three times in a row, right in front of one of the cameramen and I knew my head just wasn't in the right place. Each time I had struggled to stand on the slippery surface with my dodgy legs and motocross boots. I pulled to the side of the track, out of the mud, and got off the bike. I needed a better plan. I was riding way too conservatively and it simply wasn't working in the mud. I decided to stop overthinking it all and just ride it as I always did. I climbed back on the bike and this time got hard on the gas. I hit the mud patches with the front wheel in the air and kept the hammer down. The mud sprayed out behind me and I raced kilometre after kilometre through the mud and water without falling again.

A good while later the mud and water ended and the area became more arid and dry. The racing section became very dusty, making it impossible to overtake the riders ahead without taking some serious risks. I was racing at high speed along tracks lined with vegetation when I caught up to the rider in front of me, but because of the dust I decided rather to back off and keep a dust gap between us to keep it as safe as possible. It went against my instincts to hang back, but I reminded myself that the days of flying blind through the dust and risking it all were long gone.

My front brakes began to fail just after halfway. The thick mud had coated my bike and got under my fork seals, causing both sides to leak and the oil had run down onto the front disc. I pushed on towards the end of the racing section, allowing for the extra braking distance. The siren on my bike went off with three sharp beeps and it caught me by surprise. I looked down at my screen and it read 'CAR'. I looked back and saw a car was closing in about 200 metres behind me. The track was easily wide enough for both of us, so I pulled to the right – the opposite of my natural instinct of going to the left in South Africa. I was still doing about 100kph when the car passed me at nearly double my speed, it seemed insane! Stones and dirt from his tyres leapt up at me and stung each unprotected area of my body. In a split second, I was completely blind!

The dust cloud was thick and, still travelling at 100kph, I was totally disorientated, so I hit hard on the anchors. I was slowing down, but couldn't see past my handlebars. I ended up with my front wheel in a small thick bush as I came to a halt and toppled over. I picked the bike up, thinking that I needed a much better plan when the next car came along. It did within a matter of minutes after I began riding again. The same process of beeps played out and I pulled off the track this time. The car passed and I waited for the dust to clear.

After checking the oncoming track for other vehicles, I joined with the road again and raced on. The latter approach gave me a better chance of keeping my word to Meredith of staying alive so I decided that that was the way I would play it going forward. I loved racing off road at full speed and often back home my enduro buddies thought I was crazy taking those risks, but Dakar had me wide eyed at the speeds some guys were riding at. It was insane, the statistics of serious injuries and deaths made perfect sense.

One section was as wide as a car with thick vegetation on either side. It was like a tunnel that lasted for at least 50 kilometres. The track was sheltered from the wind which made the dust hang in the air. Visibility was low and I saw a couple of guys have close calls with some of the many cows that wandered onto the track. It was risky to say the least, but I had to keep my speed up along with the other riders to avoid being hit from behind. I had to bury my memories of the cow back in Pongola as I raced along with one finger on the front brake and my foot over the rear brake lever, peering through the dust and ready to brake at a moment's notice.

The day was really long and I managed to finish the special as the sun was setting around 8pm. I rode the final liaison and rolled into the bivouac in the dark at around 9pm. I had spent close to 16 hours on the bike; I was worn out physically and mentally from constantly focusing on the track and navigation. That day we had encountered a whole variety of terrain, from the mud and water earlier on into the flat-out gravel rural roads, and then through the thick vegetation and red soil. I had hit every waypoint and navigated well but, above all,

I was happy just to make it safely into the bivouac that night in San Miguel de Tucumán.

I had developed a blister on my hand from riding with wet gloves in the morning and I had another one on my foot from walking in my boots for so long at the start. The one on my hand was my own fault; I had a spare set of gloves for that very reason and I should have changed them sooner. I couldn't feel the blister on my foot because of my spinal cord injury and only noticed it when I took my boot off. They were hassles I really didn't want to deal with so early on, so I kept an eye on them and made sure they stayed clean so that they didn't get any worse or become infected.

Another nine bikers would not get through that day and went out on the second stage.

STAGE 3

After only a few hours of sleep since arriving in the dark the previous night, I rolled out of the bivouac and onto Stage 3, still in the dark at 5am. The day was to be one of extremes – both in temperature and altitude. We started in the hot, semi-desert lowlands with temperatures reaching over 40 degrees. It was sandy and most of the route was just based on CAP headings through the dry sandy wasteland. I wove through the bushes in the harsh terrain, dodging deep ruts and washouts. The route was mostly in thick sand and I got stuck several times along with other riders, having to haul the bike out manually. The effort had my legs going into spasm with fatigue. As the day went on, we rode up a pass where the temperature plummeted to just above freezing as we climbed to an altitude of 5000 metres. That's only about 800 metres lower than the summit of Kilimanjaro.

It started raining and then turned to snow as I rode the switchbacks. The bike's power and mine dropped as the air became thinner. I dropped the bike a few times in the slick wet turns on the dirt track, as the bike's power didn't come on as I anticipated. I felt myself get dizzy in the thin air as I tried to pick up the bike. I needed to do it in stages. I picked the bike up about halfway and rested it on my bent knee as I focused on breathing deeply and making sure I stayed conscious. After I'd caught my breath I lifted the bike up the rest of the way and just stood there resting against the bike. It felt ridiculous, as though I was a frail old man.

My mind reflected on my first race after breaking my back and the similar difficulty I had picking up my bike then. Then finally, after recovering again, I got on the bike and rode on. I stood up between the switchbacks and focused on breathing deeply, counting my breaths in and out and trying to take in as much oxygen as possible. When I got to the tight turns I sat down and put my foot out motocross style focusing on keeping enough power to take me through the corner and up the sharp incline. There were so many switchback corners and I concentrated as hard as I could to get each one right, desperate not to drop the bike.

Eventually I reached the top of the pass, where I found two of my teammates, Walter and Ronald. We had made the ascent in about an hour, forced into breaking all the rules of acclimatisation. I later heard from Walter that Ronald had fallen over when he stopped, so I knew it wasn't just me taking strain. Ronald had finished the Dakar once before, but I could tell from his pale face and the dark rings under his eyes that the high altitude was affecting him badly. They had a disposable bottle of oxygen and they shared it between them. I had one on me too but I didn't want to use it until I felt that I really needed to. We stood together for a few minutes as they breathed in the oxygen, cold and surrounded by small pockets of snow in complete contrast to the searing heat in the arid valleys we had experienced that morning.

I carried on through the pass where it started to descend, now going downhill through the familiar switchbacks. I found myself trying to keep the bike from going over the unprotected edge, as the dusty track had turned to snot in the wet weather. It was a fine balance – braking on the downhills, while not letting the wheels lock up on the slimy surface. As I came around one particularly tricky bend, I saw a mangled Quad bike in the track ahead that had clearly gone over the edge on a turn higher up. I could see the medical chopper perched on a small flat gravel area next to the cliff and the rider was lying in the track covered with a silver blanket. My heart dropped and I felt sick to my stomach as I rolled towards him in the rain.

We have all heard of the deaths that occur at Dakar and now that I was racing it, I could completely understand how easy it would be to lose your life out there. I dreaded seeing the rider's body as I passed the quad with its navigation tower broken and mangled, the equipment held on just by the wiring. The front wheels were broken off the steering struts, with the bars facing right, one wheel was flat and facing left and the other tucked under the bike. The seat was torn and the dark mud was caked on the grips and handguards where they had made contact with the ground. I tried to prepare myself for the scene I was about to face, but as I got closer I saw that the rider was still alive and on oxygen as well as a drip. The blanket had been placed over him and packed around his head to try to keep him warm as they stabilised him and prepared to medevac him out. It was huge relief to see that he was alive, but a grim reminder of the risks we were all taking.

The weather was terrible, but I had known it would be so I had planned well in advance and had my cold weather gear from KTM ready to go. I had it all on by this point and had followed the advice to put my wet weather gear on before I got wet. Others had waited too long and I could see them getting really cold. Some riders shivered as we filled our bikes from the large drums of petrol supplied by the organisers at the refuel point. It was a long day with nearly 800 kilometres to cover, making it a long time to be wet and freezing in the wind. It was another one of those small things you could learn before the race to increase your chances of finishing. I washed the mud off my face at the refuel point with water from the organisers and put on the fresh goggles in my jacket, it was only Day 3 but I could feel my face becoming tender from wearing the goggles all day.

Several cars had passed me earlier in the day when the trucks began to come by as well. I followed the rule I had made to pull over for passing cars and it went well, until my siren sounded and the screen displayed 'TRUCK' while I was on a very rocky track. The track was narrow, with rocks piled high on both sides for as far as I could see. There was no way to get off the track! As bikers, we needed to weave our way along the track, but trucks just flew flat out at more than double our speed, totally unfazed by rocks the size of rugby balls. I was in a bad place. I rode over to the right-hand side of the track, where I pressed myself up against the rock wall with my bike. I looked over at the opposite ridge and I could see it was near impossible to fit a truck between us. The truck was committed, coming towards me at full speed and I just closed my eyes, bit down hard, held my breath and made myself as flat as I could against the rocks. I was really grateful that I had lost weight leading up to Dakar.

I was getting ready to walk to the light, when the truck passed within millimetres of me, in a gush of wind that nearly blew me right off the bike. I honestly thought that was going to be the end of me – it was way too close for comfort! I thought of the scene that I had passed earlier that day and how much I had to live for. I just wanted to finish this race now, simply so I didn't have to come back. After that my pace slowed, as I was constantly looking backwards, anxious about the cars and trucks behind me.

We passed through a large muddy marsh about 300 metres in diameter. Several riders were stuck and digging their bikes out, helped by a couple of local guys. I couldn't tell the depth, but I had learned the lesson on the first stage about riding too cautiously. I picked a line, shifted my weight back and just gave it horns into the unknown. The bike snaked under me but I just kept the power on, leaving a rooster tail of mud flying off the back wheel. The depth of the thick tacky mud varied and I felt the engine labour each time the wheels started to bog, the mud now covering the axles. I just kept the throttle wide open, standing up on the foot pegs and focusing on my exit point. I made it through cleanly in one shot. I whooped in my helmet as I flew out the other side. 'Where's the damn cameraman now?' I thought.

I came across a rider who had torn his hand open, severing the tendons to his fingers, as well as another rider with a broken leg being loaded into an ambulance at a checkpoint. The scene was crazy, I was worn out physically and emotionally – the serious injuries seemed so traumatic. Memories came flooding back of the injuries that I had sustained over the years. I knew the risks before I came and, as harsh as the reality was, I needed to suck it up, so I put it all to the back of my mind and focused on getting to the finish. Head down, I pushed forward into the unknown.

It was now after 8pm, the sun had set and my body was cramping from being on the bike for more than 15 hours. My wrists ached and my hands could barely hang on to the bars. I still had more than 100 kilometres to go in the dark. I found that the bike was riding me towards the end and I was just barely hanging on. I was on the liaison now and the tar road snaked sharply through the mountains in the darkness. The rally cars cut each corner with their inside tyres on the dirt run-off. This kicked up a bunch of rocks and dirt into the road with each car that passed. The dirt quickly became mud in the rain and rocks the size of half bricks littered the road, making riding the winding downhills in the dark on the knobbly tyres as treacherous as the racing section. In the daytime, with the road dry and clean on a KTM Super Duke street bike, it would have been riding heaven, but I had stopped having fun a while back today. I was in survival mode.

After being on the bike for 17 hours, I pulled into the bivouac in San Salvador de Jujuy in the dark at 10pm. I was exhausted, and my body felt exactly how I would have expected it to feel at the end of the race. If my body had been making the decisions, I would have gone out that day for sure. As I stopped next to the pits, Gwen held on to my bike and Bart helped me get off and then helped me to remove my boots. I thought back to my first race, where I had finished one lap and Neal took my boots off. Today I had covered about 65 times that distance, but I felt the same as I had back then. I simply sat there, completely exhausted and fighting back the emotion. What I had endured that day both physically and mentally was colossal. The other riders on the team sat around with blank stares, their eyes hollow with exhaustion. Bart mixed me a shake to get some easy nourishment in and helped me with my stuff. I can't tell you what a dedicated and committed team I was part of. Each member was personally invested and shared in every rider's pain and successes.

I had long missed riders' briefing but Bart had gone and collected all our starting times and had written the important info on the whiteboard hanging in the pits. We all moved our clocks an hour ahead, as he had mentioned we were moving into another time zone. I took a cold shower on the ground behind the truck and, shivering, got into some dry clothes. Gwen worked his magic on my bike, preparing it for the next day, and I marked my roadbook as quickly as possible and made the necessary changes while eating some supper. It was midnight when I finally got into bed. Gwen worked away, still having lots to do on the bike before I left again in just a few hours. My throat was raw and I sucked a lozenge in an attempt to stop coughing as I fell asleep.

Another eight bikers had gone out that day.

STAGE 4

I had been asleep for only three hours when my alarm went off. It wasn't like at home where you could press 'snooze' and get a few more minutes. I was still exhausted, but I was here for one reason – to finish this race! So I got out of bed like a robot and started kitting up.

I was fully kitted up and sitting at the bench in the pits eating breakfast along with the other riders when it dawned on us. The message from riders' briefing had been relayed incorrectly. We should have put our clocks *back* one hour instead of forward one hour. We had got up two hours too early! It had been a really tough few days for the whole team and Bart had done us a favour by going to riders' briefing for us. It wasn't his fault, even I struggled to understand the information half the time, what with it being translated into English. And English was Bart's second language. We all knew this, so everyone just carried on as normal. Some climbed back into bed for an hour while I lay under the stars and caught up on my voice diary that I hadn't managed to do the night before. Although I had had only three hours' sleep, I appreciated the time to gather my thoughts and get my head right. I would need my head more than the sleep for the onslaught that that day had in store for me.

Over the last five hours of darkness, Gwen had prepared my bike and it was once again clean, ready and waiting for me. I loaded my roadbook and headed across the bivouac to the start. That day we would cross over into Bolivia. The total stage distance was only 521 kilometres, but the special – or racing section – was 416 kilometres at high altitude and through the sand dunes. Distance is always relative to terrain. For instance, in the mountains of Lesotho you could ride for 12 hours and cover less than 100 kilometres, whereas on a straight gravel road you could easily cover 100 kilometres in 40 minutes. Dunes, as I had discovered in Morocco, were particularly difficult to cross, but at high altitude the bikes had less power which compounded the challenge. The distance relative to the terrain was a huge ask and we had been warned that it would be one of the toughest days of the rally. It didn't disappoint.

It was really cold as I started in the dark that morning and I wore my neoprene face mask, which made me look like Hannibal Lecter, and my thick waterproof gloves. Twisting around on the bike, I took turns heating up each hand on the exhaust during the morning liaison. It worked well until I managed to melt one of my gloves. The liaison was short and it wasn't long before we started the special and entered the dreaded dune section. Shortly into the special, the roadbook got very confusing and riders' tracks went off in every direction. Riders were zigzagging all over like ants and I got lost along with most of the others and managed to miss four waypoints. Realising my mistake, I worked my way back through the dunes to a point where I would miss only one.

I would receive a time penalty for the one I missed and I knew exactly where it was, but it meant going back another four kilometres on a narrow track against the cars that were now arriving. It would be extremely dangerous and I knew the time penalty wasn't worth my life. I bypassed the waypoint on my GPS and rode through the dune field for the third time picking up all the waypoints in the correct order. I rode many extra kilometres and burnt a ton of calories, but I was still in the race and that was all that mattered.

The day was a mix of massive dunes and smaller softer dunes with a lot more vegetation. While I was riding through some smaller dunes,

I caught my foot in a thick branch that ripped my foot outwards and off the peg, causing me to fall in the sand. I tried to stand up, but my left leg was completely dead. This happened anytime I hurt my legs; I couldn't feel the pain, but my leg would go lame. After anything from ten seconds to a couple of minutes, the feeling would come back, almost like a fluorescent light switching on, and I would be able to get it working again.

So I waited until the feeling came back, but it was taking a while. I checked my boot to make sure the branch hadn't gone through into my leg, but it seemed fine. About a minute later the feeling came back and I stood to pick up the bike, but as I swung my leg over, I felt it go again. I managed to lean on the other leg with the bike still between my legs, hoping that I hadn't done anything serious. The feeling eventually came back again and I pulled off. I was fine most of the time, but if I twisted to the right while standing my leg would go dead. All this had happened at about 10am and I was worried that I had damaged something in my hip, but I pushed on through the day.

The dunes were very soft and if you lost momentum your bike would immediately sink into the sand, making it extremely challenging to get going again. One section combined the soft sand with some vegetation which made it even more difficult as you had to weave around the bushes, losing precious momentum on each turn. To add to it all, the high altitude at nearly 4000 metres robbed the bikes of power and, loaded down with 33 litres of fuel, it bordered on the impossible to ride. These conditions made it easy to overheat the engine or clutch and cause permanent damage. One rider's bike had even caught alight and was just a simmering pile of ash by the time I reached it. The rider sat on the dune near the bike with his head in his hands. Once a bike catches alight, it is an inferno in seconds because of all the fuel we carry. The fuel on my bike had begun to boil and I could see it bubbling out of the overflow tubes. I decided to stop and take a few minutes to let my bike cool down. There were stranded riders dotted all over the dunes. As I stood there I heard the roar of a rally car from behind. The rally cars had an easier job but still needed to keep momentum and they had a couple of close calls with riders as they squeezed past, unable to slow down for fear of getting stuck.

I had caught up to Walter and Ronald, who were about 60 metres away from me. They were struggling along with me and the other riders in the unforgiving sandy waves. There was little we could do to help each other. You couldn't push the bikes – they had to be ridden hard. All you could do was face the bike downhill, start going and try to get some momentum and keep on top of the sand going up the next dune – all this while avoiding vegetation and other riders and getting out of the way of the cars. It was almost impossible to recover if you got stuck in one of the dune holes. I heard the bikes revving all around me, but I just sat still to let my bike cool. Then when I was ready to continue, I rode the way I had learned to survive in the enduros. I started the bike and rode it hard, sometimes for just a few metres, stopping on a small sandy mound from which I could take off. I would then let the bike cool for a few minutes and repeat the process. Slowly I inched my way through the smaller soft dunes.

Eventually the smaller dunes with vegetation gave way to huge dunes with hardly any vegetation. I rested for a bit at the start of the big dunes, staring up at the eight-storey high sandy face. I saw a rider go up and get stuck halfway. Then another got stuck a little higher; both would have to come back down and try again once they managed to fight their bikes around.

I have always loved a good steep hill climb, often called 'widow makers', and I knew there was only one way up it – flat out. I pushed the starter on my bike and then lifted the gear lever into second for a smoother pull off. I pulled away down the final small dune where I had stopped. As my speed increased my tyres rose on top of the sand and I slowly twisted the throttle making sure to keep traction till it was wide open. I changed up to third gear and the revs climbed higher, hitting the face of the dune as the motor was about to redline. I raced aggressively up the steep face, standing up with the gas wide open, my eyes fixed on the top. I passed the other two riders and made it up first time! I kept up the momentum, my bike finally happy to have some air flow, and rode several more in the same way. I was getting through them well when, just as I was about to crest a dune, my bike's alarm went off. You're supposed to accelerate to just get over the crest to prevent the front wheel from digging in, but I let off the gas too quickly and my front wheel sank into the dune just over the top. I slid with the bike about three metres down the steep side.

The alarm on my bike had indicated that a rider was down, but he was over the next dune. My alarm then started to sound to warn others that I was down too. My engine had cut out and the bike was lying on its side, half buried in the sand. But I had bigger problems: I could hear the roar of a truck engine coming up the same dune where I was lying. There was no way he could see me, because I was just over the lip and he needed to breach right over the top or get bogged down. The sand was too soft and steep to climb up and there was no time to try to lift my bike up and get out the way. I stood next to my bike on the steep incline, with my boots sinking in the sand, my eyes wide open and fixed on the summit just a few metres from me, waiting for the beast to crest so that I knew which way I needed to dive. The roar got louder and all at once, the huge machine burst through the top of the dune, cresting about four metres to my left.

I breathed a sigh of relief and frantically fought my bike, trying to get out of there before the next vehicle came over the top. The dune was too steep to pick the bike up, so I ended up having to drag it metre by metre to the base of the dune before I could get it upright, while making sure the sand didn't run backwards down my exhaust into the motor, which was something that had happened to Darryl a couple of years back in the Namibian dunes, seizing his motor. It was another time advice from previous races had kept me in the race.

I dropped my bike many times that day and my leg continued to go dead. I knew that something was wrong with it and I just wanted the day to end. After 14 hours of fighting the bike through the dunes, I arrived at 7pm at the bivouac at Tupiza, Bolivia.

After getting off the bike, I could barely stand and had started feeling pain in my leg, which was something I didn't expect. I called Meredith on the satellite phone and told her I was in, but I had a problem with my hip. I knew I should go to the medical tent, but I was hesitant. I would get the treatment I needed, but if the doctor decided my injury was severe he could pull me from the race and there would be nothing I could do about it.

I sat on the truck weighing up the options and carefully taking off my gear. I bumped the inside of my knee and my leg immediately went into spasm. I carefully pushed it around and noticed that my knee was swollen on the inside. It wasn't my hip after all, it was my knee. I really had no choice. I was in a bad way and needed help, so I made it to the tent assisted by my crew, taking the risk of expulsion. Just before we got to the tent I told the guys to let me walk in on my own, I wanted the help but I didn't want to look as though I was in serious trouble.

There was an X-ray machine and sonar equipment in the medical tent and after moving my leg into different positions, the orthopaedic surgeon held my leg straight and pushed the knee inwards and the pain shot right through my body. I could definitely feel it but I played it down as best I could. The doctor performed a sonar scan and picked up a torn ligament on the inside of my left knee. He gave me a course of anti-inflammatory medication and strapped my knee with adhesive strapping. He reported the injury to the head trauma specialist who would decide if I could continue. They spoke for a while in French as I waited not so patiently, desperately trying to look as cheerful and as normal as possible. He showed her the sonar and I saw her lips tighten as she raised her eyebrows. It didn't look good. I was waiting for the whistle a mechanic gives before he tells you what the repair is going to cost. She looked at me and, speaking in English, recommended that I retire. My heart sank and I felt as though someone had ripped my heart out. Surely it couldn't be the end! Not now!

'But,' she continued, 'your knee is stable so I won't stop you from continuing, if you choose to.'

It was a no brainer that I would continue, I would need to see the bone protruding through the skin before I was going to give up. I'd had torn ligaments before, playing soccer in my twenties, and knew the real challenge would be the next day. The whole process had taken two hours and wearing a brace the doctor had given on top of the strapping I slowly headed back to the truck. My knee slowed me and my mind was heavy with the news and the decision I had made to continue.

When I arrived back at the truck I noticed that Ronald and Walter still hadn't arrived. Bart, along with the mechanics, Gwen, Mark and Willem were visibly upset and explained that they were both out of the race. I couldn't believe it and was totally gutted for both of them. They had been riding so well and were clearly well prepared. Walter and I had spoken for hours about this dream of ours, and the finish meant as much to him as it did to me. I could only imagine the anguish and frustration he was feeling now.

The organisation had picked them up, but they were hundreds of kilometres away and none of us knew when we would see them again. The race would move on, leaving them in its wake. A dark cloud seemed to hang over the pits that night, the two missing members leaving a gaping hole in the team. I still had to eat and sort my roadbook out, so I did that before climbing into my bunk. Walter's bunk below me and Ronald's above were conspicuously empty and I still wasn't sure whether my knee meant the end of the road for me too. Gwen worked on my bike just metres from me. The bike would be ready to race in a few hours but the big question which hung over me was: would I be ready? I still had eight days to go and now had to do it with a torn ligament. The situation was looking hopeless.

Eleven bikers, two of whom were Ronald and Walter, went out that day.

Chapter 25

STAGES 5 AND 6 AND REST DAY

STAGE 5

My alarm woke me once again in the dark and I got up, carefully putting my weight onto my leg. It was still a bit swollen, but seemed all right despite the damage to my knee. If I kept it straight, it worked fine but I couldn't twist on it or it just went dead. For the first time I was grateful that I couldn't feel the pain properly, as I knew it would have been throbbing that morning. I fitted the knee brace that the doctor had given me, along with my knee guard, and forced my foot into my boot. My team helped me onto the bike in the dark and I was off once again.

My body hurt everywhere. My lip had split at the corner of my mouth and my face was tender and windswept from the rain and snow. My finger joints ached and my wrists were painful to move. I was already chafed around my knees from the knee guards combined with the sand, and the Velcro on my kidney belt had rubbed my waist to the point of drawing blood. Every muscle in my back and shoulders was stiff and hurt with every bump I rode over.

The only thing that was easy at Dakar was quitting. All you had to do was press the recovery button on your bike and within a few minutes a chopper would land next to you and all the pain went away. I didn't allow myself even to consider it. I had made a sticker for my roadbook cover which read: 'You didn't come this far, to only come this far.' I knew it was going to be tough, but I had been through far worse and with that mindset I knew I could endure anything for two weeks. It's a little weird, I know, but I often talk to myself when I'm racing and things get really bad. That day I kept telling myself that the Dakar was tough and I was in pain but it had picked on the wrong guy this time.

'You won't break me!' I shouted as I raced, freezing cold, through the rain … dumb, I know – but I was really tired and in need of some inspiration, so it worked for me!

David Thomas, now the only other South African biker left in the race, and I spoke for a while at the start of the special after the long liaison. He had had a tough day the day before and was starting a bit further down the order than usual and was closer to me now. He is a much better rider than I am and a multi Cape enduro champion. He pulled away first into the racing section and was gone. I started soon afterwards and began knocking off the kilometres.

The track was wet and muddy and some sections were again quite treacherous as we crossed the mountainous terrain. Massive drop-offs were just centimetres from the edge of the wet slippery track as I raced through the tight corners, feathering the throttle as the back wheel drifted out behind me. There was zero room for error; a small lapse in judgement could easily cost you much more than your finisher's medal. It rained on and off and the water flowed down the mountain sides in small streams across the track which had been cut roughly into the slopes. The dirt tracks had deep ruts running diagonally across them, many of them deep and unmarked on the roadbook, since they had probably only formed in the unrelenting rain over the last 48 hours. Each time one suddenly appeared I had no choice but to open the throttle, lifting the front wheel and hoping the speed of the back wheel was enough to ride it out.

The bike bucked under me as the back wheel caught the diagonal lip on the far side, kicking left as I shifted with the bike, keeping the power on in an attempt to straighten it out. At other times the track would be broken up over a blind rise, with deep gullies running with the track rapidly becoming deeper and rocky over the next few metres. Picking the wrong line in a split second decision could have you flying over the bars. David later commented that in the wet the single cautions on the roadbook should be considered doubles, the doubles triples and the triples a matter of life or death. At times it opened up with flatter faster sections as the track wandered through the lowlands, only to head towards more mountains and their dangerous rocky tracks.

About an hour into the stage, I came over a rise to see, once again, the medical chopper, and I knew that a rider was down. I scanned the track ahead and saw a rider surrounded by three paramedics. I looked

over at the bike and my heart sank on seeing the USN decals. It was
David. I stopped next to the track and went over to him immediately.
He had taken a big fall at high speed and was in a really bad way. His
leg was badly broken and the bones were displaced. I found out later
that he had broken his leg in nine places. I went back to my bike to
press a button on my tracking unit, letting the control centre know I
was OK because my bike would be stationary for a while. I saw the
GoPro camera on my bars and decided to take it with me. I know it
sounds a bit macabre, but something I wished I had was more footage
of the time I broke my back and of the challenges I subsequently
went through. We had no pictures from the day I crashed and had
taken very few during rehab because at the time it all just seemed
so terrible. I wanted to capture that moment there with David and I
looked forward to seeing it play one day soon, alongside one of him
finishing the rally!

David was on an inflatable stretcher and hooked up to a drip.
His boot had been cut off and his leg was strapped in a splint in an
attempt to keep it stable and prevent the broken bones from moving
around any more than they already had. David was a tough guy, but
I could tell he was in severe pain because he cried out each time the
stretcher moved and shifted the broken bones in his leg. The medic
asked me to help carry David to the chopper, but I could barely walk
on the muddy surface with my legs and damaged knee. There was
no way I could help carry him in his condition. So I held the drip,
freeing up one of the medics and then I flagged down two quad riders
who stopped and helped carry him to the chopper. It was extremely
awkward trying to fit him into the chopper with his leg constantly
moving around, causing him immense suffering.

In spite of the trauma, David wasn't thinking only of himself. He
had a brother who had died in a car accident many years before and
he had put a sticker of his name, Justin Thomas, on his bike and
vowed to take it to the finish. In the middle of the extreme situation
in which he found himself, and in excruciating pain, he looked at me,
his voice strained, and said, 'Joey, take the Justin Thomas sticker off
my bike and ...' his voice broke as he struggled to get the last words
out '... put it on your bike.' It was difficult to watch, let alone have to
endure. I would later discover he had been lying there for more than
20 minutes with his leg in pieces while the chopper tried to get to him
and land in the pouring rain.

The doctor asked if he had his passport and covered the medical
procedures. I knew he was in a bad situation, not only was he out

of the race with his dream shattered, but he was in pain and badly injured, facing months of difficult healing ahead. I tried my best to console him.

'Hang in there, bro! You know there're okes who die in this race, buddy, but you are still here, you're injured but you're OK!'

I reminded him he would be able to return in the future and finish what he had started. The whole situation was very raw. He explained how he had crashed.

'I can't believe it, Joey! I just came too quickly around the corner, I was fine as I landed but the bike followed me and landed on my leg!' His voice laboured as he dealt with the pain. 'Whack! I felt my leg shatter instantly as it hit me, I've never broken anything like that!'

The pain was visible in his eyes. He didn't break down while I was with him, but the tears ran down the side of his face as he lay facing the roof of the chopper. The medics were packing the last equipment into the chopper and I asked if he wanted me to stay.

'No, you go finish your race, bro.'

I squeezed his shoulder and walked back to his bike. I felt myself well up as I removed the sticker from his bike and placed it on the inside of my front screen. He had a small green toy dirt bike cable-tied to the navigation tower so I took that too and cable-tied it to mine.

I looked over at him lying in the chopper and as the engine fired up I got back on my bike and headed off, now a lot further down the field. I had prepared for many foreseeable things I would experience at Dakar, but I could never have expected the carnage that I was faced with on a daily basis. The organisers were very safety conscious and the medical response teams were in a league of their own. It was just that in spite of every effort – the nature of the race, combined with multiple vehicles, dangerously high speeds, rugged terrain and tired competitors – incidents were bound to happen.

I still had hundreds of kilometres to cover and ticked the waypoints off one by one. I raced on and as the hours passed the landscape again became drier and the vegetation stopped. The ground was a dark grey and hard packed with rocks strewn over the surface. Everything was covered in a layer of light grey dust. It was like riding on the moon. I came up over a rocky rise and the track came to a slightly offset T-junction. There was no symbol in the roadbook for the junction and I sat at the intersection alone, not knowing which way to ride. Was I on the wrong track? I raced back in the direction I had come from to the previous point that I was sure of, matching the roadbook, and tried again. I was definitely on the right track, I could see many tracks on the hard dusty surface heading in both directions. There were only a couple of bikes behind me and I still had to catch up because of the time I had spent with David earlier that day, so I needed to figure it out alone. I took an educated guess and chose to go right. I raced along the track for a couple of kilometres but the dusty track split again, with the roadbook once again not matching. I headed back towards the original T-junction to see if the left route was a better match to the roadbook.

As I rode towards it I suddenly saw Giniel de Villiers approaching at pace in the Gazoo Toyota. I decided, against my rules, to follow him. After all, he had Dirk von Zitzewitz navigating next to him, one of the top navigators in the world. I swung the bike around and chased desperately behind them, trying to keep them within sight for as long as I could, but they were just too quick. They had passed the point where I had decided to turn back and I followed further along the track too. A couple of minutes later they appeared again, this time heading towards me. I spun around and chased them again, as we passed bikes and cars alike, all looking for the correct route. They eventually drove out of sight, heading down the left track only to come flying back towards me once again and head back in the direction we had just come from!

It was all crazy confusion with the landscape now riddled with vehicles frantically riding from one side of the horizon to the next. Everyone was lost and confused about the unclear directions. I decided to go back to a point on the map that I was sure about and put in the time to try to work it out again. It was a good thing I did, because I finally discovered where most of the guys had gone wrong. There was a faint track that continued straight, where the main route took a sharp right. There were only a few tracks heading down it and it was almost invisible. I took a chance and headed down for several kilometres and suddenly my GPS picked up the next waypoint, confirming that I was on the right track. It was the lucky break I needed! I was finally back on track in the roadbook. I pushed on, racing fast for kilometre after kilometre, relieved that I was finally heading in the right direction. Later that night there was a lot of complaining about the roadbook, as most competitors had got lost that day. I had been very fortunate to hit every waypoint that day and I didn't incur any penalties.

As the day continued the weather deteriorated, becoming worse and worse. The rain was relentless and the rivers swelled, making them near impossible to cross – everywhere was flooded and muddy.

Distances that should have taken just a few minutes to ride now took more than twice as long. The organisers realised that the last part of the day's route was simply impossible to ride because the rivers, now well over a metre deep and flowing fast, had become impossible to cross. Later in the afternoon we were rerouted and given a new liaison to the bivouac in Oruro, Bolivia.

It became 300 kilometres of misery! The rain poured down and the high altitude made it freezing cold. I had all my cold weather gear on again and tried to keep my face warm as the wind whipped through my motocross style helmet. I had my neoprene facemask and balaclava on, but I was already struggling to breathe at the high altitude and anything over my mouth just increased the difficulty. I had taken the latex gloves out of my first aid kit and added them over my riding gloves for extra insulation. Then it began to hail and things went from bad to worse. I sat on the bike with my shoulders hunched and my head dipped, my left hand tucked under my leg and kept my eyes fixed on the ICO, watching the kilometres sluggishly tick by, until eventually I arrived at the bivouac after dark again.

There was a queue of trucks and service vehicles for a couple of hundred metres lined up at the entrance and I squeezed my way between them to enter the bivouac. The entire bivouac was covered with mud and the rain was not giving up. Trucks and backup vehicles stood deep in the mud, unable to move. I rode through the deep mud struggling to stay upright, found my team and sat in the truck, finally out of the rain. It had been another really tough day but my knee had survived and, surprisingly, only gone dead a couple of times. I thought about Dave and wondered where he would be now, as well as Walter and Ronald who I still hadn't seen and had no idea where they were either.

Gwen and Mark worked away on the bikes under the truck's floodlights, splashing around in the ankle deep muddy water. They were as tough as any rider and carried on as if they were in a pristine workshop. Bart wrote the starting times for the next day on the pit board and made sure I was woken up in time. He made me some food and I remember again feeling proud and privileged to be part of such a committed team. I didn't even try to shower that night. I called Meredith on the sat phone to tell her I was in. The signal was terrible and although I got the message across, it left me feeling frustrated at not being able to communicate with her. I wanted to find Darryl, but the mud was thick and with my knee it was impossible to reach him on the other side of the bivouac, about 600 metres away. I needed to sleep more than anything, so I got out of my wet kit, shoved the food in my mouth and got into my bunk. The bed below and above me spoke volumes, still lying empty.

Another three bikers fell out that day.

STAGE 6

The rain hadn't let up the whole night and by the morning the entire bivouac was under water. The organisers had decided to cancel the stage because all the pit crews were stuck and therefore unable to leave. More than that, the rivers we would be crossing on the track were again completely flooded. To say I was relieved would be an understatement. It was a bit more complicated than that though, because we still had to ride the 300 kilometres in the rain to La Paz, the capital of Bolivia.

With the later start time I decided to make my way across the pits to find Darryl. We caught up on the last few days and he sent the voice clip back to South Africa. He could see that I was worn out and knew of the challenges I had faced over the last week. He was full of encouragement and advice which helped me to focus on what lay ahead. He still had faith in me and it inspired me to keep going.

After I got back to the truck, Walter and Ronald arrived. They had been airlifted out of the stage two days earlier and dropped off in a nearby town where they had spent the night in a motel. The next morning, now hundreds of kilometres behind the constantly moving Dakar machine, they had hired a taxi in an attempt to try to catch up to the team. They had been driving for the best part of 24 hours.

As he walked towards the truck Walter's frustration boiled over – he was angry! He is an incredibly focused rider and holds himself to a high standard, which made the situation he found himself in very difficult to deal with. Ronald was more philosophical about it. He had tasted the victory of finishing before and knew it couldn't always end that way. I dare say that he was noble in his defeat and just accepted the situation for what it was.

I gave Walter some space for a minute before walking over to him. There were no words that could make the circumstances better. I just hugged him and told him that I was sorry that it had ended that way. We both stood there, tired and worn out. He broke down and tears ran down both our faces. The time we had spent together meant we were equally invested in each other's dream. After about a minute he was able to gather his thoughts and we talked some more.

STAGES 5 AND 6 AND REST DAY

Knowing the work he had put in to being there, and now having to watch the riders kitting up and heading out, must have been torture for him. I suggested that he move on to Buenos Aires where his girlfriend Christelle was planning to meet him at the finish and just have a holiday together. But right there, on the spot, he made a decision that would have a huge effect on my Dakar journey over the next week. He decided to stay with the team and later he unselfishly made it his goal to do as much as he could to get me to the finish.

A couple of tractors had arrived and were tasked with trying to haul the service crew trucks out one by one, often getting stuck themselves. We snapped a huge tow strap trying to get the truck out. There were a lot of frustrated teams in the pits that morning, all trying to get their vehicles moving and on the road again.

I rode the 300 kilometres into La Paz mostly through miserable cold weather. Whenever I had seen Dakar stages being cancelled on TV in the past, I figured the competitors got a day off. Far from the truth!

That day it took about six hours to cover the distance to La Paz, thanks to the speed limits and riding most of the way in the rain. The highlight of the day was arriving at the race halfway point in La Paz. About 60 kilometres before the finish, there were streams of cheering people alongside the road. I figured it was another town on the way to La Paz, but the crowds grew bigger and bigger! For the last 50 kilometres, the streets were lined with spectators. Every overpass we went under was full of Dakar fans. They were all waving Bolivian and Wiphala flags at every competitor. I had never seen anything like it before. It was like doing the Tour de France! In some places, they filled the streets and parted only when you rode through them, patting your arms and back. If you stopped, the fans descended on you, pushing one another over to get to you with the usual shouts of 'Photo! Photo!' Although physically I was broken, I couldn't help smiling and waving at the incredible reception we received in beautiful La Paz.

I arrived at the bivouac located at the main army base and rode around the huge compound looking for my team. A guy in a Yamaha shirt called out to me and came running over. I didn't recognise him, but he introduced himself as a friend of Dave Griffin's. His name was Alexandre Kowalski and Dave had contacted him after hearing about the tough race I was having. He had gone out of his way to find me and was full of encouragement. I needed it at the time and it really boosted my spirits. Arriving at the halfway point was a huge achievement and a big milestone, but the thought of having to repeat the distance I had travelled again over the next six days seemed impossible.

Bart had booked us into a hotel across town for two nights, to help the riders recover as best they could. Sleeping in the bivouac with all the power tools, floodlights and engines revving through the night was not easy. I parked my bike with Gwen and took a taxi to the hotel with Walter and Ibraheem. It was dark already, but we managed to find a laundromat that was open and dropped off all our kit to be washed. I took the best shower that I'd had in years and after washing all the dirt and grime off I was probably 10 kilograms lighter! I climbed under the clean sheets and fell asleep in seconds.

During the night, I woke up with a pounding head and feeling as though someone was sitting on my chest. I had been warned it might happen and knew that it was just a side effect of the high altitude. I lay there taking deep breaths in and out for a few minutes until I felt better and the headache went away. I fell asleep again but it happened several times during the night.

REST DAY

They call it 'rest day' as there is no riding, but for the team it was hectic. The mechanics stripped all the bikes, checking every bolt and lubricating every bearing. The complete drive chains were replaced with new chains, sprockets and sliders. New air filters, oil changes, as well as new tyres and mousses were put on and the spare wheels were fitted out too in preparation for the next few days. It was the longest day of the rally for the service crew. They worked meticulously, knowing that any small undetected error could spell the end of the race for a rider.

In the hotel I got busy too, washing my boots, helmets and protective gear. I had stuff balancing all over the bathroom trying to get it dry. (Just so you know, hotel hairdryers don't last much longer than about three hours when left on continuously.) I washed out my hydration packs and took full advantage of the hotel buffet meal before heading down to the pits for riders' briefing that evening. The next two days were the marathon stage, meaning we would have to sleep the following night in a remote location and would have no service crew. Our tyres needed to be marked by the organisers to ensure that no one got any outside assistance. In the rush of the day our crew missed the cut-off time for marking by just a few minutes and were slapped with a fine of €200 per bike. The organisers ran a tight ship and enforced every rule to the letter.

The highlight of the day for me was talking to Meredith and the girls on the phone. We spoke for ages and it put my mind at ease hearing their cheerful voices and knowing they were loving the gifts I had left them. For the rest day gift, I had bought them all 'bath bombs' from Lush. For guys who don't know, they are coloured chalky balls that you chuck in the bath and they change the colour of the water and smell like flowers and stuff. A total rip-off, but girls dig them – so I bought them.

I had gone into the shop and told the assistant what I was looking for. She went on about how they relax your mind, make pain evaporate and ease stress caused by the modern world. It sounded like the stuff some of my buddies smoked. She held one up to my face to smell, but I was having none of it. How about you just pick five for me, I'll pay you and I can go. She picked five out and wrapped them up. Once I got home, I stuck them in the gift bag and was done. The girls had opened them that day and had read the names out to me. 'Frozen', 'Blue Bomb', 'Golden Wonder', 'Twilight' and 'Sex On The Beach'. Hysterical giggling followed!

'Er, that last one's for Mom!' I said quickly. Next time, I still won't be smelling them, but I'll be checking the names for sure.

Meredith told me about the support I was getting and all the calls she had received from people offering her any help she needed. Friends, family, people from church and fellow bikers all rallied around and supported us. I had opened up my WhatsApp and there were nearly 2000 messages on my support line and tons of private ones too. Somehow, I needed to pull through the next six days. I didn't know how I was going to do it, but it had to happen!

My knee was a bit swollen and I could see the bruising was coming to the surface, with the inside of my knee turning various shades of blue and purple. I was still taking the anti-inflammatory meds and had the knee strapped again by the doctor that day. At that point, I didn't care less about further damage. I needed six more days from it and I would worry about the fallout when I got home. Walter wouldn't let me complain and he was right; he would have traded places in an instant because I still had a fighting chance.

The following morning we climbed into the taxi at 4am and set off to the start, or so we thought. The driver had assured us that he knew where he was going, but it wasn't the way we had driven before. We asked him several times and each time he assured us he knew.

Walter was the one who eventually decided he'd had enough and made him pull over. After checking on his cellphone, he found that we were miles away and it was going to be touch and go to make our start time. We got the driver back on track and made the start with seconds to spare!

Chapter 26

MARATHON STAGES 7 AND 8

STAGE 7

After barely making my start time, I set out at about 5am, riding in the dark again. Today we would need to cover 622 kilometres on our way to Uyuni and it was all at high altitude, ranging between 3700 and 4000 metres. It would be freezing and I made sure I had all my warm gear on, because I wouldn't see my team until the following night.

The day started off with a long, cold liaison that took us out of the capital city and into the Altiplano, the most extensive area of high plateau on earth outside of Tibet. A couple of hundred freezing and wet kilometres later we entered the special. It was really physical riding with dunes and off-piste routes when there are no tracks or paths. We just followed CAP headings through the terrain. It was easy to get lost in some places, and once you were off the roadbook the confusion escalated quickly. The navigation was very tricky and I needed to ride smart, making sure I collected each waypoint and didn't cover any more distance than I had to.

Conserving energy and survival would be my focus in this second week. Going through more dunes, I rode outside of the sandy tracks on the smoother untouched sand where it was easier to ride, compared with the dug-up rutted main line. It wasn't the shortest route but it was easier on my body which was taking some serious strain. I rode as smoothly as I could, trying not to ask too much of the bike. Being the first day of the marathon stage, the most essential thing was to arrive with no damage to your bike. No spares would be available that evening and any time you spent working on your bike was subtracted from the amount of sleep you got.

219

Most of the twisty gravel tracks that day were also muddy and wet, because it rained on and off all day. Again, it was easy to throw it all away at a moment's notice. Rivers often cut through the terrain and that day I crossed more than I could remember. Many of them were not on the roadbook as a result of the excessive rainfall now flowing from the mountains. We rode for more than 40 kilometres in a 50-metre wide semi-dry sand and stone river bed, crossing the same stream again and again as it snaked back and forth across our path. The stream beds were filled with thousands of loose slippery rocks which made a rumbling cracking sound, shifting and knocking against each other as the weight of my wheels rode over them. I saw one rider crash as he exited the river, his tyres slipping out from under him on the icy wet rocks. His body was thrown hard into the solid jumbled ground. I stopped to make sure he was OK and after a nod and a thumbs up he picked up his bike and continued to push on.

The rivers were swollen and at some crossings the depth borderlined on the impossible because it covered the top of our wheels. I remember one river crossing in particular that reminded me of a YouTube video I saw before I left home of a Dakar rider passing through a river just like it. I had seen him pushed over by the current and the river swept his bike away, tumbling over the rocks as it was washed downstream. 'My' river had the same rushing water, was visibly deep and flowing at a serious pace. I entered cautiously, as the clip played over and over in my head. Momentum was key and I kept the throttle fixed halfway open, leaning into the turbulent flow as the bike bucked over the rocks on the river bed. My arms were like shock absorbers as the handlebars shook violently and the front wheel bounced over hidden obstacles. I had a few close calls, but I managed to keep the bike rubber side down through the rivers all that day.

Towards the end of the special there were fewer rocks, but now there was mud everywhere, which always makes things interesting. My tyres were coated in the thick red mud and gave zero traction – it was like riding on ice. I fought the back wheel, constantly trying to overtake the front. I stood up through the mud pits as much as I could, keeping my feet on the foot pegs and the throttle open, desperately trying not to put my feet down for fear of causing further damage to my knee. The cars raced past, covering us with mud, their rear wheels drifting left and right and spraying in every direction as they relentlessly counter steered.

I lost a lot of time that afternoon when the GoPro camera belonging to the organisation, came off my bike. Out of the corner of my eye I saw it fly off, but I was riding fast and by the time I stopped it could have been anywhere over a distance of 100 metres. I was in a wide sandy river bed scattered with small dark rocks. The terrain provided perfect camouflage for the camera. I searched for ages and was joined by some locals who were spectating nearby. I did my best to explain what I was looking for, using classic charade actions, until I said the word 'GoPro'. Suddenly they understood exactly what I was looking for!

About 20 of us scoured the area and pretty soon a young girl came running over with it held high above her head. I cheered along with the other locals and gave her a small reward while they took a few pictures of us holding the camera. She was all smiles and they waved and cheered as I pulled away. It was incidents like that that made me fall in love with South America. There was widespread poverty, but the people were always cheerful and happy to help you in any way they could.

Each morning in the predawn hours, the streets were lined with spectators – from young children right up to old ladies bent with age, waving and smiling and showing the last few teeth in their mouths.

My cautious approach had me finishing with the bike in good condition, but near the back as I arrived at the Uyuni military barracks, our bivouac for the night. I had been riding for 15 hours, once again arriving in the dark at about 7.55pm, only five minutes before riders' briefing. I knew time would be a big challenge tonight, so I grabbed a tray and piled it with food from the mess hall and headed over to the briefing. Riders and drivers stood around, showered and dry in the clothes supplied by the organisation. In contrast, I was still in my wet muddy kit with my hydration pack still on and my helmet on the ground between my feet. I stood there, the only one with a tray, shovelling food into my mouth to the amusement of some of the other competitors. I didn't care though, I was in and that's what counted!

After my combined dinner and riders' briefing, I headed to the army dorm where there were bunk beds lined up half a metre apart for as far as I could see. I walked along, looking for a spare bed and found what appeared to be the last one, on the top bunk in the middle of the room. It was no time to be picky and I dumped my kit on it and went off to get my marathon bag. The marathon bag was supplied by the organisation and contained some basic essentials like toiletries,

T-shirt, blanket and a lunch pack for the next stage. There were tons of extra bags, so I grabbed a second one and wrote Walter's number on it so he would at least have a keepsake when they returned in the truck the following night. I also went over to the organisation tent to get my passport stamped, as we were re-entering Argentina the next day.

Gillian, commonly known as the mom of all Africa-based entrants, saw me and checked up on how I was doing – just as she always did. She sent a message back home to let everyone know that I was in and OK. I bumped in to the Toyota guys, Giniel de Villiers, Dirk von Zitzewitz, Conrad Rautenbach and Rob Howie. It was cool hearing some familiar accents and we chatted for a couple of minutes before getting a photo together. It was the first time I had met Giniel, even though the rally was over halfway – probably because he was generally in bed before I arrived each night! The guys in my pit had decided – based purely on that fact – that a good nickname for me would be 'Night Rider'! Conrad and Rob always gave me a wave and thumbs up whenever they passed me on the stages. Really good okes.

I went over to the physio tent for some treatment because my back had been painful the whole day. They helped me out and restrapped my knee once again, this time adding some extra strapping where the brace had chafed the skin on the back of my knee. I made the necessary changes to my roadbook, marking it up as quickly as I could. Then it was back to the dorm. I cleaned up and put on some dry clothes from the marathon bag and heaved my way onto the top bunk which had no ladder. Not a big deal for anyone else, but with my dodgy knee and not being able to jump and I looked like an 80-year-old trying to climb a fence. It was 11pm and I was lights out in seconds.

Another biker went out that day ...

STAGE 8

The route that day was set to take us across Bolivia and over the border into Salta, Argentina. The total stage distance was set at a colossal 892 kilometres, with the distance of the special set at nearly 500 kilometres. The route was mountainous and we would climb to altitudes over 4400 metres several times that day.

I was up at 4am that morning, and even though I had hung my kit up it was still wet. There were no other options so I put it on and walked over to the canteen. Once again, eating was the last thing I felt like doing, but I shoved the food down my throat, knowing it was essential. I loaded my extra-long roadbook and climbed on the bike – still muddy from the day before – and started the stage at 5am in the now familiar darkness. I didn't know it at the time, but it was to be the longest riding day of my life.

The liaison was a relatively short and cold 40 kilometres to the start of the special. The riders stood around for a few minutes awaiting their start times. Every one of them was looking pretty rough. Many had hands taped to cover blisters, and their faces varied in levels of rawness from the goggle foam and wind. A few guys had parts held on to their bikes with cable ties and wire from falls the previous day and their tyres showed varying degrees of wear.

The first hundred kilometres of the special were really dangerous with more mud, water and thick fog, reducing my visibility to only a few metres ahead of me. I needed to be cautious, because at the high speeds we were running the lack of visibility made it very risky. As we rode on, the fog started to lift and the track opened up. It turned into what I like to call 'video game' racing. I hung on to the bars, steering through the bends as the track flicked left and right. The gravel roads were like WRC tracks and I raced flat out, backing into the corners and drifting round the bends. The traction varied from little to none but it was a blast to ride and I was having fun.

I remember looking around and thought how incredible it was – despite the fatigue – to be racing on my bike through South America in the Dakar Rally. I could see snow covered peaks to my right as my bike sucked up the winding path ahead like a strand of spaghetti. Over the last few hundred kilometres of the special we encountered more camel grass, dunes and river crossings and I found myself really enjoying the stage, riding smoothly and without any major problems. It wasn't easy to cover the distance but it all went well right through to the end of the special. It was early evening when I pulled up at the checkpoint and had my time card stamped.

Although it had been fun, it had still been a really tough workout riding the last 12 hours or so and I now expected, as per the roadbook, another 350-kilometre liaison to get through to the next bivouac in Salta. It was going to be a long, difficult ride. However, the marshal at the checkpoint had news for us. He explained that there had been some kind of natural disaster and that the bivouac had been moved and was now only 150 kilometres away. The marshal was French and I was not sure exactly what had happened, but the end of the stage being closer was good news in my opinion. I rode on for the 150 kilometres, wondering how they had managed a whole new bivouac – they are massive and usually set up days in advance; it just didn't add up.

At about 9 o'clock that evening, I arrived at the checkpoint of the 'new' bivouac in the middle of nowhere. It was just a petrol station and a small motel. Along the gravelly sides of the road, there were some team service vehicles – mainly for the rally cars – but my team was nowhere to be seen. I pulled up to the marshal where I was checked in and finally got the full story.

With all the bad weather and flooding, there had been a huge landslide which took out the main road up ahead, as well as part of the town. The only other route to the actual bivouac was another 350-kilometre detour through the mountains on a dirt road. The plan was for competitors to spend the night at the new bivouac and then ride the 350-kilometre detour in the morning, then to continue straight into another 600 kilometres to the next night's bivouac. Thereafter, the race would continue as normal. It all sounded completely insane, but I had learned from other cross country rallies that there was so much that could go wrong or change on a race of this length, over which the organisers had no control. It was a race that crossed countries, things were bound to happen! They simply had to do the best they could with whatever situations arose.

'Wow, so where do we sleep tonight?' I asked the marshal.

'Anywhere here,' was the reply.

Other riders were arriving behind me and I had to move on. I looked around and there was nothing, so I went over to the garage where a bunch of riders and people were standing around.

My teammate Maikel was there and he told me our team was already at the bivouac 350 kilometres away. The small motel had long since filled up, leaving us with only two choices. We could sleep on the floor in the concrete parking area, with nothing but the kit we were wearing and a space blanket, or ride the 350-kilometre detour through the night to our team. Our bikes had already gone through two full racing days without a service, so the bonus of riding to our team that night was that our bikes would get a decent service before the 600 kilometres we had to cover the next day.

It was a tough decision, though, as it was now 9.30pm and we had already been on the bikes for at least 16 hours. The detour would be easier to ride in the light the next morning, so the concrete started to look inviting. We weighed up the pros and cons and decided, right or wrong, just to go for it. I grabbed a quick bite and a cold drink at the garage, put my cold gear back on and we headed out into the night. Two other riders decided to do the same, but they were riding more slowly and Maikel and I were just keen to get it over with as quickly as possible. We decided to split up and Maikel and I shot ahead.

We took some crazy risks that night, going flat out in the darkness, riding side by side on the gravel road to create maximum light. If anything ran out into the track, we would have been tickets! We passed some rally cars and other service, press and organisation vehicles along the route. It was a dirt road, and we would have had to ride blind into the dust clouds of the vehicles. Our bikes' lights would just illuminate the dust in front of our faces, making it even more difficult to see.

We passed the vehicles that didn't even know we were there, as they wove from side to side on the track to avoid the rocks, washouts and deep sand. We couldn't tell the pockets of deep sand from the hard pack in the darkness and sometimes the bikes just bogged down as we hit them, nearly sending us over the bars on several occasions. The whole situation was completely ludicrous. We heard the next day of a service truck and a press car that had crashed over the edge of one of the steep drop-offs, rolling over and over to the valley below. By no small miracle, there were no fatalities.

Just after midnight, we stopped in a small rural town under a streetlight to take a break and warm up a bit. Both of us were wide eyed and glad still to be alive. There were still fans on the street and the usual 'Photo! Photo!' requests. We obliged and posed for photos while I ate the rest of the sandwich I had bought at the petrol station. We were there for about 20 minutes, with still no sign of the other two riders. We climbed back on our bikes, still less than halfway there and rode on side by side into the night.

The same scenes played out again, taking crazy risks and pushing blindly through the dust – we were running on pure adrenalin. My eyes stung with each blink. I was so tired, but the only way it was going to end was to cover the distance. The fast pace, combined with the visibility we had that night ranked right up there with some of the most dangerous things I have ever done. I had raced a mountain pass on the tar with knobbly tyres against Neal a few years back in Lesotho, which had us both come very close to going over the cliff edge, down to certain death. That now paled in comparison!

Eventually, we arrived at the bivouac just after 3am, those last 350 kilometres taking us nearly six hours. Walter was at the gate of the bivouac to meet us, about a kilometre from the truck. He hopped on the back of my bike and directed us. Gwen was there and ready to get to work, as he had been every single day. I had ridden a total of 1150 kilometres that day, over a period of 22 hours. I can't tell you how relieved I was to have finished the marathon stage – and a marathon it certainly was! I had been on my bike for 36 of the last 48 hours!

I climbed into my bunk on the truck at 4.20am.

Another two riders didn't make it that day and were out of the race …

Chapter 27

STAGES 9 AND 10

STAGE 9

As a result of the landslide the day before some teams were still stranded on the other side of the disaster, and so the Stage 9 racing section was cancelled. However, all the competitors still had to ride the 680-kilometre route from Salta to Chilecito.

I had only slept for two hours and was still half asleep and feeling groggy when I entered the start queue ready to ride out. Gillian spotted me and came over again to check up on me. She could see that I was exhausted and told me to ride safe and stop whenever I felt as though I was drifting off.

'Make sure you drink enough!' she said, checking that my hydration pack was full. 'Where's your hydration pack?' she exclaimed, feeling nothing on my back.

I was so tired and out of it that I had left it back at the truck. I shot back there and sheepishly picked it up. (Like when you have to walk back into a store to pick up your car keys.) Crisis averted!

There was no racing that day, but it was still a very long day in the saddle and I spent ten hours on the bike. It rained on and off again during the morning, but we were descending in altitude and so it started to warm up as the day went on.

Those liaisons were often pretty dangerous. Some of the roads were closed to traffic, but the majority were not. Everyone wanted to get a photo of the riders, so cars would ride up right next to you, often with one hand on the steering wheel and the other holding their phone trying to get the shot of you. Sometimes kids hung out the windows to give you a high-five, or the car in front of you slowed down for them to get a better look. People in the towns would step out to see the bike that had passed ahead of you, not realising they were stepping right into your path. You always had to be wide awake!

I had seen hardly any wildlife the whole rally, apart from llamas and they were always far off the track. But that day I had a close call that nearly ended my rally. It would have been a terrible way to go out, and on a liaison on top of it. I was riding in a 60kph zone going through a town. The streets were closed to all other traffic and were lined on both sides with spectators waving flags and cheering. A stray dog crossed the tar road ahead of me from right to left. He was fairly big and looked like a ridgeback. I moved a little to the right, where there was plenty space and no danger. Then someone from the side he was heading for, yelled at him, making him turn and bolt back towards the side he had come from – straight into my path. There was no time to brake, so I accelerated and swerved to squeeze past and miss him. My front wheel missed him by millimetres, but my boot and the side of the bike connected with him. I nearly went down, but fortunately managed to keep control of the bike. I stopped and the dog ran off uninjured. It was one of those moments where it could all have gone wrong so quickly. Falling on tar at 60 kilometres an hour could easily be a race ender.

The first 300 kilometres went well, as we rode through twisting valleys with brown rocky cliffs on either side. The road followed a river valley and as it descended we shed altitude with each passing kilometre. I wound through the jagged peaks on the road that had been creatively carved between the river and the mountains. It was incredibly beautiful as we moved into the lower regions where the vegetation increased.

I tried to focus on the scenery and kept looking around to stay awake, constantly swapping between sitting and standing. I still had to stop often when I felt my eyes get heavy, each time getting off the bike and walking around a bit. I splashed water on my face and ate something from my jacket pockets. All I wanted to do was pull over, lie down in the beautiful surroundings and fall asleep. Once I stopped at a viewpoint where there were some other people. I was so tired that I managed to fall over with the bike on top of me, just as I had done the first time I rode after the accident. The people standing there helped lift the bike. Seeing me fall and now stumble around in my exhausted state and not knowing about my dodgy legs, I'm sure they wondered if I had been drinking a bit!

The knee brace the doctor had given me had been chafing and cutting into my leg over the last five days. I couldn't feel the pain, but my leg kept going into spasm, so I knew it was becoming a problem. It was the least of my worries though. By now my whole body was a mess. I had known it would happen and I had done everything I could to prevent what I could control. Before coming to Dakar, I had put extra foam on my chest protector to stop chafing. I had worn sunblock and UV protective lip balm every day. I had worn earplugs and even safety glasses on the early liaisons to help my face recover from the hours of the foam goggles rubbing against it. Each night, I made sure my feet dried out and I washed and treated all my cuts and blisters.

In spite of my efforts, my face was raw and the inside of my ears felt bruised from the plugs. My lip was split and my neck was rubbed raw from the collar of my jacket. My throat was sore and hurt each time I swallowed. My shoulders were chafed from wearing a bag every day and my nipples bled from wearing the chest protector. My stomach was chafed from the kidney belt where the Velcro had not lined up properly and my knuckles ached. I had blisters on both hands and my left foot and my clutch fingers were bruised from the constant pulling. I had the pillow on the bike for the liaisons and it had helped, but my butt was still bruised and raw from the hours in the saddle which was often wet from the rain. My back ached and my right elbow throbbed where my triceps had been reattached. I really wanted it all to end.

'Only three days to go,' I thought, just three more days.

As the day went on, the road straightened and the long tar sections became really boring. They did nothing to help me in my battle to stay awake. At one point I rode up next to Lyndon Poskitt, a rider from England. He had his left hand across the bike holding the throttle open to give his right hand a break. I had an extra rubber band, so as we rode alongside each other I passed one to him to put over the throttle. We were both being used as part of the Dakar Heroes show and so we both had GoPro cameras from the organisers. With the throttles held open by the elastic bands, we goofed around filming each other to pass the time and keep ourselves awake. I'm sure the guys downloading the footage that night, were like 'What the hell is this crap?' But it kept us awake and alive and we both arrived at the bivouac in one piece.

It was the first dry bivouac we had had in a long time and the temperature was warmer. We were down to 910 metres – much lower than the 3500 metres the night before. For me it was unusual to arrive at a bivouac in the light and I took the opportunity to grab something to eat at the catering tent and to mark my roadbook properly for the next day. That day it was my team's turn to arrive well after dark and they parked the truck next to the fence where crowds of spectators had gathered, all asking for caps and shirts. We were no factory team and unfortunately had nothing to offer. The shower was attached to the back of the truck and I stood there showering with only a thin curtain separating me from hundreds of people. I kept one eye on the curtain, certain that one of the crew would unhook it at any minute. They didn't and so the crowds missed out, clearly disappointed.

Walter went to riders' briefing for me and got my start time for the next day. It was really good of him, as there were so many other things he could have done, walking around the pits and meeting all the famous racers. I needed to know my start time, but I never cared what my position was and I did not look at the standings once during the whole rally. I was there to finish and I didn't want to be tempted into racing other guys or trying to climb the ranks. You were allowed to claim back any time you spent helping injured riders, but I never bothered. I just ignored the time that I had spent with David and other injured riders; it didn't matter to me.

I got to bed at 10.45pm, the earliest in a while. I had marked my roadbook, but hadn't loaded it on to my bike yet. This time, I put it safely in my jacket pocket and zipped it up, not wanting a repeat of Morocco! I took a sleeping tablet, recorded my voice diary on my phone and then fell asleep.

STAGE 10

The total distance we had to cover that day was 751 kilometres on our way to San Juan. The stage would be hot and dry and I was relieved to be finally done with all my cold weather gear. I had slept for about five hours, which by Dakar standards was a good night. Going through the roadbook the night before I could tell that it would be tough and I was glad I'd had the time to mark it up properly. The complicated drawings close together with lots of warnings and CAP headings meant it was going to be tricky to stay on the right route.

The morning started off hot and the temperature climbed steadily the whole day. The early navigation was difficult, as I had expected, along dry river beds and rocky paths and through canyons. I focused on executing each navigational instruction to the letter. I simply couldn't afford any unnecessary riding in terms of time or effort. At one particularly difficult section the dry river bed we were riding in was at times over 100 metres wide and split many times which made the navigation very challenging. Riders and cars often took the wrong split and had to turn around and head back to the split against the flow of other competitors. The sand was thick, making it difficult to turn and there was a fair bit of vegetation that reduced visibility. I arrived just after Slovenian KTM rider Simon Marcic had a head-on collision with the Peugeot of Stéphane Peterhansel. The car had stopped on top of him and in the process his leg had been badly broken. The chopper hadn't arrived yet and the biker sat there in pain being attended to by Peterhansel and his co-driver. It was yet another reminder of the dangers we all faced on a daily basis.

The riding was very technical and it took its toll on the bike as well as my body. The whole Dakar was a balance to get both bike and body to the end. Just as you could eliminate yourself from the race with an injury, your bike could equally be eliminated. As your body grew fatigued it was easy to seize a motor in the dunes by excessive revving without enough movement, or to damage a motor casing by dropping the bike in the rocks. Even a simple low speed crash could be a race ender if you or your bike landed awkwardly.

Over years of racing I have seen guys sustain horrific injuries from slow enduro crashes. Not long before, Tristam had snapped his Achilles tendon on a rocky climb while riding at walking pace, resulting in major surgery and many months of recovery. Gary broke his leg with a complicated spiral fracture in the same way. On the other hand, Neal once overshot a high speed corner and cartwheeled through the rocky veld, completely destroying his bike although he stood up uninjured. It was just the luck of the draw.

The day Neal crashed we played probably the cruellest joke I had ever been part of. The standard rule when riding in groups is you make sure the guy behind you is OK and still following, which meant glancing back every few minutes to make sure he's still there. This way the whole group stayed together and was safe. Neal's brother Brad was the worst when it came to this rule. Outside of riding, Brad would help anyone in need and had been a huge support to me when I was in hospital and throughout my difficult recovery, but for some reason he forgot about everyone else once he put the helmet on. He just raced on, oblivious of the riders behind. On numerous occasions Neal and I had been frustrated with him as the group rode around trying to find one another in vast riding areas.

The day Neal crashed we dragged his mangled bike back to the main track and stood it up. The bars were bent and the front wheel twisted. The broken plastic shrouds hung off the bike along with the torn seat and missing rear mudguard. Neal and I stood there with Clinton, who was riding with us, wondering what we could do to make it rideable. Twenty minutes after Neal crashed there was still no sign of Brad returning. Finally we heard his engine coming back towards us through the bush. In a cruel 'teach him a lesson' joke, Neal lay flat on his back next to the bike with his eyes closed, while I knelt beside him, my arms straight and my hands together on his chest simulating CPR. Brad came round the corner and at the sight of us jumped off his bike, throwing his helmet down – only to be met by the three of us roaring with laughter. For some reason Brad struggled to see the humour.

That day, on Stage 10 of the Dakar, I was tired and worn out and I made a number of riding mistakes that resulted in two crashes. The first happened on a sweeping bend in a fast sandy river bed section. My front wheel washed out and with my hands on the bars, I face planted with my helmet leaving a line in the sand a couple of metres long. I was surprised my peak didn't break off but my goggles were torn off, giving me a face and helmet full of sand. I stood up spitting out the sand and talking to myself again.

'What the hell was that, bro? Do you want to finish this race or what, man? Focus!'

My neck was painful as I twisted it left and right while trying to pick the heavy bike up out of the sand. I was OK and had reprimanded myself so I pushed on. It was a dumb mistake and was the result of being exhausted. In soft sand, you have to be on your game and ride the bike aggressively or it just doesn't work.

The second fall that day was a big one. I was alone on a hard pack single lane dirt road and the speeds were high. The road wound through the semi-desert region, turning and twisting with the landscape. I glanced down and then back up, constantly checking my roadbook for cautions and turns. One twist in the track caught me off guard as I was looking down and when I looked up I was drifting wide. What I should have done was look through the corner, weight the outside peg and get on the gas. I would normally have ridden it out easily, but being so tired I just fixated on the large rock I was heading for a couple metres ahead of me. Locking up the brakes I hit the rock hard and went flying over the bars; the bike followed me, both of us cartwheeling through the air. I landed in a huge thorn bush and the bike landed on top of me, the 180-kilogram weight knocking the wind right out of me. The momentum we were still carrying rolled both the bike and me out of the bush and onto the hard rocky ground. I lay there on the ground, motionless and unable to breathe.

Once again, I eventually got that first breath and started to move. I heard voices and saw a local man with what appeared to be his two sons running towards me; they had been watching the race as it passed through. The father and his boys jabbered away in Spanish as they helped me stand up awkwardly, my body not only fatigued, but now really sore. My wrist had taken a big hit and my ribs felt bruised. I assessed my body. Everything hurt, but that was normal by now. Fortunately I couldn't feel any major injuries. That thorn bush had saved me big time. I looked around at the rocky ground and I knew it could so easily have ended the same way it did in Pongola only two and a half years earlier.

My rescuers picked up my bike and I could see the front end was twisted. They only spoke Spanish, gesturing at the front wheel and shaking their heads. It was totally buckled up against the side of the front mudguard and unable to turn. There were 15 more kilometres to the next checkpoint and a few hundred more kilometres after that to finish the stage. It could easily be a race ender. Perhaps even *should* have been a race ender, but even though my body was ready to quit I knew I still had fight left in me.

I got my tools out and loosened the triple clamps and lined up the bars with the front suspension as best as I could. Then I laid the bike on its side and found a sizeable rock. The local guys stood on the wheel as I pounded the rim with the rock to get it straight enough to clear the mudguard. I worked on the bike and buckled rim for at least half an hour. Once I got it cleared, I picked my bike up, packed my tools away and rode on. The wheel was terrible and I had no choice but to ride slowly. Riders kept passing me as I crawled to the next checkpoint. Some of the marshals knew me by now and they cheered as I pulled up next to them. They saw the wheel and helped me off the bike. They could see I was completely fatigued. They offered me a chair and insisted that I sat down for a while. They gave me some meat and energy bars to eat, as well as some much needed cold drink. I had always heard how rigid and uncaring the marshals at Dakar were, but I found the complete opposite. They were fantastic and each check-point was like reuniting with old friends. They even helped me get the wheel straighter and I left recharged with nourishment and hope.

The wheel was better but still far from straight and wobbled as I rode on, unable to do more than about 40kph. I limped on, my mind preparing me for another long night. I had ridden through the night in Lesotho and had done it again just a couple of days ago. If I had to do it again, then that was what I'd do. I continued on the dusty gravel track, all alone. There were only a couple riders, if any, behind me after all the time I had lost. The handlebars vibrated as the shuddering front wheel fed through into my blistered hands. I started to wonder how long the wheel bearings would last over the hundreds of kilometres I still needed to cover. I would ride for as long as I could and if it broke completely then I would drag it. There was no ways I was stopping or going back to the marshals only a couple of kilometres behind me. I would rather be picked up the next day in the middle of the bush than be sitting waiting at a checkpoint. I rode on feeling determined, but I knew my chances of getting through the stage were slim to none.

Several kilometres later, completely out of the blue, I saw Peter from my team run into the road to flag me down in front of a small rural petrol stop. I pulled in and there, with a couple of other team vans, was our race van and my trusty mechanic Gwen. It was a designated service point (DSP) that I hadn't even noticed on the roadbook. A DSP is a point where you arc allowed to be helped by your service crew. The top guys used them to get a fresh rear tyre or to refuel so they could keep the bike lighter on the racing stage. As far as I knew there were only one or two in the whole race, so its positioning couldn't have worked out better for me.

Gwen noticed my wheel and immediately pulled a new one from the van. I couldn't believe it! I felt so emotional that I nearly kissed him! He smiled broadly when he saw the relief and renewed hope in my eyes. Peter and Gwen lifted my bike over a tree stump and together set about changing the wheel. I was back in the race! So many times over the past ten days I had got close to the point of not being able to continue, only for something to happen to make it possible. Someone was definitely looking out for me! I left Gwen and Peter with huge thanks and still a long way to ride before even entering the second racing section of the day.

It was already late in the day when I entered the second racing section. I was near the back of the field again because of my crashes, but I was still in. The second section was incredibly tough with lots of soft sand and fesh-fesh. I got stuck in the deep rutted section filled with fesh-fesh and my bike fell in such a way that I just couldn't pick it up. My legs were completely exhausted and kept going into spasm and after about 20 minutes I had made no progress. Years ago, when my legs worked properly it would have been a struggle, but still doable. Now it was just impossible and the frustration started to consume me. I tried to flag down a couple of riders who had passed me, but they had just ridden on. I didn't blame them, we were all in the same sinking boat and at the limit of what we could handle. I gave up trying to stop guys and carried on trying to get the bike up on my own when a rider stopped. He saw I was struggling and he came over to help. It was rider number 167, Matteo Olivetto from Italy. He helped me lift the bike up, once again putting me back in the race. He rode on and I passed him on a sandy track a couple of kilometres later when I waved and thanked him again. He waved back and we both continued with our race.

The route was incredibly difficult. At times it was thick deep sandy tracks that were rutted and whooped out in mounds of sand just a couple of metres apart for as far as I could see. I rode for as long as I could and then stopped in little patches of shade to recover for a minute or two. I made sure I drank enough, as the hot temperature remained constant, even as the sun set.

I again came across another fallen rider with the medical helicopter parked next to him. This time the rider was number 164, Ricardo Martins from Brazil. He had stopped his bike and collapsed from dehydration. Another rider had pressed his emergency button and possibly saved his life. He was lying on a stretcher and on a drip and was being loaded into the chopper. I stopped, knowing there was always water on the choppers, refilled my dusty hydration pack and drank another 500ml bottle. I poured water over my head and I wet my legs to help my body keep cool.

I rode on as the day turned into night once again, ticking away the kilometres in the dark. My bike was losing power and at first I thought it may have been because of a dirty air filter from all the dust and sand. I soon realised it was my clutch that was failing. As soon as the revs picked up it lost traction. I kept gearing up and nursed it to the end of the racing section, where I arrived just before 10pm.

At the checkpoint, the marshal told us that there had been a change in the last liaison route to the bivouac and he had the amended roadbook. We had about 50 kilometres to travel and the area was fairly flat. They were short of copies, so he gave the roadbook to the guy in front of me and told us to stick together. Now on the flat tar my clutch pulled a bit better and I figured I would try to ride it to the end. I knew that as an absolute last resort I could strip the whole clutch and break one of the friction plates in half to make the clutch engage permanently, but that would take a fair amount of time and I was so close to the end.

We rode on through the night, with me following the other rider. But with still about 20 kilometres to go, the gradient of the road increased and my clutch started to slip again. The rider in front kept going, unaware that I was falling back. The clutch deteriorated further until I stopped on the side of the road in the dark and watched the other rider's tail light disappear in the distance. I was so close that with a working bike I would have reached the bivouac in ten minutes. A couple of minutes later, having given the clutch a chance to cool, I started the bike up and pushed with my legs to get it going again. The road turned downwards and I picked up some speed and another few kilometres clicked by.

Eventually, my clutch gave in completely and the rider in front was gone. I was alone, my bike was properly broken and now I was lost as well.

'Really,' I thought, 'you couldn't make this stuff up!'

Could it get any worse? I saw some people, called out to them and signalled to ask which way the riders had gone. They pointed out the direction and I started pushing my bike. After a while I got to another downhill and once again could ride it for a short distance, frequently signalling for directions from people in the town. Eventually the bivouac came into sight at the top of a steep hill. I could almost feel the warm welcoming floodlights on my face as I had felt the sun when I came out of the hospital all those years ago. Still about a kilometre away, it was painfully close.

'Come on, boet!' I encouraged myself in my helmet. I never worried much about the fact that I talk to myself on endurance events, it's when the second voice starts and they argue that I get really concerned.

With the clutch completely gone, the engine off and the bike in neutral, I pushed the bike as best I could up the start of the hill. My boots now felt as though they were filled with lead and dragged against the tar between each step. It was 11pm and I had been on the bike for 18 hours. After seeing me struggling, I was joined by an army guy who was assisting with race security. I pushed on the handlebars and he pushed on the rear mudguard up the hill that became steeper with each step, until we were in sight of the gate.

Walter was once again at the gate waiting for me and he ran down the last hundred metres to meet me and we pushed the bike through the gate together. The marshals smiled in disbelief at the sight of a bike being pushed across the finish line of a stage while they stamped my time card and patted me on the back. We went over to our truck where Bart and Gwen were waiting and I was welcomed as if I had won the race. Bart mixed up a shake and Gwen immediately got working on the bike; he would have to fit a new clutch on top of his usual midnight maintenance schedule. Darryl came over to hear what had happened and record a daily report for back home. He shook his head and laughed as he had done each time he saw me arriving after dark. Once again offering encouragement, he left me feeling optimistic that the next day would be better. That day had been really ugly, but I was in and that's all that mattered.

Another ten bikers didn't get through that day and were out of the Dakar.

Chapter 28

STAGE 11
– END OF THE ROAD

The alarm on my phone went off. It was 3.45am, just over three hours since I had fallen asleep. I opened my eyes narrowly and they stung and battled to focus in the light of my phone screen. I knocked my head as I climbed out of the small bunk on the truck and stumbled around to the opposite end where the toilet was and drained my bladder with one of the disposable catheters I had grown to accept. I put it into a plastic bag and shoved it deep into the dustbin outside, like something I was trying to hide. I then climbed the metal tread plate steps up the truck, sat on a bike stand and began putting my dusty riding gear on. I was numb to everything around me. I just wanted to stay on the truck and for it all to end.

Never in my life had I felt so completely wasted and hollow in every way. Every part of my body hurt, both inside and out. Greg had told me that when he finished the Dakar in 2012 it took him six months to recover fully. At the time, I thought it seemed like an exaggeration, but at that moment it sounded really quick to me. It's not only stiff muscles and a few bruises, it's every joint, every tendon and ligament that feels damaged.

Generally when you work out you push yourself hard, but if you have an injury like shin splints while running, or you pull a muscle or sprain an ankle playing soccer, you take a break and heal up. At Dakar there was no time to heal or recover, it was relentlessly in your face and if you couldn't hack it then the race went on without you. It's not a rational approach but that's because it's not a rational race. I knew I was doing my body no favours and that I would suffer later, but I would deal with that later. At that moment reaching the finish was the only thing that mattered. If you started thinking about what was reasonable and whether it was wise to continue, you would have been out on the second day. I had come to finish the race. Full stop.

'Two days left,' I kept telling myself, 'two days left.'

Walter was awake and had marked my roadbook for me the night before, allowing me to get a little extra sleep. He sat next to me and gave me a breakdown of the route and what to expect, as well as the warnings given at riders' briefing the night before. It didn't sound good: today was going to be a huge test and would weed out any riders at the edge of their resolve. It was a 754-kilometre stage ending in Río Cuarto, consisting of two specials. The first special started with 50 kilometres through the San Juan dunes, the final dunes of the rally and tipped to be a sting in the tail. After that the route went into the flatter lowlands for about another 70 kilometres through the fesh-fesh filled rutted tracks to the first checkpoint.

Walter pointed out three climbs on the roadbook in the dune section that were in thick sand with vegetation, and were very steep. They had been warned at riders' briefing that they would be difficult to climb. The cars' route would miss that section and it would be touch and go whether most bikers could ride up them. The roadbook had alternative routes around them so that the riders who were unable to go over them could continue. He had marked all the alternative routes and told me to take them first time. It was sound advice; he could see the state I was in. His only goal was to get me across that finish line the next day. I looked at the route and agreed that it was the right approach.

I force-fed myself once again and climbed on my faithful KTM, perfectly prepped by Gwen while I had slept. I slung my hydration pack which Walter had prepared over my back and lined up once again in the dark. I remember thinking that at least it was dry that day. I would take hot and dry over cold and wet any day. I pulled out of San Juan with the 754 kilometres ahead of me that day, until I arrived in Rio Cuarto.

I didn't know that when the calendar ticked over that night, I would not be in that next bivouac.

The day started with a relatively short liaison of about 50 kilo-metres and a fuel stop to fill the bikes. Even before dawn, the petrol station was packed with fans wanting photos and autographs. I was less accommodating than I had been earlier in the race, but I did my best to smile and be approachable. After all, they had made the effort to come out and support us, the least I could do was be friendly.

After the liaison, I lined up once again at the start of the special. Because of the crashes the day before and the problems I had had with my clutch, I started 98th out of the remaining 99 riders in the race. Second from the back. The marshal held up his hand in front of me and by tucking his fingers in one by one, he counted me down.

Now I was awake! No matter how little sleep you had had or how you felt, when that marshal counts down, you know it's go time! I twisted the throttle and dropped the clutch, clicking through the gears as I sped off. The track turned to deep sand and the vegetation was similar to that in the Kalahari dunes when I had raced in the Northern Cape. The route was whooped out again, with big rolling mounds of sand. They were too far apart to double two at a time, but too close together to get enough speed, making it difficult to ride. If I rode too slowly, my wheels would sink into the sand, but if I rode too fast I would be getting air off the top of each roller and landing into the face of the next one, nearly sending me over the bars. It was taxing on both my body and the bike.

When the bigger dunes arrived, the cars began to catch me. Stopping in the thick sand was easy, but pulling away again was where it got tricky. I struggled through kilometre after kilometre as the sun climbed higher in the sky. I stopped, exhausted, on the top of a large dune where some local riders were spectating. They came over and took some pictures and we shook hands while I sat on the bike. I thought it would be cool to get some footage for the Dakar Heroes channel with some local riders, so I clipped the GoPro off my bike and held it up as they gathered around me and we all shouted 'Dakar!' They were a good bunch of guys and they wished me luck as I rode off.

The car and bike track split up ahead, just before the big sandy climbs I was to bypass. I saw the climbs come up on my roadbook and I looked ahead to see a narrow track heading what seemed almost vertically up a dune several storeys high. It was intimidating and if you didn't get up the whole way in one go you were in for a world of pain. I looked down again at the alternative routes marked in my roadbook. The alternative route was the sensible choice, but I hadn't come to race the Dakar to be sensible.

'Stuff that!' I thought. 'I didn't come all the way to South America to take the chicken line!'

I raced through the mounds towards the base of the climb forcing my back wheel down into each dip like a BMX racer for maximum speed and I hit the base of the first climb with the bike pinned. I stood up and kept the throttle wide open up the face of the climb, with the sand peeling off my back wheel and flying metres into the air. I crested the top and was pumped.

'That's how it's done, boys!' I shouted to myself in my helmet.

I did the same for the other two climbs, feeling proud to have taken on the worst the route had to offer. I wanted to stand on that finishers' podium and say that I rode the whole race, every metre.

The cars' route joined ours once again and my alarm went off several times. Each time they gave me plenty of notice and I obliged by pulling aside to a stop each time they sped by. I noticed my GoPro was gone from the mount on the front of my bike. I looked around but it had clearly fallen off earlier and I had no idea when. I considered going back to look for it, but I didn't have the energy or time and going back against the cars over the blind rises would be suicide.

'Great! Now I have to explain to the organisation that I've lost their camera!' I thought.

The route then flattened out with more vegetation, becoming a rough twin track that snaked through the scrub. The area had been very muddy at some point and the constant hammering by vehicles had eroded the ground, forming two deep parallel ruts. The deep ruts were almost full of fine fesh-fesh sand, blown there by the wind. The centre island was narrow and pointed making it impossible to ride on, so the wheels of the bike ran along the bottom of one rut that often varied in depth and roughness. The fesh-fesh concealed the ruts like muddy water, making it almost impossible to predict what the wheels would do. I rode cautiously along the rutted track on the left, trying to keep my speed constant and looking up ahead to keep my wheels in the rut. The trucks had also started to catch me now and I needed to pull out of the ruts from time to time as both cars and trucks passed me.

The alarm on my motorbike burst to life once more with three sharp beeps. Its sound was clear even with my earplugs in and over the growl of the large titanium Akropovic pipe sticking out the back of my KTM 450RR rally bike. Then, in just a matter of seconds, my entire race came to a violent end. As the siren went off I turned to see the approaching vehicle through the dust but this time it wasn't 200 metres behind me, it was only 30 metres back and was closing in at double my speed. I had only three or four seconds to get out of the way before impact.

I tried to get out of the deep rut, weighting my right foot peg and pulling hard on the bars, twisting them to the left and keeping the power on. The front wheel just pushed hard into the left side of the rut compressing my forks, the wheel unable to climb out. The bike tucked as I exited left off the track parting from the bike in a last ditch effort to escape from the car behind me. The car missed me by inches only to drive right over my bike, its two-ton weight crushing it as its tyres ripped through my tanks and navigation tower. Blinded by the fesh-fesh filling the air I heard the impact a metre or so from me. I knew exactly what had happened, the crunching sound was unmistakable over the roar of the vehicle's engine.

The car had continued on, the incident a minor detail in their books, but for me it was everything. I knelt down next to my mangled bike, struggling to accept the situation and my shattered dream.

I was seething as I dragged the mangled wreck that was my bike out of the petrol soaked track and stood it up. The full extent of the damage was now apparent. The carbon fibre navigation tower was broken in several places, with the roadbook holder completely crushed and the bracket ripped from the mountings. Two of the ICOs showing my distance and CAP headings were blank, with some wiring ripped out. The bars were bent and unable to turn, because the tower was bent into them. The bottom triple clamp was mangled and the front wheel was skew. There were three petrol tanks on the bike and the one at the rear as well as the front right one was crushed and the petrol had run out. The front left tank was the only one still working and that had only a few litres left. The seat had been ripped off and the cover was torn. The exhaust pipe was completely flattened and the silencer bent into the back wheel, making it unable to turn. I noticed the right foot peg was also missing and I searched for it in the track, finding it hidden in the fesh-fesh. It had broken off at the mounting, with the broken aluminium still attached to the foot peg. The rear mudguard and tail lights were smashed and the wiring was ripped open and exposed.

The bike was destroyed, unable even to start, and I was out of the race.

I had been fighting to keep it together for days, the pain and fatigue had been eating at me and now it just all spilled over. The tears streamed down my raw dusty cheeks just as I had cried nearly ten years earlier, alone and paralysed in the hospital bed at night. Everything I had worked towards and poured my life into for the past year was gone. I had fallen just short of the goal. It was an intense feeling. I was completely gutted that I wouldn't get the finish, but at the same time there was a twinge of relief that the pain would now end.

Through my tears, I could see the butchered bike in front of me, covered with names and fesh-fesh. At my feet lay the broken cover of my roadbook with the quote I had stuck on it just that morning. It read 'If all you can do is crawl, start crawling'. It certainly was appropriate for the dire situation I found myself in.

I looked at the bike again and, like a shot of adrenalin to the heart, my body surged with resolve. I decided it would not end here – this would not be the end of my story! I thought about everything – from lying in the hospital right through the years to this moment. The melted mousse and tyre in the Richtersveld, the cow in Pongola, the physio sessions, the hours in the gym, my buddies who had helped me raise the money, the sacrifices my family had made.

NO! It would not end here! I hadn't come all this way to finish in the middle of the bush just a day and a half before the end. That would not be my fate. I was going to fight back!

Kneeling in the dirt I took my tools out of the bashplate and put them on an old rag that had been stuffed in with them. I had to get the bike to run. I started by taking the bottom ICO off the tower so that the bars could turn. I loosened the triple clamps and kicked the front wheel, lining it up as best I could. Then I removed the exhaust and silencer. I disconnected the front damaged tank that was now full of dirt and tried to force the seat back on. I then realised the whole frame was bent and where the seat fitted between the front tanks was completely mangled. I hammered on the tank with the broken foot peg, trying to force it out enough to fit the seat in. Eventually I managed to do this. I reattached the foot peg as best I could with heavy duty cable ties. I ripped off the remainder of the rear mud-guard and disconnected the broken cables at the plugs. With the bike covered in petrol, I didn't want any sparking. I cable tied the broken exhaust on the back where the mudguard had been and just hoped it would fire up.

My thoughts turned to Meredith, back home following me on the live tracking, waiting for me to pass the next checkpoint. She would be worried beyond belief when my race number didn't come up on the screen. I pulled out my satellite phone and opened up the aerial, dreading telling her the news. I knew she would know that there was a problem the moment the number showed up on her phone. She answered the call and I immediately blurted out that I was fine and unhurt. Then I explained how the car had driven over my bike and it was near impossible to continue. She probably would not see me pass another waypoint.

'NO! NO! NO!' she cried as she burst into tears and we wept together, thousands of kilometres apart. I would have given anything to be with her at that moment. The signal wasn't great and the delay made it even more difficult to talk. I told her I would not be pressing the recovery button even though I was sure I was out, I would not be quitting. I was going to continue until the moment the sweeper truck caught me. I would be moving when I went out, even if I was just crawling. I hung up the phone and was once again alone.

MEREDITH:

Not seeing Joey pass through the waypoints on the tracking system on the second last stage of Dakar was my breaking point. I was on edge from hardly sleeping or eating for the past two weeks. Eating anything hurt my stomach and I was pretty sure I was starting to develop an ulcer. The 'From Para to Dakar' WhatsApp chat line started pinging non-stop at about 4pm with everyone wanting to know if Joey was OK or if there was any news about him. The last I'd heard from Joey was a phone call early that morning at 2.43am that lasted less than a minute, telling me he had finished the previous day's special. The exhaustion in his voice did nothing to calm my fears and Joey telling me that he had had two really bad falls just added to the stress and anxiety I was already feeling.

At 5pm my cellphone rang and Joey's satellite phone came up on the caller ID. My heart sank because I knew this couldn't be good news. Joey told me that a car had driven over his bike. I could hear the anger and despair in his voice when he told me it looked as though he was out of the Dakar. I was furious shouting, NO, NO, NO! Feeling totally devastated, I told Joey how much I loved him, my heart breaking at how cruel and unfair life can be, and we cried together. As we hung up, our girls, hearing me shouting, ran up to my bedroom, freaked out and wanting to know what had happened. Up until that point I had been Wonder Woman for my girls but it all crumbled within seconds. My daughters, through their own tears, tried to console me and one another. I phoned Verity, sobbing my heart out, and she arrived a few minutes later to five distraught weeping girls.

As usual, Verity was amazing and had me go through exactly what Joey had said on the phone. She told me that she just didn't feel that it was over, she put Shawna on her lap and cuddled her and told us all how Joey just didn't give up, she reminded us of when he had a hole in his tyre at the Amageza and how he made a plan and finished, and that he would find a way to finish Dakar too. Within 15 minutes she had changed the mood from despair to hope. My parents arrived and they too felt that we weren't to give up hope.

A couple of pushes of the starter later and my wreck burst to life. It didn't sound great without the exhaust and its parts were rattling, but it was running. I swung my leg over, forgetting the exhaust silencer cable tied on top of the rear tank. My foot connected with it, I lost my balance and fell over, once again, with the bike on top of me. I wriggled out through the dust and picked the bike up. I made sure the stand was down and climbed on from the left, using the foot peg as a step. I fired it up once again and pulled off. The right foot peg broke off again the moment I put weight on it. The sudden failure sent my foot hard into the ground and I swerved into a bush and fell – again. Once more, I picked the bike up and reattached the silencer that had broken off the cable ties. I walked back a few metres and picked the foot peg up out of the fesh-fesh. Another car came hurtling by, covering me in the fine dirt. It didn't bother me though; I had bigger problems. I had already lost about an hour by now, meaning that I was stone last in the bike category with not a single bike behind me. It was just after 10am and I still had 660 kilometres to cover that day.

I knew that often in survival type situations like this, guys get frantic and miss obvious solutions. So I took a moment to think about how the day could play out. The next checkpoint was about 60 kilometres away. After that was a 'neutralisation zone' before the final racing special. A neutralisation zone was a non-racing section similar to a liaison. If by some miracle I managed to get that far, perhaps my team could meet me there and give me the parts I needed. I was pretty sure it was allowed because it was out of the racing section. They weren't parts they would normally carry, though, and they would have to get them from the KTM truck. I pulled out my satellite phone and this time I tried to call my team. I couldn't reach them on any of their numbers, so as a final resort I called their bike shop in Holland and explained the desperate situation I was in. They said that they would try to contact my team and I hung up. I had only a few litres of petrol – it wouldn't be enough even to get to the next checkpoint where I might be able to get some, but I had to keep going.

I pulled off again without a right foot peg.

'Of course it is!' I thought, as I realised that the one foot peg I had was on the side where I had torn the ligaments in my knee. With one foot on the left foot peg and my right knee on the seat, I rode off.

The bike lacked power and there was no way I could ride in the track so I zigzagged through the bush, keeping the track in sight and following the dust clouds of the occasional car or truck. Time kept ticking away and my progress was unbelievably slow.

I was a dead man walking, not able to navigate properly and rapidly running out of petrol. In reality, I was already out of the race, but at that moment I was still in, pushing back the inevitable. I rode like that for over an hour, covering only about 15 or so kilometres, and my petrol was all but gone. Then the most incredible thing happened – something that I will still smile about one day on my deathbed, with a twinkle in my eye.

In the middle of the vast dusty wasteland, miles from any town or settlement, somewhere between San Juan and Rio Cuarto, Argentina, stood a KTM rally replica in perfect working condition.

I often joke that there was a pillar of light that lit it up along with heavenly choruses. I pulled up next to it and three Argentinian guys on old dirt bikes who were watching the rally came over to me. I could see all the tracking equipment had been stripped off the bike, as they always did when a rider was medevacked out of the race. The three guys couldn't speak English, but mimed that the rider had broken his arms and been taken out in a chopper. The standard procedure was to fly the injured rider out and the bike would be collected later when the sweeper truck came through. I couldn't swap bikes because the regulations stipulated that you had to finish on your own frame, suspension and various other major parts. What I could do, though, was 'borrow' the parts I needed and get my bike to the end.

In true biker fashion – and typical of the South American way – the three guys, Raul, Abel and Mario – pitched in and helped me as we went about stripping the bike. I noticed one of them had only one leg and smiled at the thought of him defying his own disability, unknowingly helping me to defy mine.

We took the exhaust and fitted it to my bike. Then we had to strip the whole foot peg holder off the bike, which meant taking off the whole rear brake assembly and lever. I had every tool we needed on me, except a size 17 spanner which we needed to remove the final bolt that went through the swing arm and foot peg holder. Without the spanner it was impossible to remove.

Unbelievably, one of the Argentinian riders had a big shifting spanner cable tied to his bike. What were the chances? He brought it over and I tried to loosen the bolt, but it was on tightly. I slid the damaged mid-section of the exhaust over the back of the shifting spanner for extra leverage, being careful not to strip the nut, and eased it off. Then we realised that we had to take the exhaust off my bike again to fit the foot peg holder on, so we did it all over again. We siphoned the petrol out of the bike and poured it into my bike. In retrospect, we should just have taken the tanks but at the time it was difficult to think rationally. After some time, my bike was again rideable. I still needed the whole navigation tower, roadbook holder and ICOs but it would have taken hours to swap all of that and I was already running the risk of missing my start time the next morning.

On the final day the bikes started in reverse order, meaning I would probably be first out at 4am. I had to reach the bivouac before then and a lot of the second special would be in the dark, making the pace extremely slow. I had to get a move on. I thanked my new friends and we took a couple of pictures together. Then I was off and more pumped than I had been throughout the whole rally.

I was back in the crazy race, now with a fighting chance!

After all the time lost between the two repairs and zigzagging through the bush I was now near the back of the cars and trucks as well. The one advantage was that I could keep up with some of the vehicles, so I followed a truck for a while, relying completely on his navigational abilities. I picked up several waypoints, but had to be careful as I didn't know where any of the cautions were. The truck pulled away in the dust as the track opened up and I was alone again. I followed the tracks of the vehicles ahead, stopping where the trail split and scanning the surface for tyre tracks. I slowly bungled my way through the navigation, eventually arriving at the checkpoint.

My friends the marshals greeted me once again like an old buddy, patting me on the back and full of smiles. They had heard a bike had been ridden over by a car and were shocked at the state of my bike and the way I had managed to finish the special. They gathered around inspecting the bike, jabbering away in French and shaking their heads. I was given water and I refilled my hydration pack and ate the energy bar they gave me. I still had about 600 kilometres to go and it was already well into the afternoon.

Riding on the tar showed how obviously damaged my bike was. The frame was bent and where I sat didn't line up with the front. My bars were bent with one hand lower than the other and my wheel pointed forward but I was steering to the left. My blood boiled as the kilometres passed and I thought of ways to hide the bodies once I had slaughtered the occupants of the car.

MEREDITH:

At about 7pm I had a phone call from Bart's wife Mariska. It was a hard conversation to follow as she doesn't speak much English and I don't speak a word of Dutch. I think she told me that Walter and Gwen were on their way to meet up with Joey and if Joey phoned me again I was to tell him where he should meet them. At 9pm I had a phone call from Walter to say they had seen Joey and he was still in the race. For Walter to have taken the time and money to phone me was absolutely incredible of him; I don't think he will ever realise how much that phone call meant to me.

Walter just said, 'He's got a long way to go but he can do it!'

I finally put a message on the WhatsApp chat line detailing what had happened and instantly got flooded with messages of hope and encouragement that 'Joey has got this'. It was going to be a very long night ahead of us and so I assured Verity and my parents that they could go and we would be OK. I would let them know the second I heard any news. The girls slept in my room that night so that if I heard anything I could let them know. They were all determined to stay awake until they heard their dad had finished the stage, but exhaustion took over and they were all fast asleep by midnight.

I had been riding for a long way on the tar when my team's vehicle appeared, coming towards me. I had never felt so grateful to see a car headed towards me! They pulled over next to me and Gwen and Walter climbed out. We shook hands and embraced and then they stared at the bike. Walter loves his bike to be perfect and he looked at mine with the expression of someone viewing a mangled body.

Gwen shook his head as he walked around the bike and assessed the damage. I told them about the car going over the bike and the challenges I had been through and then about how I found the other bike. They shook their heads in sheer disbelief. I asked if they had been nearby and they said, 'Not really.' They had the spares in the van and I asked whether or not they were allowed to help me. Gwen said that according to the rules this wasn't a common liaison section so, strictly speaking, no. I didn't want any reason to be disqualified so I told them not to do anything to the bike and they agreed. Gwen reminded me of the distance I still needed to cover and within a few minutes I rode off, pushing towards the second special.

I had managed to get one of my ICOs working, so I knew the distance that I was travelling, but the roadbook holder was completely crushed and unable to turn. I tore out the roadbook scroll and stopped to pull several instructions out then tore them off and kept them in my pocket, checking them as I rode. Once I had passed them all, I stopped and tore off several more and that was how I navigated the rest of the stage. Along the way, I opened the small bags on my handlebars to get out something to eat but all my food had been destroyed by the petrol which had soaked the bags when the tanks were damaged. It had gone through the wrappers leaving the energy bars and sweets sticky and reeking of petrol.

After I had ridden for a couple of hours, it dawned on me that Walter and Gwen had driven all the way from the bivouac back to me. The round trip would have been about 700 kilometres and then I had refused their help. I felt terrible because they hadn't said a word. It was a real face palm moment and I couldn't wait to see them again to apologise. As usual, I spoke to myself again. 'Joey, you're such a chop!'

It was late in the evening when I started the twisting climb up nearly 1800 vertical metres to the start of the second special on top of the Sierras de Córdoba – a mountain range in the Córdoba region. With my body weary and my eyelids heavy, I lost concentration as the route twisted and drifted off the track. I saw it all happening, but seemed unable to correct myself. I hit the rocks on the edge and with millimetres to spare I managed to regain control, stopping myself from plummeting off the edge and down the mountain side. I pulled over, took off my helmet and rested my head on the bars. That had been too close!

'Come on, Joey, keep it together, boy!' I told myself.

The wind blew the way it had done in the Cape on my solo adventure a couple of years back and the long grass was bending right over. The views were spectacular and I reflected on the many close calls I had experienced because of my worn-out state over the last 48 hours.

I started the bike back up and pushed on up the mountain range to arrive at the start line of the second special as the sun disappeared at around 8pm. I had already been riding for 15 hours when I reached the start of that second special and was now about to start a racing distance typical of a full national off-road race back home. I still hadn't seen another bike or quad in the ten hours since the crash. I climbed off my bike to put on an extra layer of clothing as the temperature was dropping. I stumbled, struggling to keep my balance.

A medic came over, took me by the arm and led me to a seat. I could tell he was worried about me and was reluctant to let me continue. I explained about my spinal cord injury and said that I was still OK, I could continue. Again, I felt like a boxer with jelly legs nodding at the ref as he held my wrists counting 7, 8, 9 … He wanted to know how much I had had to eat and drink during the day and I told him. He brought me an extra lunch pack. I ate it and stuffed my jacket with some more energy bars. I had to climb on from the left as I almost always did. It was my stronger side since the accident but I barely managed. With the medic watching I knew that if I fell over it would be the last straw. With my hydration pack now refilled, I lined up at the start once more.

The marshal held out his hand in front of my bike and I was counted down. I pulled away cautiously in the strong wind and fading light. This was not a special to *race*, but one to *survive*. The gravel track once again wound through the mountains, crossing several streams and switching back on itself with sheer drop-offs. But it was now dark. I couldn't see how deep the rivers were nor could I see the dirt track further than the reach of the bike's headlight. The ground was hard and tops of rocks broke up the surface. To the side of the tracks lay piles of rocks that had been cleared over the years as the narrow road had slowly eroded. The edges of the mountain tracks held no forgiveness, free from barriers and run off, one mistake would send you airborne into the dark abyss. I rode carefully, not wanting to go over the steep rocky edges. My eyes stung and watered as I struggled to see in the darkness and there were no more fans asking for photos and autographs; the stylish decals on my bike and the brands I was wearing meant nothing that night. There was no racing glamour, no trophies and no cheering. It was just me and my bike trying to pull off the impossible, completely alone somewhere in Argentina in the middle of the night.

I rode for hours, still winding through the mountains, stopping again and again to tear off more directions and cautions from the roadbook. I memorised them in the light of my dim torch and then rode on. Alone in the night, under the full moon, the beauty of the area wasn't lost on me and I decided I would go back there one day with Meredith and drive the route in the daytime. But that night, my headlight danced around ahead of me as I chased the clock, just as it had through the Richtersveld along the Namibian border less than two years before. More than four hours later the calendar ticked over as, after midnight, I left the mountains and arrived in the lowlands to ride along farm roads next to barbed wire fences. Mud pits had been churned up by the trucks to the point where they were nearly impossible to cross. Then followed more thick sand but in the darkness I was unable to tell the difference between wet sand and ruts. I had a few close calls, but managed to keep the bike upright.

I crossed wide sandy streams and climbed steep riverbanks filled with deep muddy ruts from the trucks ahead of me. Over the last five hours and approximately 200 kilometres, I had seen only three vehicles in the race, two trucks and a car. Their headlights and LED bars had illuminated the entire area as they sped past, only to leave me alone again with my small beam casting light just a few metres ahead of me.

I would like to say that I thought about many things that night, but my mind was consumed with trying to stay alive, navigate the track and reach the bivouac. I fought the physical obstacles the track laid out ahead of me. I fought the pain as my failing body hurt and cramped with each metre. I fought the urge to push the button on my bike that would bring a swift rescue. I fought the race that is designed to expose every flaw and every weakness and leave you short of the finish.

'You messed with the wrong guy!' I shouted to myself in the darkness. Over and over again, willing myself on, the words muffled by the roar of my rally bike.

At about 1.30am I looked at the torn roadbook sheet in my hand in the dim light of my torch. I was at the finish of the special, but there was no one there. I double checked as I sat on my damaged bike alone in the darkness. It was definitely the right place, my GPS had picked up the waypoint that confirmed it. I realised that the marshals had packed up already and headed along the liaison to the bivouac.

Did that mean I was excluded from the race? There was no cut-off time on the torn off roadbook I held in my hand. There was no one to ask and I had the waypoint registered on my GPS. They would be able to confirm my finish and so I started out on the liaison to Río Cuarto.

At 2.11am, I saw the lights and marshals at the gate of the bivouac. There had been so many times that day when I had thought this moment would never arrive. Walter was there clapping his hands above his head and then he grabbed a fist full of my jacket sleeve, smiled and said, 'You did it, boet!'

My eyes glistened as I shook my helmet and smiled. I had no words. That day the Dakar threw everything it had at me, the full arsenal, and I had somehow pulled through. I hadn't done it with grace and poise, it had been messy, with mistakes, tears and shouting. But that day I had dragged a broken body along with a broken bike across the finish line.

MEREDITH:

I refreshed the tracking app every 30 seconds and watched the WhatsApp chat line like a hawk. So many people stayed awake through the night and the early hours of the next morning, SMSing messages to Joey, myself and our girls. I was overwhelmed by all the love and support that just kept pouring in. It was all too stressful for my parents, making it impossible for them to sleep, and at 3am they got up and started doing some housework to keep themselves busy. At 4am Mike, Gary Rowley, Verity and I were still messaging and updating one another on what we thought could be happening with Joey. I could no longer take not knowing what was happening and in the early hours of Saturday morning I SMSed Darryl to find out if there was any news of Joey. He replied that he wasn't in yet. I was working myself up into a flat-out panic again when my phone beeped at 7.11am with an SMS from Darryl to say Joey was in, he'd completed the stage. I let out a squeal of excitement and again burst into tears which woke up the girls. I was over the moon to let them know that this time they were happy tears and that their dad had done the impossible and finished the stage. I'm sure our neighbours must have wondered what all the screaming was about as we celebrated the unbelievable news. We then opened our final gift bag from Joey.

The message on the front of the bag read: 'A shortish racing section followed by a long liaison. Should be a formality but I will keep my guard up. Bringing it home, baby!'

Walter climbed on the bike behind me. I warned him I could barely hold the bike up and he made sure to keep his legs down till I pulled away as he guided me to our truck. We pulled up at the truck and Darryl was there waiting for me, as well as the Red Bull TV crew. I had seen the Red Bull guys around the top teams during the race, but had no idea why they were at our truck after two in the morning. It turned out Darryl had told them about the car, what had happened and how I was pushing on to reach the finish. They wanted to get the story first hand.

As I stopped, Darryl held on to the bike. I tried to get off and just collapsed, caught on the way down by Walter and Gwen. I couldn't apologise fast enough for what I had put them through, driving out to me that day. They brushed it off as though it was nothing. The triumph of finishing that day was shared by the whole team, along with Darryl and the Red Bull guys. They interviewed me for their Dakar Daily Report and congratulated me on the accomplishment. I walked up the truck's metal steps, this time on all fours, not wanting to collapse again and sat on the bike stand. I was grinning from ear to ear.

I no longer cared who was driving the car that crushed my bike, it no longer mattered. I had just survived one of the craziest days of my life. I called Meredith on the satellite phone and this time heard tears of joy.

Another two riders had gone out that day, but I was not one of them.

Chapter 29

STAGE 12 AND PODIUM

I had arrived with my broken body and bike in the bivouac less than two short hours earlier but it was already time to wake up again. I had slept for just one measly hour but that day it was easier to get up. It was the final day of the 2017 Dakar Rally and against all possible odds I was still in. I had paid the price to be there in every way. I ignored all the pain and focused single-mindedly on one goal: to get to that finishers' podium.

The final stage consisted of a short liaison of only a few kilometres followed by the final racing special of 64 kilometres and then a mammoth liaison of nearly 700 kilometres on tar into the capital Buenos Aires.

During the last two hours Gwen and Mark hadn't stopped working on the bike and were still busy as I got dressed. I never once doubted that the bike would be ready when I needed to go. My team were as solid as they come. I smiled at them and they smiled back, shaking their heads, none of us able to take in the unbelievable events of the last 24 hours. They had been over at the KTM factory's rally truck and organised a new front tank for me, a navigation bracket and new roadbook holder. They had them fitted to the bike along with the new rear mudguard. The damaged wiring had been sorted out and my ICOs were working again. My bike needed about two weeks' work but there was no time now. All I needed was for it to last one more day. The wheel was a bit straighter but the bars were still bent. My torn seat now also fitted a little better with the new tank. Bart made me something to eat and I stuffed some energy bars in my jacket. Walter had taken my roadbook when I arrived in the early hours of the morning and it was marked, corrections made and loaded on the bike. He handed me my filled hydration pack and I was off once again, pulling out of Rio Cuarto.

Next stop Buenos Aires!

As I rode the liaison to the start of the final special, I thought about riding up the finish ramp later that day just as I had imagined it lying in my hospital bed nearly ten years earlier. My bloodshot eyes narrowed and my split lips widened as I smiled at the thought of what the day held. All I had to do was somehow get through it, just one more day.

I pulled in at the designated service station just before the start of the special to fill up with petrol. There was an older guy there who was having a problem with the pump. He fumbled around for the key and went in and out the building mumbling something to himself in Spanish. I saw the time ticking by and I could see I was going to miss my start time. I didn't have a choice, though, so I sat tight and waited. The worst that could happen was that I would get a time penalty for a late start and at this point in the game it was neither here nor there. The riders behind me were getting agitated and eventually the old boy got the pump going. I let a couple guys go before me and then filled up and headed to the start.

As I expected, I was late and was sent out by the marshal right away. The route was between farms and small forests, crossing rivers with 90 degree turns sandwiched between barbed wire fences. The track was made up of soft sand and rutted hard pack eroded by the rain and farm vehicles. The weather was dry and hot with no wind, making the dust hang heavy in the air. I rode through at a safe speed, neither my body nor my bike were exactly 'race ready'. Just like the last day in Morocco, I had nothing to gain and everything to lose. Some riders flew past me, racing blind in the dust and taking crazy risks. It seemed so insane at this point in the race. I kept out of their way and nursed the bike through the special. After what felt like the longest hour of the race, the end of the special came into sight. The relief was tangible, like a heavy load lifted off my back.

I shouted in my helmet and punched the air. 'You did it, bro, you did it!'

I pulled up next to my marshal buddies as they cheered me in. They recorded my number and stamped my timecard for the last time. I rode through to the large field where all the riders and press were waiting to watch the leaders cross the line. We all still had the 700 kilometre liaison to get through to the final finish but this was the end of the racing and everyone was walking around and celebrating the finish.

My buddies Vincent and Lyndon had both finished and with our arms over each other's shoulders we spoke into Lyndon's GoPro for the last time. It turned out Vince had also lost a camera and Lyndon had lost two, so I didn't feel so bad about losing mine. My friend Fernando from Portugal had also crossed the line and was welcomed home by his proud parents, both there to support him. John Comoglio who had been puking through his helmet in the Morocco dunes crossed the finish line too. We congratulated and hugged one another. Maikel, my crazy Dutch teammate, ran over and jumped on me. He's a skinny oke but there was no ways I could support his weight at this stage and we both fell over in a pile, laughing and whooping. It felt great, but I knew the 700-kilometre liaison would still be a big challenge for me and would take at least ten hours. After about 20 minutes we all started heading out on the liaison.

In the craziness of the night before and that morning, I had left my phone on the truck and so I couldn't take any pictures. I looked around for my truck but they had moved off to the finish already. I got on my bike and started the long haul to Buenos Aries. After a few kilometres I realised I had also left my inflatable seat cushion behind; it would really have come in handy that day.

I rode through towns and villages lined with fans and waved as they cheered us on. But then we hit the long desolate roads and I felt my eyes drooping once again. Each time this happened I stopped and woke myself up, once again walking round the bike and splashing my face with water. After two hours I was really struggling and my stops became more and more frequent, and there was still so far to go. I pushed on and on, constantly making sure I didn't kill myself by falling asleep on the last day.

Because of all the stopping to stay awake, I was once again lying at the back with about 200 kilometres to go. Suddenly the warning light started flashing on my bike, indicating a problem with the motor. I immediately pulled over to the side of the highway. The light gives a certain number of long and short blinks similar to Morse code to show what the problem is and so I had saved all the codes on my phone in case it happened. That would have been a great plan if I hadn't been stupid enough to leave it on the truck. I looked over the bike trying to figure out what the problem could be. I had no idea and was hesitant about continuing in case I seized the engine. If I did, I would be out the race.

The fact that it was the final liaison made no difference. It simply wasn't worth the risk. The truck of a KTM team from Bolivia saw me on my knees next to the bike and pulled over to help. We had a look together and at that point I noticed that the radiator was cool but the oil cooler was hot. There could only be a blockage in the radiator or it was empty. We opened up the radiator slowly and it was bone dry. I could only think it had been slightly damaged by the car the day before and had slowly leaked out over time. I filled it with bottled water from the Bolivian team and started up the bike. The light went off and after I downed a Red Bull from the team and stuffed a couple more water bottles under my jacket, I rode on. I stopped a few more times to check on the level and top it up which made my arrival at the finish later and later.

During the last couple of hours my mind reflected back on the journey that had brought me to this point. I had always wanted a full life. It didn't have to be a long life (although that would be preferred) but a life filled with adventure and rich experiences. It occurred to me that a full life was not only filled with good experiences but with the full palette of what life offers. That meant experiencing the bad as well as the good. The challenges I had faced over the years, along with the successes, had made me who I was.

I don't always feel this way, but in that moment I was honestly glad I had broken my back. It had made me see life differently, it had made me think differently, and it had allowed me to tap into strength I didn't know I had. I may have been broken outside, but inside I was titanium.

I didn't care any more if my kids or anyone else saw me cry, or if they saw me fail, because they will always see me finish, even if it's at the back. The last ten years along with the last two weeks, had been a long difficult journey for me and my family but in that moment it was all worthwhile. I thought of Meredith and how the challenges we had faced had brought us closer together. I thought I loved her when we got married nearly 20 years ago but that was a primary school crush compared with what we had now. She had raised four incredible children, despite me being involved, and when it was all added up, I had my full life.

Late in the afternoon I entered the outskirts of Buenos Aries and again had cars on the highway riding alongside me, taking photos, kids waving from the back windows. They crowded around me on the highway in what felt like the most dangerous part of the whole day. I was joined by a few guys on their scooters, a couple of them with girlfriends on the back, who shadowed me all the way to the finish area. Thousands of people lined the streets behind the crowd control fences. The music was pumping and flags were waving. I had been so stressed for the last couple of hundred kilometres that my bike wouldn't last to the end, so much so that the moment just didn't seem real.

I was stone last, once again, and had missed my allotted podium time but the marshals hurried me through the cars and trucks that were queuing at the finish ramp. I was stopped just before the finish ramp and stood at the base looking up at the finish. I scanned the crowd looking for my team. My bike side stand was down and I stood on the foot pegs for extra height.

'Come on guys, where are you?' I thought, with only seconds remaining before I was to be called.

Then I spotted Bart waving frantically along with Walter and his girlfriend Christelle. I waved back and then was called up to the ramp. It all happened so quickly that I never even had a chance to get my South African flag out of my hydration pack. They came running up the ramp behind me. I stopped the bike on top next to Xavier as they announced my name to the crowd. Xavier gripped my hand and rubbed my head like a proud dad as my team arrived.

Before he got to hang the medal around my neck, Walter, who had been a stranger I had helped load into an ambulance a couple years before, grabbed hold of me and hugged me tightly. We were brothers now. Along with Darryl, he knew my history best and together they had witnessed first hand over the last two weeks the high price I had paid to get there. Darryl slapped me on the back and threw his arm around me. We both knew the odds were stacked against my finishing, yet somehow I had pulled off the impossible. He whooped and cheered as much as he would with the winner, KTM factory rider Sam Sunderland, later that evening. Bart, the rock and leader of the team hugged and congratulated me like a brother.

The whole team stood on the finish podium ramp with me and it was so right that they did. Each one had helped me reach that point. Gwen smiled widely, we embraced and I thanked him for his super-human support. He deserved a medal of his own. I was the Night Rider, and no doubt the most challenging rider he had ever been a mechanic for. Maikel and Ibraheem congratulated me and stood alongside with their medals. Mark and Peter had both put daily effort into helping me and also shared in the moment.

Xavier finally got to hang the medal around my neck, my final overall position was 94th out of 96 finishers. My racing time was more than double that of the winner. Not exactly an impressive result, but in my mind I had won the race, just like the one I had won all those years back shadowed by Tristam and Johan.

I stood on that finishing ramp surrounded by real men – not because we had just finished the toughest off-road race in the world, but because of the way they had done it. Each of them was part of the team, tempers never flared, nobody had shied away from jobs, whether it was their responsibility or not. Each of them had given their all and left nothing on the table. I had made friends for life and I felt proud to be part of that team. The only thing that would have made the team moment better would have been to have Ronald and Walter alongside me with their own finisher's medals.

The race had been everything I had hoped for and more. It had been tougher than I had expected, more beautiful than I had imagined and the finish was sweeter than I had hoped. I had seen riders cross that finish ramp many times over the years and could hardly believe I was standing there myself, now a Dakar finisher. My raw dirty face, bloodshot eyes and broken grimy body hinted at what I had been through. I really needed a good scrub but nothing was going to wipe that smile off my face. I looked down at the medal around my neck and wondered how I was going to bath because I wasn't going to be taking it off.

After about a minute I rode down off the ramp and stopped just after the base. I looked at my screen and saw the sticker from David. It read 'Justin Thomas' and I was honoured to have been able to take him to the end. I had heard that David had had two helicopters and one plane ride to get to the hospital in Bolivia where they had operated on him. Toby Price, the previous year's winner, who had shattered his femur the day before David had broken his leg, had been taken to the same hospital. Both of them were on the way to recovery, to race once more in the most demanding off-road race on the planet. The little green toy bike I had taken from the front of David's bike belonged to a friend's young son Gabriel who had tragically drowned just a couple months before the Dakar. I would later get to return the toy bike to his parents.

I would also later track down Juan Sarmiento, rider number 101 from Colombia, and explain why his bike was missing a few parts. He was stoked I had been able to finish and totally cool about it. Once my bike arrived back in Europe my team sent all his parts back to him.

The podium in Buenos Aires was spectacular and a few days later I arrived back at OR Tambo International Airport in Johannesburg.

Meredith had warned me that a lot of people had been following my progress and some of them would be at the airport.

'Make sure you come back with all your teeth this time!' was the advice.

I collected my bags and walked towards a moment that made the finish podium in Buenos Aires pale in comparison.

I heard the chants 'Joey! Joey! Joey!' before I was even out the arrivals door. The doors opened and Meredith ran into my arms as my daughters Kayla, Jenna, Tyra and Shawna wrapped themselves around us. The crowd cheered and the moment sent my legs into spasm.

I had never seen so many people at the arrivals terminal before – all of them were more than supporters, they were part of the dream. A huge KTM banner with my picture on it was held high and cameras flashed away. A couple of days before I had felt that I was riding alone in the dark, but it was far from the truth. Each person I thanked and hugged had contributed to and lived the journey with me, along with many others around the world. I had a number of interviews right there for television, radio and various biking magazines. It was all overwhelming and utterly incredible at the same time.

'Wow! You're so lucky to have such a cool story!' someone commented.

'Cool story?' I thought.

Ten years ago, lying paralysed in a hospital bed with little chance of recovery, I certainly didn't feel lucky. No one ever said it was cool back then! But the truth is, it *is* a cool story and I *am* lucky, I just didn't know it at the time.

I've realised that when things are really tough and there seems no hope for the future, it's sometimes just Chapter One of a really cool story and the ending is entirely up to you.

Finishing the race after the car rode over my bike made my Dakar even more epic, just as breaking my back had done the same to my life.

From Para to Dakar.

ACKNOWLEDGEMENTS

had only been back from Dakar for a couple of months when I met with Tracey, the publisher of this book, in a coffee shop one morning to discuss the possibility of writing a book. She loved the story and asked if I had any writing experience. Apart from a couple of small articles for the *Enduro World* magazine, the extent of my writing was what teachers had made me do in school. I knew it was probably beyond my capabilities and we spoke about the possibility of a ghost writer. She gave me a few days to consider my options.

I met with a mate, GG Alcock, who had written a couple of books and we spoke about the ghost writer stuff. In the end it just didn't sit right with me. If my name was on the book I wanted to say I had written the whole book myself, every word. GG encouraged me just to go for it and said he would be happy to mentor me along the way. I spoke to Meredith about it too and, as always, she had full faith in me that I could pull it off. (Basically what I'm saying is, if you don't like the book it's their fault.)

Anyway, I mulled it over in my mind and a couple of days later I was lying awake in bed at about two in the morning and I thought, 'Stuff it, I'm gonna write this book!' I got up and started writing right then until the sun came up. I got back to Tracey that morning and told her I was keen to write it myself. She took a huge chance on me and the contract was signed. I had three months to hand in a finished manuscript.

I spent the next three months, day and night, hunched behind my laptop typing away with two fingers, occasionally showing off by hitting the space bar with my thumb. I enlisted the help of Robyn Williamson, a good friend of ours, to correct my spelling and poor grammar and sent chapters back and forth to GG who made content suggestions and told me what he loved and when it was crap.

Three months later I sent off the finished manuscript to Tracey, just less than two hours before midnight on the day it was due – squeezing it in just before the cut-off, just like I had raced the Dakar. My thanks to GG and Meredith for the push and to Tracey for taking a chance on me. Also thank you to Robyn, as well as Pam Thornley, the final copy editor, for making sure the text is readable!

Almost every time I have had the opportunity to share my story, people comment that it's Meredith who deserves the medal. They're right! She has equally shared every challenge I have faced, and even more, without the recognition. Her love is totally unconditional and without her support and encouragement I would never have been able to reach my dream. Every time I have felt doubt, or felt like giving up, she has pushed me forward and her belief in me makes it impossible to quit. She has almost no interest in worldly possessions and values me and our girls above everything. I say *almost* because we had one deal. She has always wanted a Mini so the deal was if I raced the Dakar then she would get her Mini. It's on order and so by the time this book is published be aware of a short blonde girl racing around in her brand new Mini Cooper with a Dakar sticker on the back. *Thank you* just doesn't cut it; you are my everything.

Then thank you to my daughters, Kayla, Jenna, Tyra and Shawna for allowing me to chase my dream. No dream is too big and you are capable of reaching anything you put your mind to. I will continue to compare the challenges they face growing up with the challenges I faced reaching the Dakar finish line. For the rest of my life I will take every opportunity I can to mention the word *Dakar* and no amount of eye rolling and 'yes Dad, we know!' shall deter me. I know secretly they love the story of how Dad got to the finish of the Dakar Rally. And I'm currently working on four wedding speeches on that very topic. I love you girls more than you will ever know!

After that where do I even start?

Over the past 10 years, literally thousands of people have contributed to helping me achieve my dream to race the Dakar Rally. As much as I get to keep the medal, there has never been more of a team effort in the history of the race.

First, thank you to all our family: to Meredith's parents, John and Coral Elks, for raising the girl of my dreams, for all their help while I was in hospital and for their support throughout the years; to David and Verity Bester and their boys for countless acts of selfless service over many years and for always looking after my five girls whenever I'm away; to my parents, Ian and Jacqui Evans, thank you for the sterling job they did raising me! Actually, it would be more appropriate to apologise to them for the challenges and many scares I've given them over the years. Well done on surviving my upbringing. I love you.

ACKNOWLEDGEMENTS

Thanks to my three brothers, Matt, David, and Mike and their families for the donations and support, to my sister Kerri in Holland for one of the first donations, and to my other sister Julie for her huge support over the years, and especially for helping us through the dark early days. And to Brad and Melissa for their support during the tough hospital days. The support from all of you during the darkest times has been incalculable. Despite the challenges we have faced over the years, we have never once felt alone in our struggles.

Thank you to all my friends who visited and supported me and my family when I was in hospital and in that first most difficult year. Thank you for the prayers, kindness and service from my friends at church.

Thank you to all the doctors, therapists and nursing staff who have helped me over the years. The job you do can often be a thankless task, but you should know that just like what you did for me, you change people's lives, give them hope and a chance at living a full life.

Thank you to all my riding buddies, the guys I've ridden with over the years, the guys I've raced with and against, the race organisers, the marshals, the racing media and all those who form part of the brotherhood of bikers. I am honoured to be part of you.

Thank you to everyone who believed in my dream – those who gave of their time as well as those who donated financially, and all those who helped at the fund-raisers and who attended and supported me. The money to race in the Dakar wasn't made up of one big sponsor but of literally hundreds of people and often small amounts. Thank you to each one of you who gave what you could. I truly appreciated every donation irrespective of the size.

Thank you to KTM South Africa as well as Raceworx and RAD KTM for supporting and backing an underdog. This boy's blood is orange.

Thank you to all the companies that sponsored my kit, donated money, prizes for our fund-raisers, publicity and time. Behind every company there are people and I thank you all.

Thank you to Bart, Gwen, Walter and the BAS/Van der Velden team that I was privileged to be a part of at Dakar. I would go into battle with you any day.

Thank you to my brother Mike and all the staff at Lex Pools for running the business and giving me the chance to live my dream.

Thank you to everyone who sat up late at night watching me pass each checkpoint on the computer during the race. I apologise for the sleepless nights and lack of productivity at work. Your support was felt thousands of kilometres away.

Lastly, thank you to my mates Gary Rowley and Phil Prentis. Your belief in me was incredible and I loved making you proud. Gary gave me the biggest hug at the airport on my return and visiting Phil in hospital just a couple days later I showed him the medal. 'I knew you would do it,' he whispered. I miss them both. Till we meet again, rest in peace.